OXFORD MEDICAL PUBLICATIONS

What is Clinical Psychology?

What is Clinical Psychology?

Edited by

John S. Marzillier

and

John Hall

Department of Clinical Psychology,
Warneford Hospital, Oxford

OXFORD NEW YORK TOKYO
OXFORD UNIVERSITY PRESS
1987

Oxford University Press, Walton Street, Oxford OX2 6DP
Oxford New York Toronto
Delhi Bombay Calcutta Madras Karachi
Petaling Jaya Singapore Hong Kong Tokyo
Nairobi Dar es Salaam Cape Town
Melbourne Auckland
and associated companies in
Beirut Berlin Ibadan Nicosia

Oxford is a trade mark of Oxford University Press

Published in the United States
by Oxford University Press, New York

British Library Cataloguing in Publication Data
What is clinical psychology?——
(Oxford medical publications)
1. Clinical psychology
I. Marzillier, John S. II. Hall, John, 1944–
157'.9 RC467
ISBN 0-19-261516-5
ISBN 0-19-261521-1 Pbk

Library of Congress Cataloging in Publication Data
What is clinical psychology?
Includes bibliographies and index.
1. Clinical psychology. 2 Clinical psychologists.
I. Marzillier, John S. II. Hall, John, 1944 Apr. 9–
[DNLM: 1. Psychology, Clinical. WM 105 I619]
RC467.I58 1987 157 86-31189
ISBN 0-19-261516-5
ISBN 0-19-261521-1 (pbk.)

Typeset by Colset Private Ltd, Singapore
Printed in Great Britain by Biddles Ltd
Guildford and King's Lynn

To Mary and Sonia

Preface

Many people—friends, patients, professional colleagues—often ask us about our work as clinical psychologists. What exactly is a clinical psychologist? What do you do? How does your work differ from that of a psychiatrist or psychoanalyst? It was partly to answer these questions that this book was written.

We are aware that there are several 'good books' on clinical psychology and some excellent ones. But they do not serve our need, for two reasons. First, the vast majority are American. Although there are many parallels between the practice of clinical psychology in America and that practised in Europe and elsewhere, there are also significant differences. To take one important example: in the UK clinical psychologists work in the National Health Service and are essentially public employees responding to the health care needs of the community. In the USA many clinical psychologists work in private practice and respond to market demands. This difference affects how the clinical psychologist works and what he or she does. Second, most of the books on clinical psychology are lengthy, detailed expositions of theory and practice. The reader needs to be prepared to take the time and the trouble to read through them. We wanted a book that was more readily accessible, or 'user friendly' as the current jargon goes. But above all we wanted the book to describe practice, to tell the reader what clinical psychologists actually do.

The book is divided into chapters describing the work of clinical psychologists in various settings and with different patient groups. This seemed the most sensible division as it closely accords with existing practice. There are clinical psychologists who work predominantly with children, others who work with the elderly, and others who work in psychiatric hospitals, for example. The book has also allowed us to invite a number of experienced practitioners to provide accounts of their work. There is overlap of course, though we have sought to minimize needless repetition, and we have in our final Chapter brought out some common themes. The variety of settings and practices are significant since they illustrate how much clinical psychology has developed over the 20 years or so that we have both been working as clinical psychologists. We both began our work in psychiatry, carrying out psychometric assessments and some selected, mainly behavioural treatments. That was then the main role for clinical psychologists. Now, as this book illustrates, there is much more to the work of clinical psychologists and the scope of their practice has vastly expanded. It is an exciting time to write about our profession and we have sought to capture the variety of ways that clinical psychology is practised.

Almost exactly 10 years before we wrote this preface, Don Bannister, a noted British clinical psychologist, wrote about the sort of professional who was needed in clinical psychology. He said, writing in visionary mood, it should be someone who could:

cope with a warring therapy group, excite a class of dead-tired nurses, investigate by test and/or conversation the dynamics of a family, devise a revealing and helpful attitude survey for a unit split by interprofessional differences, coax and bully a hospital committee into democratising its wards, introduce a machine teaching programme into a subnormality hospital, understand and counsel a virgin chronic patient on the joys of sex, act as a link man for a community anti-suicide programme and take a bunch of very old ladies for a really enjoyable trip to the zoo.

Trips to the zoo are relatively rare these days, but clinical psychologists appear to be involved in all these activities and more, as the various chapters of this book illustrate.

The book does not need to be read from beginning to end, although most readers will find it helpful to start with the first chapter. A glossary of key terms is included at the end of the book to explain the various technical terms used, although we have tried to keep these to a minimum. At the end of each chapter there is a short list of further reading on the material covered by each chapter: these titles have been chosen to be relatively accessible to the non-specialist reader.

We are grateful to the people who helped us in writing this book, especially those who have commented on chapters: notably Sid Bloch, Hilary Edwards, Godfrey Fowler, Mike Hobbs, Joan Kirk, Ian McPherson, and Geoff Shepherd. Most of all we would like to thank Julia Jones, for her tireless efficiency on the word processor and good temper in coping with our editorial foibles.

Oxford   J.S.M.
June 1986   J.N.H.

Contents

Contributors

Professor Chris Cullen
S.S.M.H. Professor of Learning Difficulties, University of St Andrews, Scotland

Dr Dorothy Fielding
Head of Department of Clinical Psychology, St James University Hospital, Leeds

Dr Jeff Garland
Principal Clinical Psychologist, Littlemore Hospital, Oxford

Dr John Hall
District Clinical Psychologist, Warneford Hospital, Oxford; Clinical Lecturer, University of Oxford

Dr John Marzillier
Top Grade Clinical Psychologist, Warneford Hospital, Oxford; Regional Tutor in Clinical Psychology, Oxford Regional Health Authority

Di Staples
Principal Clinical Psychologist, Mary Marlborough Lodge, Nuffield Orthopaedic Centre, Oxford

Laurence Tennant
District Clinical Psychologist, Coleshill Hall Hospital, Birmingham. Unit General Manager Mental Handicap, North Warwickshire Health Authority

Dr Louise Wallace
Principal Clinical Psychologist, Monyhull Hospital, Birmingham

Dr Barbara Wilson
Senior Lecturer in Rehabilitation Studies, University of Southampton

1

What is clinical psychology?

John Hall and John Marzillier

Clinical psychologists are health care professionals who work predominantly, though not exclusively, in the field of mental health. Among their main activities are: (a) *Psychological assessment*, that is the use of psychological methods and principles to gain better understanding of psychological attributes and problems. Intelligence tests and personality assessments such as the famous Rorschach "ink-blot" test are very well known examples of psychological methods of assessment. But there are many, as illustrated in this book. (b) *Psychological treatment*, that is the use of psychological procedures and principles to help others to bring about change. There are many forms of psychological treatment ranging from brief, practical procedures for overcoming specific fears to lengthy and complex treatments such as some forms of psychoanalysis. (c) *Psychological evaluation*, that is the use of psychological principles to evaluate the effectiveness of treatments or other forms of intervention. Clinical psychologists have been particularly involved in developing methods of evaluating psychotherapies and to a lesser extent physical forms of therapy.

Although these are the main activities of clinical psychologists, there are also others. Training of other professional staff, involvement in administration and advice, involvement in health service policies, and collaborative research, are activities that some clinical psychologists engage in as part of their work. This diversity is well illustrated in the subsequent chapters of this book.

WHAT IS PSYCHOLOGY?

The term psychology is derived from two Greek words: *psyche*, which means 'spirit' or 'mind', and *logos*, which means 'study'.

'The study of the mind' is therefore the literal, though not now the customary, meaning of psychology. Up to the end of the nineteenth century psychology did not exist as a separate academic discipline but was part of philosophy. Philosophers such as Locke, Descartes, Hume, and Berkeley addressed themselves to understanding mental processes via philosophical discourse and analysis. Descartes' famous dictum 'Cogito, ergo sum' (I think, therefore I am), Locke's conception of the mind as a *tabula rasa* (blank slate), Hume's careful elucidation of the principles of causation via mental association are all examples of a philosophical approach to understanding human behaviour. Psychology departed from philosophy in two fundamental ways. The first was the development of a *scientific* approach rather than a philosophical one. In 1879 Wilhelm Wundt opened the first psychological laboratory in Leipzig, Germany. There began a period of experimental study in which Wundt and his students sought to gain a scientific understanding of conscious experience by a systematic and carefully documented examination of their experiences and sensations when specific stimuli were presented, such as certain colours and sounds. This method of inquiry was known as introspectionism and its aim was to capture the essential quality of sensations through scientific experimentation. Although introspectionism proved a short-lived approach in psychology, mainly because of its reliance on idiosyncratic, personal accounts of experience, it embodied the experimental scientific tradition that has predominated in contemporary twentieth century psychology.

The second departure of psychology from philosophy came in the extension of the subject matter beyond mental processes. In 1913 J. B. Watson, an American psychologist, had a profound effect on twentieth century psychology with his call for psychology to be concerned not with internal mental processes, which he regarded as unverifiable and hence unscientific, but with observable behaviour. Behaviourism became the dominant creed of early twentieth century psychology. Strongly emphasized was the need to place the science of psychology firmly on the bedrock of observed behaviour; experimental studies were conducted upon the behaviour of pigeons, rats, and other animals in the laboratory setting. B. F. Skinner pioneered the use of the famous Skinner box, in which rats pressed levers or pigeons pecked discs in response to various conditions of reward and punishment. These and many other laboratory experiments upon animal behaviour provided the basic psychology of conditioning and learning.

Psychology, therefore, had in the twentieth century moved from being a section of philosophy to a scientific discipline in its own right. It had ceased to be the reasoned study of mental processes and became the experimental analysis of behaviour, animal and human. By this change psychology established links with other sciences such as biology, physiology, and biochemistry. The interrelationship between psychology and these sciences could now be studied by examining the link between observed behaviour on the one hand and its biological basis on the other as, for example, in the relationship between brain waves and sleeping, or cardiovascular systems and emotions such as anxiety.

Modern psychology is still very much rooted in the behavioural biological tradition. However, the narrow adherence to observed behaviour in the laboratory that characterized Watson's behaviourism is long gone. The psychology of the present day is a flourishing and popular academic discipline which embraces a broad range of topics and activities. It requires knowledge of basic biological processes such as hunger, thirst, sex, sleeping, and waking, and of how these processes affect behaviour. Its central feature is the study of basic psychological processes such as perception, learning, memory, language, thought, and emotion. Psychological study seeks to describe and understand these processes as, for example, how memory processes work or in what ways people construct and organize their perceived world. The experimental method remains an important part of the psychological approach, although it is not the only method of inquiry. Developmental and social aspects of human behaviour are also vital features of modern psychology. Understanding human behaviour necessitates the study of its development and change from early infancy to old age. Developmental psychologists study, amongst many things, how children acquire and use language, the effects of early attachment and separation from parents, the processes and functions of play, and the effect of ageing on basic processes such as memory and thinking. Social psychologists study behaviour in its social context, which can be done experimentally in artificially created social encounters in the laboratory or naturally by observation and analysis of the individual in society. Finally, psychology merges into other academic disciplines, biological sciences (such as biology and physiology) on the one hand, and social sciences (such as sociology and anthropology) on the other.

In the example below the psychological approach is illustrated in the example of *pain*, which has an obvious biological and physiological basis in its relationship to tissue damage and the transmission of pain signals in certain nerve fibres to the brain. But it is not enough to describe pain in biological terms. Psychological factors play a significant part in our experience and expression of pain. The contribution that psychology has made in furthering our understanding of pain has led to one of the most influential theories of how pain is processed, the 'gate control' theory of Melzack and Wall (1982). Further, it has led to the development of new and promising treatments for chronic pain as well as effective methods of preparing individuals for necessary painful experiences such as surgery. It is the combination of basic research and theory and applied methods of assessment and treatment that characterize the branch of psychology that is the subject of this book, clinical psychology.

THE PSYCHOLOGY OF PAIN

As we can all testify pain is a response to injury or hurt. The more we are hurt the more likely we are to experience pain. Despite its unpleasantness pain has obvious survival value; it has the vital function of protecting us from serious injury. Thus a child's first contact with a hot stove will cause distress and pain but will rapidly lead to adaptive learning. Pain also sets limits on activity when a part of the body is injured. We learn to rest damaged ankles and knees rather than to continue to exercise them and injure them more.

Yet there are some intriguing facts about pain that cannot be explained solely in biological terms. Severe tissue damage, such as that produced by a deep wound, will in some people not produce any immediate pain despite the severity of the wound. Chronic and unremitting pain can occur in certain people long after the initial injuries have healed, the most dramatic example of which is 'phantom limb pain', pain localized in the place of an amputated arm or leg. The capacity for some people to undergo extremely painful experiences such as major surgery while hypnotized and not report or show any signs of pain has been well documented. The psychology of pain is concerned with understanding and influencing the psychological aspects of the experience of pain.

Psychological experimentation

Psychologists have contributed to our knowledge of pain in several ways. Firstly, by means of scientific experimentation they have clearly shown how psychological factors can affect when people will report pain (pain threshold) and how much pain they will bear (pain tolerance). The 'cold pressor test' is a laboratory test involving the immersion of a hand in ice cold water. The use of this test has shown, for example, that people can learn to tolerate pain for longer periods of time by adopting deliberate strategies such as distraction. Other experimental studies have shown that if people believe they have control over the amount of painful stimulation they are receiving (e.g. painful electric shock), they can tolerate more pain (even if their perception of control is illusory).

Secondly, reliable measurements of the experience of pain have been developed. One of the best developed is the McGill–Melzack questionnaire (see Fig. 1.1), which presents a series of adjectives to describe the different sensations of pain experience. The adjectives can be categorized into three groups, namely those describing the sensory qualities of experience, those describing the affective qualities (e.g. tension, fear), and those that evaluate the intensity of the total pain experience. Studies of different types of pain using this questionnaire have indicated characteristic adjectives for different syndromes. For example, toothache tends to be described as throbbing, boring, and sharp, whereas menstrual pain is described as cramping and aching. Not only is a questionnaire such as this useful in gaining a better description of what painful experience consists of: it also helps in classifying different sorts of pain.

Thirdly, theoretical models of pain experience have been proposed, the best known of which is the 'gate control' theory. The theory proposes the existence of a neural mechanism, located in the dorsal horns of the spinal cord, which acts like a gate, modulating the flow of nerve impulses from peripheral fibres to the central nervous system. The 'gate' is also influenced by descending influences from the brain, representing the influence on pain of such psychological factors as attention, memory, and emotional states.

Finally, psychologists have developed a variety of treatment

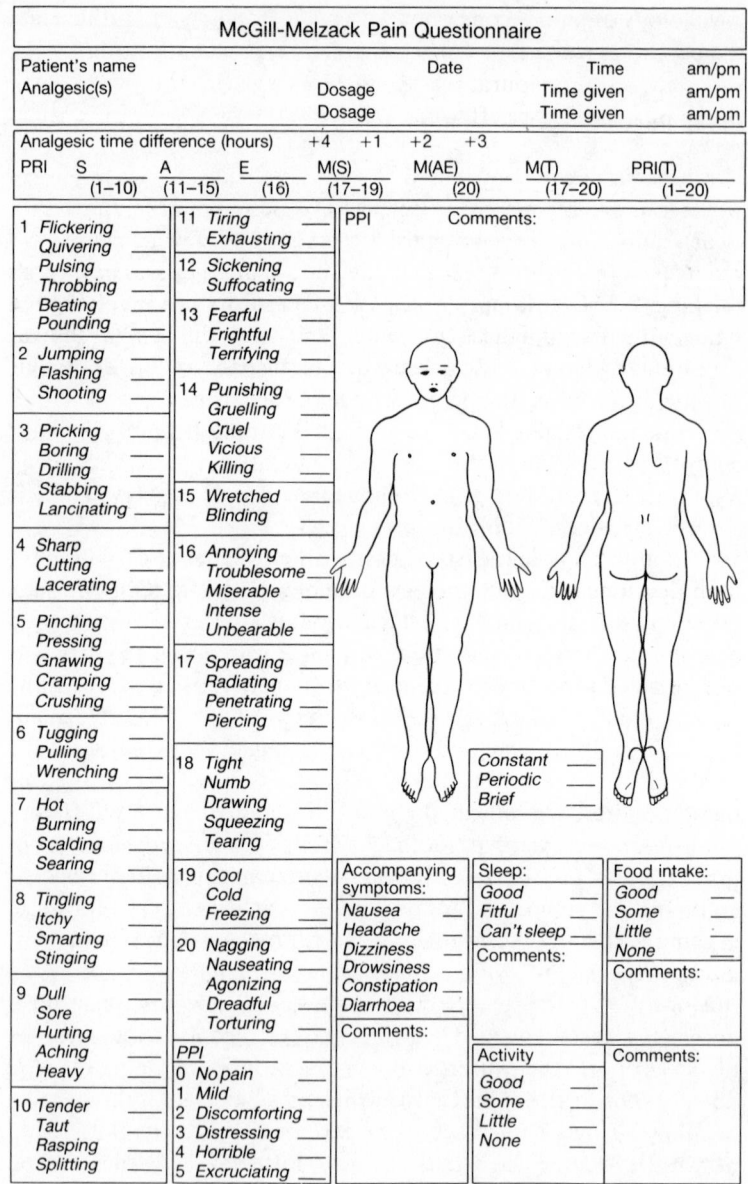

McGill-Melzack Pain Questionnaire

Patient's name ... Date ... Time ... am/pm
Analgesic(s) ... Dosage ... Time given ... am/pm
... Dosage ... Time given ... am/pm

Analgesic time difference (hours)   +4   +1   +2   +3

PRI   S _____   A _____   E _____   M(S) _____   M(AE) _____   M(T) _____   PRI(T) _____
      (1–10)   (11–15)   (16)   (17–19)   (20)   (17–20)   (1–20)

1 Flickering ___
  Quivering ___
  Pulsing ___
  Throbbing ___
  Beating ___
  Pounding ___

2 Jumping ___
  Flashing ___
  Shooting ___

3 Pricking ___
  Boring ___
  Drilling ___
  Stabbing ___
  Lancinating ___

4 Sharp ___
  Cutting ___
  Lacerating ___

5 Pinching ___
  Pressing ___
  Gnawing ___
  Cramping ___
  Crushing ___

6 Tugging ___
  Pulling ___
  Wrenching ___

7 Hot ___
  Burning ___
  Scalding ___
  Searing ___

8 Tingling ___
  Itchy ___
  Smarting ___
  Stinging ___

9 Dull ___
  Sore ___
  Hurting ___
  Aching ___
  Heavy ___

10 Tender ___
   Taut ___
   Rasping ___
   Splitting ___

11 Tiring ___
   Exhausting ___

12 Sickening ___
   Suffocating ___

13 Fearful ___
   Frightful ___
   Terrifying ___

14 Punishing ___
   Gruelling ___
   Cruel ___
   Vicious ___
   Killing ___

15 Wretched ___
   Blinding ___

16 Annoying ___
   Troublesome ___
   Miserable ___
   Intense ___
   Unbearable ___

17 Spreading ___
   Radiating ___
   Penetrating ___
   Piercing ___

18 Tight ___
   Numb ___
   Drawing ___
   Squeezing ___
   Tearing ___

19 Cool ___
   Cold ___
   Freezing ___

20 Nagging ___
   Nauseating ___
   Agonizing ___
   Dreadful ___
   Torturing ___

PPI ___
0 No pain ___
1 Mild ___
2 Discomforting ___
3 Distressing ___
4 Horrible ___
5 Excruciating ___

PPI   Comments:

Constant ___
Periodic ___
Brief ___

Accompanying symptoms:
Nausea ___
Headache ___
Dizziness ___
Drowsiness ___
Constipation ___
Diarrhoea ___
Comments:

Sleep:
Good ___
Fitful ___
Can't sleep ___
Comments:

Food intake:
Good ___
Some ___
Little ___
None ___
Comments:

Activity
Good ___
Some ___
Little ___
None ___

Comments:

Fig. 1.1 The McGill-Melzack Pain Questionnaire. (Reprinted, with permission, from Melzack and Wall 1982.)

strategies for acute and chronic pain. These are described in more detail in Chapter 9. Relaxation, distraction, hypnosis, biofeedback, and planned behavioural programmes have shown promise in helping people cope more effectively with painful experiences.

WHAT IS A CLINICAL PSYCHOLOGIST?

One of the commonest questions put to psychologists both by patients and professional staff is 'What is a clinical psychologist?' or 'In what way is a clinical psychologist different from a psychiatrist, a psychotherapist, or a social worker?'. In Table 1.1 we have listed some, though not all, of the health care professionals whose work may in some way overlap with or touch upon that of a clinical psychologist as they relate to each other in Britain.

The main differences between clinical psychologists and other professionals occur (a) in training and (b) in the formal structure of their work. Psychiatrists, for example, receive their initial training in general medicine, which provides a solid basis of biological, anatomical, and physiological knowledge of human functioning. By virtue of this training they have a particular expertise in physical and pharmacological treatments. Of all the professions listed in Table 1.1, psychiatrists are the only ones with the right to practise medicine, i.e. prescribe psychotropic drugs or carry out surgical or physical treatments such as ECT. This right is protected in most countries by formal statute or registration.

Clinical psychology training involves specialized knowledge of psychological functioning and psychological methods, which provides particular expertise in carrying out psychological assessments such as psychometric tests, psychological treatments, and psychological methods of research and evaluation. In some countries the right to practice psychology is embodied into statute, usually by registering the title of 'psychologist'. But this is not true of all countries, and the protection of the title does not prevent others from practising psychology as long as they do not call themselves psychologists.

The confusion between clinical psychologists and other professions therefore arises in part because of a real overlap between their respective activities. This is most evident in the case of psychotherapeutic skills, which are part of the activities of all the profes-

Table 1.1 Health care professionals in mental health

Profession	Training	Type of work
Clinical psychologist	First degree in psychology plus two to three years postgraduate training on university or Health Service Course	Psychological assessment and treatment, including psychological testing and psychotherapy (various). Specialist in cognitive–behaviour therapy. Research and evaluation
Psychiatrist	First degree in medicine plus three years postgraduate specialization in psychiatry	Psychiatric diagnosis, pharmacological and physical forms of treatment, psychotherapy (various). Certain statutory responsibilities *re* admission and discharge to psychiatric hospitals
Psychotherapist	No formal training or qualification necessary. May take one of many specialist courses at various institutes or centres. Common for other professions (e.g. psychiatrist, psychologist) to take such courses after initial qualification. But need not be professionally qualified	Psychotherapy—type will depend on training and experience of individual
Social worker	Two-year professional training, which may follow a first degree in sociology, social administration, or an unrelated degree	Social casework, involving the detailed assessment of family and environmental circumstances, and understanding of provision of social welfare benefits, housing, etc. Gives close support to individuals and families, practical guidance and advice, and may include psychotherapy
Psychiatric nurse	Three-year training. In-service training at Nurse Training School for Registered Nurses, or two-	Direct nursing care of patients, both in hospital and in the community, including physical care

Table 1.1 *Continued*

Profession	Training	Type of work
	year practical training for Enrolled Nurses	—giving medication— and social support, and providing a pattern of daily living for patients
Occupational therapist	Three-year training at College of Occupational Therapy	Provision of varied range of day activities, emphasizing rehabilitation, and creative activities, specifically aimed at improving patients' functioning
Counsellor	Variable. One to two-year courses in counselling psychology	Psychotherapy/counselling for less disturbed individuals. Some specialist forms *viz.* marriage guidance, careers

sions listed in Table 1.1. Clinical psychologists have specialized in some forms of psychotherapy, notably behavioural, cognitive and client-centred therapies (see Chapter 2 for a description of these approaches). And, to make matters worse, some clinical psychologists will *not* have trained in these methods but in other forms of therapy, or in fact may not practise psychotherapy at all! To the unsuspecting public the lack of a clear-cut description of clinical psychology, psychiatry, and other professions is not surprisingly a source of puzzlement and at times annoying confusion.

Towards a definition

Clinical psychologists tend to define their profession in terms of (a) the basic science of psychology and (b) its application to the understanding and resolution of human problems. The clinical psychologist is first and foremost an 'applied scientist' or 'scientist–practitioner' who seeks to use scientific knowledge to a beneficial end. Thus, in practising psychotherapy clinical psychologists are concerned to base their practices on what is scientifically known about problems such as depression, anxiety, schizophrenia etc. and to use psychological principles that have been well established in experimental studies. They are also particularly concerned to develop and use only those psychological treatment methods that either have been shown to be effective or are in the process of validation. These attributes are well summarized in a recent American text on clinical psychology:

> . . . clinical psychologists share several common attributes. They are *psychologists* because they have been trained to use the guidelines of knowledge of psychology in their professionals work. They are *clinicians* because they 'attempt to understand people in their natural complexity and in their continuous adaptive transformations' . . . They are *scientists* because they utilise the scientific method to achieve objectivity and precision in their professional work. Finally, they are *professionals* because they render important human services by helping individuals, social groups and communities to solve psychological problems and improve the quality of life. (Kendall and Norton-Ford 1982, p. 4)

The development of clinical psychology

Clinical psychology emerged as a recognizable profession at different times in different countries. In many countries clinical psychology does not exist as a distinct profession and this is particularly the case when the academic discipline of psychology has only recently been established. In Britain clinical psychology was not formally recognized until after the Second World War and it then took until 1966 before a Division of Clinical Psychology was formed in the British Psychological Society. In the USA and the UK a significant impetus to the development of clinical psychology came from the two world wars. The need to recruit and select suitably qualified service personnel led to the development and use of psychological tests and other assessments. In the UK the Second World War saw the development of Raven's Progressive Matrices and the Mill Hill Vocabulary Scale as tests of intellectual ability. Psychologists were confronted with real-life problems and thereby required to apply their knowledge and skills. In the United States the psychological trauma caused by battle and injury resulted in psychologists becoming involved in treatment as well as assessment, and the wartime emergency hospitals in Britain became interested in similar problems.

The formation of the National Health Service in 1948 is an important landmark in the development of clinical psychology in Britain. The few clinical psychologists that existed were brought under the NHS umbrella and employed directly by Hospital

Management Committees, the vast majority working in psychiatric hospitals. In the USA clinical psychologists found fertile ground in the Veterans Administration Hospitals that were formed after the end of the Second World War.

The role for clinical psychologists in Britain from 1948 until the early 1960s was predominantly that of a laboratory scientist, carrying out psychometric and other types of tests. There was little direct therapeutic practice. Dissatisfaction with this limited role and the desire for a more active clinical role, particularly in psychological treatment, eventually resulted in a major change in the structure and content of clinical psychology. The evolution of *behaviour therapy*—methods of treatment founded upon psychological principles and procedures—gave clinical psychology the entree into therapy. By the end of the 1960s clinical psychologists had established themselves as clinical practitioners rather than laboratory scientists and had pioneered many successful new psychological treatments.

In Britain the profession was formally recognized in the health service as an independent profession with therapeutic functions and skills with the publication of the Department of Health and Social Security report on psychologists in the health service, known after its chairman as the Trethowan Report (Department of Health and Social Security 1977). The Trethowan Report recognized the independent status of the profession of clinical psychology. It also formalised its organization in relation to the then reorganized health service, bringing clinical psychologists together into larger departments. This led to greater cooperation and a sense of professional identity. It was also recognized that clinical psychology had specialist functions outside of mental health, for example, in primary health care, in care of the elderly, and of the physically handicapped. This heralded the expansion of the profession both in numbers and in activities. Currently clinical psychologists in Britain are enjoying a broad role in the health service far beyond that envisaged in 1948.

Training and qualifications

Training in clinical psychology falls into two stages. The first stage consists of the basic science, that is, the academic study of psychology in the form of an undergraduate degree. In most countries this is a three or four year course of study resulting in the award of a

Bachelor of Science (BSc) or a Bachelor of Arts (BA). The second stage consists of professional training in clinical psychology. The first degree is not a vocational or professional training in itself although it may include a number of vocational courses or specialities.

Professional training in clinical psychology

Professional training in clinical psychology varies considerably from country to country. A recent survey of 23 countries revealed a variation in total length of training (including first degree) from four years in Italy to nine years in the USA (Fichter and Wittchen 1980). Qualifications differ too. Several countries offer training to doctorate level; others (e.g. New Zealand, Britain) have Masters courses of two or three years' duration. Yet others have specialized Diploma courses or courses leading to a formal license to practice. This variability is a reflection of the stage of development achieved by clinical psychology in different countries. In the United States, where clinical psychology is a well-established profession, training is rigorous and lengthy, and courses are stringently monitored and accredited. However, in a number of European countries (Spain, for example) there is not as yet a specialist profession of clinical psychology. Psychology graduates will therefore obtain training by attending specialized courses in psychotherapy or by attending training courses in other countries. They may set up in practice as clinical psychologists, but there is as yet no professional career structure for them. Table 1.2 illustrates the similarities and differences in clinical psychology training between three countries. One major difference is that in some countries (e.g. Britain, Australia, New Zealand, the USA) training is carried out on specific postgraduate courses which only a minority of psychology graduates enter, whereas in other countries (e.g. Norway, the Netherlands, West Germany) clinical psychology training is incorporated into the initial degree. In Norway, for example, it constitutes a second part of the Cand. Psychol. This means that many more clinical psychologists are produced in those countries where clinical psychology is 'embedded' into a general degree. However, it is likely that postgraduate courses, particularly to doctorate level, offer a more extensive and comprehensive training.

Another point of comparison concerns the extent to which

Table 1.2 Different patterns of clinical psychology training in three countries

Country	Description of clinical psychology training	Qualification	Time in training
UK	First degree in psychology (three or four years). A small percentage of graduates go on to postgraduate training, usually after one or two years relevant practical experience (e.g. as nursing assistant, psychology technician). Training is either on MSc course (normally two years) or Health Service course (three years). Training combines further academic study, supervized practical work, and clinical research	M.Sc. or M. Phil. in Clinical Psychology; Diploma in Clinical Psychology, British Psychological Society	*Min.* five years *Max.* seven years
USA	First degree in psychology (four years). Graduates seek admission to four or five-year doctorate programme in clinical psychology. Academic training is provided in general and clinical psychology. Students also carry out practicum placements, which are brief periods of supervized clinical work. The final year of training is an internship of one year in a hospital or similar centre. A doctoral dissertation in the form of an extended research project must be submitted. Some US	MA *or* MSc PhD *or* PsyD	*Min.* six yrs (masters) *Max.* nine yrs (doctorate)

Table 1.2 *Continued*

Country	Description of clinical psychology training	Qualification	Time in training
	programmes are only of two years' duration and lead to a Masters' qualification. Recently a few universities have offered a Doctor of Psychology (PsyD), which emphasizes clinical work and training and de-emphasizes research training		
Norway	Clinical psychology training is part of general psychology degree. After an initial introductory course, students take a psychological 'embetsstudium' which is divided into two parts, each of 2 ½ years. The first part is basic psychology and the second is practical training (academic and clinical). During the latter students carry out brief practicum placements as well as receiving formal tuition. All graduates are qualified to do clinical and psychotherapeutic work. The Norwegian Psychological Association accredits specialists in clinical psychology, who must have had at least five years' practice in at least two different institutions	Cand Psychol	6 ½ years

academic teaching or clinical training are emphasized. The British courses generally offer clinical and academic training in parallel. In other countries, notably the USA, clinical supervision and academic teaching are kept separate by means of periods of 'practicum placements' and 'internships'. There is considerable variation in the amount and content of clinical psychology training from country to country. This has meant that, as with other professions, clinical psychologists who wish to practise in countries other than those in which they received training need to obtain the relevant qualifications for the country in which they wish to practise. In the USA and Canada this usually entails formal examinations for the licence to practise as a psychologist. In Britain, there are procedures whereby foreign clinical psychologists may take the British Psychological Society's Diploma in Clinical Psychology and, depending upon the individual case, receive exemption from parts of it.

Professional training in Britain

There are two main routes to a qualification in clinical psychology training:

(a) Masters courses at Universities or Polytechnics, which are mostly two years in duration and lead to a postgraduate MSc or MPhil Degree.
(b) In-service training courses organized within the National Health Service by Regional or District Health Authorities. These are all three years in duration and lead to the Diploma in Clinical Psychology, a national examination organized through the auspices of the British Psychological Society.

Generally, university and polytechnic courses have tended to place greater emphasis on academic study, whereas health service courses have been stronger on professional training and clinical practice, although this difference has tended to become less obvious in recent years. All training courses, whether health service or University based, combine further academic study of clinical psychology with supervised experience and training in clinical work. Table 1.3 illustrates the academic courses available in a two year University MSc course in Clinical Psychology. There are core courses in adult psychiatry, child and adolescent psychological problems, mental handicap, quantitative methods (applied statistics) as well as a range

Table 1.3 Outline of academic syllabus for two year MSc course in Clinical Psychology, The University of Brimingham

First year	Second year
(a) *Preparatory training* Five weeks' intensive training workshops	(a) *Core Courses* Psychological problems Professional skills Clinical seminars Quantitative methods, Level 2.

(b) *Academic and clinical courses*
Psychological problems
    (a) adult
    (b) child
    (c) handicap
Therapeutic issues
Professional skills
Psychological treatment
Clinical seminars
Research method
(c) *Support Courses*
Quantitative methods, Level 1
    learning
Clinical psychopharmacology
(d) *Personal discussion group*
	(b) *Optional courses*
	(Students select six options)
	Behavioural medicine
	Clinical neuropsychology
	Criminal behaviour
	Community psychology
	Group behavioural interventions
	Learning
	Legal and sociological aspects of
	    delinquency
	Pschophysiology
	Sociological, Epidemiological and
	    social psychological aspects of
	    psychological disturbance

Clinical placements: Students work three days per week on clinical placements during term time, (four days per week outside terms).
Project: students are required to submit a substantive research project in the second year of the course.

of further core or optional courses on specialist topics. This will give trainees a thorough grounding in theory and knowledge on the populations and problems most commonly met in clinical practice. Particular emphasis is placed on theory and methods of psychological assessment and treatment.

Professional training is achieved through a combination of supervised clinical work on placements in hospitals, clinics or departments and clinical skills training by means of workshops and courses. The British Psychological Society has specified that all trainees must have supervised experience of adult psychiatric patients both chronic and acute, mentally handicapped adults and children, children and adolescents with psychological problems, and at least one specialist group (e.g. the elderly, delinquency). Placements vary from three to six months in duration and in most courses academic study is concurrent with clinical practice. In addition to academic study and clinical training trainees are required to carry out an applied research project which is written up and examined in the form of a dissertation. The acquisition of research skills is seen as a significant feature of clinical psychology training. Assessment of trainees is by a combination of academic course work, written examinations, ratings of clinical performance on placements, case reports of clinical work, and formal examination of the research dissertation.

A qualified clinical psychologist is expected to have acquired the necessary academic knowledge and professional skills to work as Basic Grade clinical psychologist in the National Health Service, a position for which the award of the MSc or the Diploma makes him or her eligible. However, it is recognized that further specialized experience and training is a necessary post-qualification requirement, particularly if a position entails working with a specialized population (e.g. in the neuropsychologically impaired) or acquiring specialized skills (e.g. family therapy, psychosexual counselling). In Britain post-qualification courses are few and far between and as yet there is no formal structure for such training, but the need for such training and experience has been recognized.

WHAT DO CLINICAL PSYCHOLOGISTS DO?

Clinical psychologists are asked to assess and intervene in a wide range of problems where they are believed to have special expertise. The range of problems where psychologists probably have a distinctive and prime contribution cover psychological conditions such as phobias, obsessional and compulsive disorders, problems of disturbed and disruptive behaviour, deficits in everyday skills such as dressing and communicating with other people, discrepancies between ability and attainment, and disorders of mental processes such as memory. In all these cases the psychologist is trying to understand or change an essentially psychological problem of an individual or group.

Secondly, a psychologist may be asked to help with the secondary consequences of a medical or physical problem, such as the sexual difficulties which may follow a spinal injury, when either a medical or other approach is appropriate for the primary problem. For some people, nothing can be done for the primary problem, but the individual still has a major and perhaps progressive handicap, as with some of the problems of old age.

Thirdly, a psychologist may be involved with an issue which does not primarily relate to identified patients, but affects the health care system as a whole. For example, many of the women who may potentially benefit most from advice on caring for their newborn baby find it difficult to understand some of the relatively sophisticated literature put out both by commercial firms and Government agencies. How can health literature be designed to maximize recall of its contents, and application of the recommended procedures? Many hospital staff may have to deal with extremely aggressive people from time to time, even though most of the time their work is routine and even dull. How can non-clinical staff such as laboratory technicians and secretaries be given some guidance or training in how to cope with this sort of infrequent event? In this third category of task, the psychologist is understanding and trying to change aspects of the health care system itself, or the way in which care is delivered, independent of the needs of individual patients.

A psychologist may respond to this array of problems in a number of ways. Firstly, by attempting to understand and define the problem as clearly as possible, perhaps making use of standardized psychological measures. Secondly, by intervening in the problem, with the specific intention of changing the problem in some specified ways. Thirdly, by evaluating what has been done to change the problem. Most of what clinical psychologists do is covered by these three categories of assessment, intervention, and evaluation. There are a number of other functions a psychologist may carry out; one of these major functions is to train or supervise others in the understanding and use of psychological methods, and this is covered in particular in Chapter 10, concerning work with other professions.

ASSESSING AND UNDERSTANDING PEOPLE

Probably one of the most common stereotypes of the psychologist is as 'tester'. Ever since Binet became interested in the attainments of Parisian schoolchildren before the First World War, formal psychometric testing of general ability, specific abilities, and of educational and occupational attainments has been viewed as one of the central professional tasks of a psychologist. Yet this attempt to assess the *maximum* performance of individuals, on apparently rather artificial tasks, is only one aspect of the modern psychologist's contribution to assessment.

Testing is indeed an important type of assessment. Educational tests for children have come to be widely used both to see if there are any discrepancies between ability and educational attainment, and to predict the probable level of attainment of a child. Most ability or attainments tests for children and adults consist of a number of sub-tests, with all items carefully selected, arranged in order of successively greater difficulty, and with information painstakingly obtained on many hundreds of subjects for comparison.

Another major group of assessment procedures are those known as personality tests, which fall into two main subgroups. The first subgroup of personality measures are the 'projective' techniques. These all rest on the assumption that when an individual makes a response to a stimulus that is essentially ambiguous or unstructured, the detail and structure elicited tell us something about the individual's inner structure, or personality. These tests have continued to have a place in the hands of skilled practitioners : an example of such measures is the Thematic Apperception Test (TAT) cards. Second is the subgroup of 'objective' personality measures, which take the form of questionnaires completed by the patient. These questionnaires contain up to several hundred items covering different areas of functioning, such as getting on with other people or the tendency to dominate or be submissive to others. Some of the major work on these questionnaires has been done by personality theorists such as Cattell and Eysenck, who have thus given their name to some personality inventories. Some other related measures are not strictly personality tests, but give a clearer idea of how an individual views himself : the personality theory of George Kelly for example, has given rise to the 'Repertory Grid', a method of exploring an individual's view of his own world that can be represented graphically.

With both ability tests and personality tests, the psychologist's job is to administer the test on a one-to-one or group basis, carefully following the standard procedure. Many tests have 'norms' available, so that the performance of any individual can be compared with others. By contrast, some assessments are not 'norm-referenced' at all, but assess individuals against an explicit criterion of everyday performance. Criterion-referenced assessments of this type are very helpful in gauging the progress of the individual, when knowledge about other people is irrelevant.

Apart from questionnaires used to assess personality in a global sense, many specific questionnaires are available, looking at tendencies such as conservatism, and at psychiatric or psycho-pathological dimensions such as depression. A wide range of checklists and rating scales exists, again mostly related to specific conditions or problems, and often completed by someone who knows the patient well, such as a family member. For example, there are several rating scales for use with mentally handicapped people which are completed by a nurse or care worker on the ward or hostel where the person lives. These typically have carefully graded items, so that an action such as 'doing up buttons' itself consists of several stages viz. 'opposes button-hole to button' and 'inserts button into hole'. A psychologist will often be involved in training and supervising nurses and others in the use of this type of scale.

Another last category of assessment instruments consists of behavioural methods. These make use of direct observation of behaviour, often in a 'natural' setting, without the necessity of the patient even being aware that he is being assessed. They yield measures of the exact frequency or length of time of a piece of behaviour, such as an outburst of aggression, and may require the psychologist to be physically present in a ward or home for several hours. Physiological measures are not strictly behavioural measures, but have the same characteristic of producing a numerical index of functioning, relating to such physiological parameters as heart rate, blood flow, or skin resistance.

Psychological assessment instruments need to fulfil several different requirements. Most important of all, they should contribute unique information which will be helpful to the people intimately concerned with the care and treatment of patients. They need to be acceptable to the people who use them: not too complex in administration and scoring for the test user, nor too threatening or demanding for the subject. Additionally, they should be psychometrically sound. This means that they should conform to technical standards of validity and reliability. The validity of a measure is the extent to which it measures what it says it measures. This means that the content of, for example, a reading test should be made up of words that are a reasonable sample of the sort of words that children of a particular country or locality use in practice. Validity is also evaluated by examining the relationship between the measure in question, and another measure of the attribute. Thus one index of the validity of a measure of depression would be the relative proportion of high scorers who present for treatment of depression, compared to the proportion of high scorers who do *not* present. Reliability is the extent to which a measure gives similar results under differing conditions of use. The administrator of a test or check-list may give it in slightly different ways, or pay attention to different characteristics of the patient's behaviour, so that different testers or raters give slightly different results. The similarity of results across two different sets of raters then gives an index of inter-rater reliability. The other important form of reliability is test–retest, or repeat reliability, indicating the similarity of results across two different occasions.

Clinical psychologists are shifting their interest in assessment from general measures of ability and personality to more specific measures of opinion, self-report, and behaviour that are more directly related to the patient's clinical problems and to their care and management. A comprehensive series of chapters on different aspects of assessment theory and practice is included in Mittler (1970) and Table 1.4 illustrates the major categories of assessment method that have just been outlined.

INTERVENING IN PEOPLE'S LIVES

Clinical psychologists were not originally seen primarily as treaters, but were used mainly as assessors. Partly in reaction to this 'test-basher' role, and partly because of the encouraging results of the first attempts to intervene in patients' lives with methods derived explicitly from psychological theory, the role of psychologist as therapist has developed rapidly over the last 20 years. Before this point only a small number of psychologists, mostly those practising as psychoanalysts or those working with children, spent the majority of their time in treatment. Since then, a range of psychological therapeutic methods have been introduced. A few, such as aversion therapy, have not been widely adopted, but many have been refined to such an extent that they have become the treatment of choice for some conditions.

Quite apart from those therapeutic techniques derived from psychodynamic, behavioural, or other theories, most encounters

Table 1.4 Major categories of psychological assessment

1. Self-description. Refers to those measures where the subject describes his own current feelings and behaviour, either in an open-ended way (as in interviews) or in a forced-choice way (as in personality questionnaires).

Example: personality questionnaire items.

Do you sometimes feel lonely?	Yes	No	Unsure
Are you easily upset when people criticize you?	Yes	No	Unsure

2. Ratings or judgments by others. Where a person other than the subject describes the subject's current emotions or behaviour, again either in an open-ended way or in a structured way (as in a standardized rating scale or checklist)

Example: A checklist item

Prepared for checking the early morning routine of mentally handicapped people in a hostel, and requiring the observer to tick each item if that act has been performed.

wakes up when alarm rings
get out of bed (feet outside bedclothes) within 10 min of alarm
washes unprompted before breakfast
toilets unprompted before breakfast
chooses appropriate clothes unaided
dresses unaided
goes to dining room unprompted

3. Life-History. Refers to the recording of *past* factual information about the subject, from whatever source, such as details of education, and of occupation.

4. Simulated real-life measurement. The subject is asked to demonstrate, or rehearse in practice, what is requested, in as real a way as possible.

Example: role-played test of social skills

5. Physiological. Refers to measures directly monitoring physiological functions of the subject's body, such as heartrate or rate of sweating, by electronic sensors attached directly to the skin surface.

Example: EEG (electro-encephalogram) and EMG (electromyogram)

6. Performance tests. This category includes the classic concept of the 'test', and includes all assessment methods where the subject is asked to complete intellectual tasks by use of standard questions.

Example: cognitive or ability test items

Pick out the word in the list below that does not go with the others
Brig   Yacht   Steamer   Schooner
Write in the next two numbers in this series
3   6   14   27   45   . . .   . . .

with patients involve the use of general therapeutic skills. These enable the patient to feel relaxed, to have confidence in his therapist, and to be able to recount events, experiences, and relationships which may normally make him feel embarrassed or stigmatized. Psychologists have examined the major attributes of the 'good' counsellor or therapist in constructing this basic therapeutic relationship, and drawn attention to the three key attributes of 'positive regard'—valuing the patient as an individual—'accurate empathy'—understanding the reality of the patient's experiences — and genuineness. A proportion of patients referred to psychologists — or indeed psychiatrists—may require nothing beyond counselling at this level, and correspondingly a psychologist may usefully spend some of his time training both professional staff, such as health visitors or community psychiatric nurses, and volunteers, such as Samaritan members, in these counselling methods.

Those clinical psychologists who spend most of their time in psychotherapeutic work will probably enter advanced training with one of the established psychotherapy organizations, such as the Institute of Group Analysis. Their clinical work may then be defined more by the nature of their therapeutic training and interests than by their initial training as a clinical psychologist. Psychotherapeutic approaches derive from the seminal work of Sigmund Freud, from the modifications to his theories of his early associates and later defectors such as Jung and Adler, and from later and contemporary workers such as Melanie Klein and Freud's own daughter, Anna Freud.

The therapeutic procedures which are most characteristic of clinical psychologists are those generally known as behavioural methods. Behavioural methods of treatment require a psychologist first to engage in a behavioural analysis of the problem. A behavioural analysis, or 'functional analysis of behaviour', involves looking at the central problem, or 'Behaviour', in the light of its 'Antecedents'—those prior events or determinants such as time of day or place in the room where the behaviour occurs—and in the light of the 'Consequences'—those events following the occurrence of the behaviour in the actual environment. Antecedents–Behaviour–Consequence (ABC) analysis is a defining characteristic of the behavioural approach, and has similarities with the Nursing Process, the influential goal-oriented model of nursing which is changing practice in many fields of nursing. Detailed examples of behavioural methods of treatment with adults are given in Chapter 2.

Apart from behavioural methods of treatment, there are a number of other treatment methods that are based on psychological concepts. As physiological measurement techniques have become more reliable, and can now be used without any direct wiring between patient and recording apparatus, so they can be used to provide the patient with immediate feedback of his own physiological response, contributing to the development of those treatment procedures collectively known as biofeedback techniques. Other treatment methods have been based on theories of memory, or on notions of the rational expression of emotion. For example, a prize-winning book by Rowe (1983) describes a psychological approach to the understanding and treatment of depression. The book draws on a wide range of concepts and models, but is very much informed by a personal-construct theory approach to understanding depression, followed by a cognitive theory guiding approaches to treatment. An example of the use of mixed approaches to both assessment and intervention is given by the case of Mrs Adams.

PSYCHOLOGICAL APPROACHES TO AN INDIVIDUAL PATIENT

Mrs Adams is a 46-year-old married woman, employed as an assistant in the technical library of a major industrial concern, who has had contacts with three different clinical psychologists over a 16-year period. Her case illustrates the changing role of the clinical psychologist over this period, the use and some limitations of standard assessment techniques, and the appropriateness of psychological treatment techniques.

Mrs Adams had failed to achieve well academically. Although she did well at school when younger, she scraped through her A levels and failed a degree-level qualification. While a child she had been seen for a year or so at a child guidance clinic, but her life was more seriously affected by the sudden onset of diabetes at the age of 23. Her diabetes has been well controlled since then, although she has had hypoglycaemic episodes which have contributed to her persistent complaints that she is deteriorating mentally. Over the years she has had continuing contacts with physicians and with psychiatrists. She feels intellectually superior to her colleagues at work including those who have obtained degrees, and constantly ruminates about the psychological implications of her diabetes. Her first contact with a clinical psychologist occurred at the age of 30, when a psychiatrist referred her to see if there was any evidence of diffuse brain damage. The psychologist reported a Verbal IQ of 141 and a Performance IQ of 110 and on the basis of other additional testing found no evidence of deterioration, but made no recommendations about treatment. Thirteen years later she was seen on referral from another psychiatrist by a second psychologist who repeated the same testing, obtaining a Verbal IQ of 144 and a Performance IQ of 106 and also gave some standard memory tests. The psychologist on this occasion discussed with Mrs Adams' ways of concentrating on her successes at remembering things, not her failures, and some guidelines on improving her memory were discussed. The psychiatrist also referred her at this period to a psychotherapist. The psychotherapist felt she would benefit from psychotherapy especially in view of her difficulty in maintaining adult relationships with others, but Mrs Adams did not take up this offer.

The third contact arose three years after the second on referral from a physician who was seeing Mrs Adams for her diabetes, who was concerned both to reassure her yet again about her mental state, and about Mrs Adams' meticulous ways of coping with her job. Since Mrs Adams had already completed some of the standard tests twice, these were not presented again as complete tests, but some of the sub-tests from them were repeated, imbedded in other new specific tests of memory function. Yet again, there was no evidence of deterioration, indeed some of the sub-tests showed remarkable consistency over the 16-year period, and Mrs Adams scored at a level equivalent to the top 10 per cent of mature students of her age. Since she continued to complain about the difficulties she was having at work, some time was spent with her, following the recommendations of Powell's (1981) text on 'Brain Function Therapy'. This gave her some specific strategies for coping with her alleged memory problems. In addition, some time was spent with Mrs Adams examining the effect that her hypochondriacal beliefs about the consequences of her diabetes was having on the relationship with her colleagues at work, and with her spouse. Although she continued to reject the possibility of psychotherapeutic help, there was some evidence that Mrs Adams was not so preoccupied with everyday lapses of memory, and had limited the expression of her ruminative thoughts so that people around her were behaving more positively towards her.

Many psychological techniques can be used with individuals or with groups. Controlled studies have shown that group application of some procedures, with carefully selected patients, can make more effective use of psychologists' time than seeing patients individually. The psychologist's task may then involve interviewing and assessing the patients, and supervising the conduct of the group. Many of these techniques can be used by the family member or prime carer looking after the patient, without the psychologist needing to intervene directly with the patient. This may be more time-consuming than seeing patients directly face-to-face, but can create a more skilled parent or nurse, who can then use the principles and procedures they have learned at other times and with other patients.

HOW TO EVALUATE PSYCHOLOGICAL PRACTICE

There is no point in using psychological methods of treatment if they do not work. There are many examples of well-established therapeutic procedures being shown, on formal evaluation, to be of little or no value. Two of the most instructive examples for clinical psychologists working in the psychiatric field are insulin coma therapy, where a 20-year period elapsed between the introduction of the method and the final controlled outcome study, and pre-frontal leucotomy, where an adequately controlled trial was never carried out. Psychological methods do not have the risk of irreversible side-effects of these two examples, but they may have some side-effects, and certainly their effectiveness should be established.

A common first step in evaluation is to show that the treatment under question is better than the routine treatment available as an alternative, or at least better than doing nothing. After that, evaluation usually takes the form of 'unpacking' the treatment package which is involved in all psychological procedures. For example, one approach to the treatment of chronic psychiatric patients involves a 'token economy', when the patient is given a token immediately after performing some desirable act. This token can then be spent on 'goodies', such as sweets, tobacco, or a magazine. However, observation of the moment when the token is given to the patient indicates that other things are going on at the same time. The patient is often praised verbally ('well done') and perhaps physically (a hand on the shoulder), informational feedback may be given ('you have got the token because . . .'), and the patient has an individual social encounter in the midst of an otherwise solitary day. Which of these events is the key therapeutic ingredient?.

The example of evaluation of a token economy focuses on looking at the outcome of individuals or groups who have completed that treatment. However, there are other outcome criteria that can be used to evaluate the effectiveness of a treatment, such as the amount of resources that have to be devoted to a patient to achieve a given outcome. For example, if treatment A produced a given level of therapeutic response after 10 h of professional time, then it would be more efficient than treatment B if the latter required 20 h of professional time for the same level of response.

Even when resources are adequate, it is important to find out whether particular procedures are effective. In times of stringency, it is even more important to be able to show that a treatment regime meets stated objectives. Fig. 1.2 presents a model of a health-care programme (from Holland 1983), and indicates the possibility of two types of evaluation of the programme. Process evaluation compares the proposed objectives and activities of a programme with the objectives and activities that are actually implemented and accomplished: it presupposes an operational plan of a programme, and makes it possible to pick up flaws in a programme before it has been completed. Outcome evaluation, on the other hand, is more difficult to perform than process evaluation, because there are often different levels of outcome, such as the patient's use of a treatment, or the impact of change in the patient upon the caring family. The

Fig. 1.2 A model of health care evaluation.

particular contribution of psychologists to health care evaluation is twofold. Firstly, by translating overall service objectives into operational objectives, and secondly, by devising measures that may need to be used by relatively unsophisticated staff.

KEY PROFESSIONAL ISSUES

As a relatively recent health care profession, clinical psychology has had to find its own niche amidst the array of doctors, nurses, remedial therapists, social workers, and other workers helping people with medical and personal problems. Different countries have imposed different constraints upon the development of the profession, so that, for example, in France only doctors can practice psychotherapy, and in Britain patients seen by psychologists in the NHS normally have to be referred by a family doctor or other medical practitioner. Other professions are understandably concerned to know how clinical psychology fits into the health care system, and what assumptions they may make about this new professional group. There are three main issues which probably require some explanation at the outset.

Professional independence

Most health care professions have emerged and developed largely as the consequence of doctors identifying a practical task which needs to be performed, but which does not require a medical training to perform it. Bit by bit, these professions have become more independent of medical supervision, as indicated in Britain, for example, by doctors no longer acting as examiners of professional competence for nurses. Nonetheless, there may still remain an argument that doctors possess an encompassing knowledge of other professions. By contrast, some of the newer health care professions owe their development to scientific disciplines which cannot be said to be encompassed by medicine. Speech Therapy and Medical Physics are examples of such professions. Like clinical psychology they may owe part of their development to pressure and interest from medical colleagues, but those colleagues cannot claim an encompassing knowledge of the procedures used.

Another criterion of professional independence is the existence of a standard of training and clinical competence which permits independence of action. For most European countries the period of clinical experience required for qualification as a clinical psychologist is comparable to the clinical experience required of medical students, and similarly follows a degree-level preclinical qualification, suggesting that individuals entering clinical psychology are as likely to be able to practise independently as medically qualified people.

The expressed aspiration of a profession to achieve independence may not, of course, be consistent with the wishes of other colleagues, who far from wanting independence want close co-operation. In some forms of clinical practice, most notably perhaps child psychiatry, teamwork has been highly valued, so that team members value loyalty and commitment to their teams above commitment to members of their own professions. Co-operation with other colleagues is an essential part of the professional commitment of clinical psychologists, although the exact way in which this is worked out locally and in particular circumstances may need close examination.

Responsibility of clinical psychologists

In many health care professions, responsibility is closely bound up with the legal registration of the profession. In many countries the major health care professions have some form of registration procedure, which essentially prescribes minimum standards of training and competence, which may protect titles or functions of that profession, and which ultimately may lead to members of the profession being 'struck off' if they fail to meet standards of professional competence. For example, all the constituent states of Australia have a requirement for legal registration of clinical psychologists. Apart from this form of legal responsibility, every practitioner also owes a legal duty of care towards the patients he sees. Quite apart from the specific implications of any registration procedure, an aggrieved patient may have recourse through the courts of law to correct alleged negligence or harm resulting from bad treatment. Professional bodies may also impose their own standards upon practitioners, independent of the standards imposed by courts.

It is consistent with a model of an independent profession to say that the psychologist's first responsibility is to his patient. The patient's needs and wishes should, from this point of view, dictate the psychologist's actions. On the other hand, when a psychologist is employed by a public agency there is no doubt that the policies of that agency may affect how a clinical service is delivered. The question of who is paying—whether patient or employer—alters basic assumptions about responsibility, and indeed in some schools of thought is believed to be an important component of the therapeutic relationship.

There is some ambivalence among British clinical psychologists about the advantages of becoming a fully fledged 'profession' with all the trappings of registration and defined responsibilities. Sensible of the evidence that professionalization may benefit the profession rather than the client, psychologists have hesitated before plunging along this path. In Britain this hesitation has been supported by the fact that the major professional body for psychologists, the British Psychological Society, was originally a learned society. It still functions as a learned society so that views of academic psychologists, and of applied psychologists who do not work in health care, have equal weight with those of clinical psychologists. The resulting caution in pursuing registration of applied psychologists may thus result in a procedure that offers genuine protection to the public, without undue protection of the profession. In Britain this has led the British Psychological Society to set in train a process whereby psychologists can become chartered and a register of Chartered Psychologists can be formed.

The role of clinical psychology in the health care system

Most developed countries attempt some overall planning of health care. The separation of primary from secondary health care is vague in some European countries, so that in Belgium, as in other countries, the family doctor or general practitioner may often also practice as a specialist in a particular branch of medicine. In Britain there is a very clear separation between 'primary' services, and the specialized 'secondary' services, which has a marked effect on the work done by clinical psychologists.

Health care systems differ considerably in the extent to which there is central planning and funding of resources, the degree of choice available to the public, and the proportion of care provided by private or voluntary agencies. In practice, most Western countries have a degree of state control, via funding, of the majority of specialized health care facilities, so that, for example, in the Republic of Ireland services to mentally handicapped people are predominantly provided by religious orders, but are Government funded. The increase of 'socialized medicine' has had an important consequence, in that it has encouraged the planning of health care services on a population basis. If the size, age distribution, and morbidity of a population is known, then health facilities can be planned on some sort of rational plan. If, however, private practice develops in an uncoordinated way and forms a major component of the overall service, it is difficult to plan in this way.

As preventive medicine has been effective, and as antibiotics, corrective surgery in children, and better care of the aged have developed, so the health problems presented in the population have changed. As health care moves to a more preventive role, so issues of compliance with advice, and personal 'health care routines'—essentially psychological issues—will become more important. As a population ages and contains more people with chronic handicaps which no longer respond to medical intervention, so the emphasis of health care will need to change to emphasize coping with disability. It seems that further improvement in the health of a population will rely as much on change of lifestyle as on the ministrations of high technology medicine.

The role of clinical psychology in a health care system is thus determined by a number of factors. The capacity of clinical psychologists to contribute independently and responsibly is one major factor. The availability of psychological knowledge along the 'primary care'–'specialist' dimension further influences the number and nature of the problems seen, and by implication the demand for psychologists. The capacity of a health care system to identify need and to plan provision also implies planning the type and numbers of staff to make that provision. At present, there are growing expectations of clinical psychologists that they will be able to contribute to several points of the system. This book describes both what they are doing at present, and what developments lie ahead.

REFERENCES

Department of Health and Social Security (1977). *The role of psychologists in the health service* (Chairman : Professor W. H. Trethowan). HMSO, London.

Fichter, M. M. and Wittchen, H. U. (1980). Clinical psychology and psychotherapy. A survey of the present state of professionalization in 23 countries. *Am. Psychol.* 35, 16–25.

Holland, W. W. (1983). *Evaluation of health care.* Oxford University Press, Oxford.

Hundleby, J. (1973). The measurement of personality by objective tests. In *New approaches to psychological measurement.* (ed. P. Kline). Wiley, London.

Kendall, D. C. and Norton-Ford, J. D. (1982). See 'Further reading'.

Melzack, R. and Wall, P. (1982). *The challenge of pain.* Penguin, Harmondsworth.

Mittler, P., ed. (1970). *The psychological assessment of mental and physical handicaps.* Tavistock, London.

Powell, G. E. (1981). *Brain function therapy.* Gower Publishing, Aldershot.

Rowe, D. (1983). *Depression. The way out of your prison.* Routledge and Kegan Paul, London.

FURTHER READING

Kendall, P. C. and Norton-Ford, J. D. (1982). *Clinical psychology. Scientific and professional dimensions.* Wiley, New York.

Liddell, A. ed. (1983). *The practice of clinical psychology in Great Britain.* Wiley, London.

Winefield, H. R. and Peay, M. Y. (1980). *Behavioural science in medicine.* George Allen and Unwin, Beaconsfield.

2

The psychological treatment of adults

John Marzillier

All clinical psychologists work to some extent with adults. Some provide a direct service to adult patients in the form of psychological assessment and treatment. Others work indirectly with adults as, for example, those who work with children will also work closely with parents, teachers and other professional staff. This chapter describes the therapeutic work of clinical psychologists concentrating on the services that they provide to adult out-patients. The therapeutic work carried out by psychologists in psychiatric hospitals (in-patient work) is described separately in Chapter 3, and their role in general medicine is the subject of a further chapter (Chapter 9).

Psychological treatments take many forms and are characterized by various labels (e.g. psychotherapy, behaviour therapy, psychoanalysis etc.). There are many different 'schools' of psychotherapy and practitioners differ in their allegiance to a particular theory as well as in their methods of treatment. Clinical psychologists have, on the whole, practised the briefer and more pragmatic types of treatment such as the cognitive and behavioural therapies and these methods are described in detail in the main section of this chapter. But some will also have received specialist training in other forms of psychotherapy, notably psychodynamic psychotherapy. Illustrations of the various therapeutic approaches are provided in the main body of the chapter.

THE SETTING

Clinical psychologists will most commonly see patients for treatment in some form of clinic. The site of the clinic will vary depending on the nature of the service as a whole. In Britain, for example, where clinical psychology has had a close historical association with psychiatry, many clinics are attached to psychiatric hospitals. But clinics may be set up elsewhere, such as University psychology departments, general practices, community mental health centres, or even over shop fronts in city centres. Where a private health service flourishes, as in the USA, psychologists will set up their clinics alongside other professions and indeed compete for customers.

The word 'clinic' is used to describe the service, although its medical connotations sometimes make it an unpopular term. But in practice most clinical psychologists act like their medical colleagues. Patients are referred by others, most commonly the family doctor or a psychiatrist, are sent appointments, attend at a centre with a receptionist and a waiting area, and are usually given a fixed series of appointments until the 'treatment' has been completed. The 'clinic' approach so described is not however the only way for psychologists to provide a treatment service. But it is undoubtedly the commonest approach and is therefore the one people (other professionals or potential patients) are most likely to encounter.

COMMON PSYCHOLOGICAL PROBLEMS

Clinical psychologists vary in the problems they treat and the types of treatments they provide. This variation arises partly from the differing theoretical orientation and experience of the psychologists, and partly from the different demands placed upon them in different settings. Some psychologists spend the bulk of their time in treating out-patients with emotional problems such as anxiety and depression. Others concentrate on applying their skills to the rehabilitation of chronic psychiatric patients in hospital. A few develop specialist therapeutic skills, usually as a result of further training courses in psychotherapy, or specialize in treating certain populations. Table 2.1 lists the problems for which psychological help is commonly sought.

This is not a recognized system of classification since none exists, but simply a means of identifying and labelling common psychological problems. There is inevitably overlap between categories. For example, a person with a psychosexual problem may also be depressed and experiencing marital difficulties. An alcoholic may

Table 2.1 Common psychological problems seen by clinical psychologists for psychological treatment

I.	*Emotional problems*
	1. Fears and phobias
	2. Generalized anxiety
	3. Obsessions and compulsions
	4. Depression
	5. Other emotional disturbance, e.g. anger, guilt
II.	*Addictions and habit problems*
	1. Alcoholism and problem drinking
	2. Drug addiction
	3. Eating problems, e.g. anorexia, bulimia, obesity
	4. Miscellaneous, e.g. smoking, stuttering, gambling, tics
III.	*Psychosexual problems*
	1. Sexual dysfunction, e.g. impotence, vaginismus
	2. Problems of sexual orientation
IV.	*Social and interpersonal problems*
	1. Loneliness, shyness, and social isolation
	2. Aggressive and antisocial behaviour
	3. Marital conflict
V.	*Psychomatic and medical* (described in Chapter 9)
	1. 'Psychosomatic disorders', e.g. asthma, headache
	2. Cardiovascular disorders, e.g. hypertension, coronary heart disease
	3. Pain
	4. Chronic, physical illness

behave aggressively towards his family and friends. The labels used in Table 2.1 are simply convenient means for the patient or the referring professional to identify the major problem for which help is sought. It is part of the job of the clinical psychologist to assess the case in greater depth to establish the nature of the problem and whether treatment can be provided. An example of how clinical psychologists practise psychological treatment is given in the case of Catherine and Henry. In this first case the process of assessment and treatment has been deliberately simplified in order to highlight the basic procedures and principles.

THE TREATMENT OF A MARRIED COUPLE WITH SEXUAL PROBLEMS

Catherine and Henry are a married couple in their early 30s with two children of school age. Henry approached his local GP complaining of impotence and lack of sexual satisfaction in his marriage. The GP suggested that he might benefit from seeing a specialist in the treatment of sexual problems and referred him to a psychosexual clinic run in a local Clinical Psychology Department. As is the normal practice of the clinic Henry and Catherine were both invited to attend the clinic for an initial assessment interview with a view to beginning a course of treatment.

In the initial interview the couple are seen together in the first instance. The problem that they present is one of impotence on Henry's part with the consequent breakdown of their sexual relationship. The first part of the interview is taken up with an account of the sexual problem, its origin, its nature and how it affects their relationship. Some background information is also sought concerning their work, way of life, their children, their social activities etc. Then Catherine and Henry are seen separately for a detailed interview of their sexual history and to explore their attitudes and feelings about the marriage. Each also fills in a questionnaire on their marital and sexual relationship. Finally, the couple are seen together again for a further discussion which focuses on possible treatments and their expectations concerning therapy. An agreement is reached that they will go away and talk together about the problem and the possibilities for treatment. A brief hand-out concerning psychosexual problems and their treatment is given to them to take away and read. Advice is given to refrain from sexual relations for the time being. Another appointment is made in a week's time at which time a final decision on treatment will be made.

The next appointment begins with a general discussion arising out of their reactions to the first interview, the information in the hand-out and the talk they had between interviews. Catherine and Henry are eager to go ahead with treatment and the psychologist spends some time describing what would be involved both in terms of specific treatment procedures and the general requirements of therapy. It is explained that the treatment is based upon the work of the American researchers Masters and Johnston and in essence entails the re-learning of their sexual relationship with the help of specific psychological procedures (see Hawton 1985). The possibility that Henry's impotence is caused by performance anxiety is raised and that a gradual and undemanding programme of resuming sexual activity is a way of overcoming anxiety, allowing potency to return. The first of a series of practical exercises is presented to them and they are asked to implement the exercise at home. Appointments are made on a weekly basis with the possibility of telephone contact between sessions if necessary. At first treatment progresses reasonably smoothly and Catherine and Henry gradually increase the intimacy of their sexual contact. However, Henry still has difficulty in maintaining potency and, after further discussions, is given some training in relaxation and advised not to be concerned with potency or sexual arousal, but to concentrate on remaining relaxed and on enjoying the intimacy of sexual contact. This results in successful sexual intercourse, the first time for many months, and leads to increased optimism and confidence on their part. Further satisfactory progress is made over the next few treatment sessions until treatment is formally ended after 12 weekly sessions. Catherine and Henry are seen for a final assessment and given a follow-up appointment in three months time.

BASIC PRINCIPLES OF PSYCHOLOGICAL ASSESSMENT AND TREATMENT

The case of Catherine and Henry is a hypothetical case used to illustrate how psychological treatment can operate in an uncomplicated fashion. Few cases are perhaps as straightforward as this, but the basic principles are the same. Treatment is always preceded by a period of assessment whose prime purpose is to gather information concerning the nature of the problem so that the psychologist may arrive at an informed decision about treatment. The initial assessment also allows the patients and the psychologist to get to know each other and establish a relationship of mutual trust and confidence without which treatment is unlikely to succeed. The decision on treatment should be a mutual one and therefore the patients must be informed about what the treatment involves and its likelihood of success. The active involvement of the patient in therapy is also something of importance as treatment is regarded as a co-operative venture in which therapist and patient work together to achieve change. Treatment takes place over regular weekly out-patient sessions, although this will vary according to the type of problem treated. Some cases need to be seen intensively at first and others require a period of in-patient treatment. In some cases patients may be seen in groups and in others the psychologist works closely with other professionals, e.g. doctors, nurses, health visitors, social workers. Finally, the effects of treatment are monitored by regular assessments and a final evaluation of the extent of improvement. Patients are often given one or more follow-up appointments to assess whether improvement is maintained.

Psychological treatment is not always as straightforward as this example suggests. For example, it is not always possible to define psychological problems simply or to use well-established treatment methods. An important part of psychological treatment is working with the patient to establish what exactly the problem is and working out an individually tailored way of treating it. In the hypothetical example, Henry's impotence could have been an expression of more fundamental marital difficulties and, if that were the case, the psychologist would need to shift his or her attention to that problem and consider whether he or she could provide help to resolve it. Psychologists differ too in how they conceptualize psychological problems, and this affects what treatment is offered. To some psychologists impotence may suggest unconscious conflicts about one's own sexuality, and treatment will be concerned with exploring such conflict in an attempt to make it conscious and resolve it.

The case of Catherine and Henry can be seen as an example of behaviour therapy. This is a school of therapy which developed in the 1960s out of experimental studies of psychological principles in the laboratory, principles of learning in particular. The basic tenet of behaviour therapy is that emotional and other problems are learned and that by applying learning principles to their problems patients can learn to resolve them.

Behavioural treatments tend to be brief, a few weeks or months at the most, and can in some instances be as short as four to six sessions. Their aim is to help the patient change his or her problem behaviour directly rather than explore its possible meaning. Although a good therapeutic relationship can be important in behaviour therapy it is not regarded as essential or as the main vehicle of change. The approach is best described as an educational and problem-solving one with the therapist using his or her specialist knowledge to guide the patient towards a solution to his problems. Another characteristic of the behavioural approach is the emphasis on the systematic assessment of change using scientifically derived assessment measures and carefully evaluated techniques. The following sections illustrate some applications of the behavioural approach.

THE BEHAVIOURAL TREATMENT OF ANXIETY PROBLEMS

Anxiety is commonly defined by subjective feelings of distress, often persistent and intense, in which there is a dread or apprehension about some unpleasant and uncertain future occurrence. There is little doubt that anxiety is in itself a normal experience which all of us encounter from time to time. The prospect of difficult examinations, a visit to the dentist, the vicissitudes of a difficult personal relationship, having to make a speech at a formal reception, are all examples where the experience of anxiety would be quite expected. In clinical practice, anxious patients seek help if their feelings of anxiety are so persistent and intense that they interfere with their daily lives or if they experience the sensations of anxiety without fully understanding what they are or why they occur.

Laboratory studies of the acquisition and treatment of fear have shown that fears can be acquired as a result of conditioning and that they can be removed by deconditioning. Deconditioning, or desensitization as the clinical method is known, involves two processes of change: a graduated approach to the feared object or situation, and the inhibition of the emotional state of anxiety by relaxation or a similar emotional state that is directly contrary to anxiety. These principles have been successfully applied in the clinical treatment of fears and anxiety as the case of Jean illustrates.

THE BEHAVIOURAL TREATMENT OF AN AGORAPHOBIC WOMAN

Jean is a 33-year-old married woman with a young son of 7 years old. She is neatly dressed, pleasant-mannered and articulate, but rather reticent and soft-spoken. She complains of a fear of leaving her home on her own and of crowded places such as supermarkets in particular. Even at home on her own she experiences 'panics' and has to ring her husband frequently for support and help. She has very few friends and very little social life except for her mother, who she tends to see most days. She can recall having experienced her fear and panic for several years and has sought help now because she worries that her son may be experiencing similar anxieties; he has reported feeling nervous at school and on occasions has been reluctant to go.

Jean has a problem that is commonly called 'agoraphobia', which literally means (from the Greek) a fear of the market-place. The main characteristics of agoraphobia are: (1) fear about leaving home or any place of safety on one's own; (2) a fear of crowded places; (3) a 'fear of fear' itself; and (4) avoidance of confined places, where escape is difficult. In this instance behavioural treatment consists of: (a) a systematic programme of increasing exposure to the situations that provoke fear and anxiety; (b) teaching Jean to become more confident in her ability to manage difficult situations on her own, i.e. restoring her confidence in herself.

In the first two sessions Jean and her therapist drew up a list of the most anxiety provoking situations and worked out a graded programme of 25 steps ranging from '(1) Opening the door of her house and standing alone on the doorstep for 30 seconds' to '(25) Travelling by bus to the centre of town on a Saturday afternoon and visiting a supermarket.' Jean was also taught progressive muscular relaxation and given a rationale to the effect that her fear of going out had been acquired as a result of the panic that she had first experienced and was now being maintained mainly by her 'fear of fear', i.e. the panic recurring. Successful treatment entailed her regaining confidence in her ability to be out on her own and to cope with symptoms of anxiety and panic.

There are two possible strategies that the therapist and Jean could adopt at this point. The first is the graduated approach whereby the easiest situation in the hierarchy is tackled first until Jean can master it without undue anxiety. This may be done first in imagination and then in reality. Once Jean is confident in this situation, she progresses to the next, each time using relaxation to combat her feelings of anxiety. And so on until each situation in the hierarchy is successfully tackled. This method is known as 'systematic desensitization'.

The other method, known as 'flooding', entails tackling the most difficult situation first and persisting in it until Jean's anxiety decreases, a procedure which may take several hours. In Jean's case this meant visiting a crowded supermarket on a Saturday afternoon and spending the whole afternoon in the supermarket, resisting the urge to escape even if anxiety became intense. Although this is an unpleasant procedure, it can have a rapid and dramatic beneficial effect. In Jean's case, she realized that none of the awful things she feared actually happened, and her anxiety feelings eventually diminished so much so that she was able to do her weekly shopping. The therapist and Jean repeated the treatment a couple of times and each time it proved much easier for Jean. She was encouraged to tackle less difficult situations on her own and thereby began the process of successfully counteracting her agoraphobia.

Jean's success in the behavioural programme helped to counteract her worries about possible catastrophe since she could see how her 'panicky' symptoms were due to anxiety and that she could manage them herself. In addition, on the advice of the therapist she joined an assertiveness training group, in which she and other patients discussed and practised ways of being more assertive, i.e. standing up for themselves and taking an independent line. The group boosted Jean's confidence further and enabled her to deal more effectively with the demands of her family, her mother in particular. At the end of her treatment, she had not only become confident enough to go out alone but had also become a more outspoken and confident person who, as she put it, had learned that she was not there 'just to make up the numbers'.

Jean's case illustrates the way in which behavioural principles can be used in a practical and effective way to reduce anxiety and restore confidence. Many agoraphobic patients have been helped by behaviour therapy and research studies have confirmed the value of this approach (Mathews, Gelder, and Johnston 1981). Behavioural methods have also been used in the treatment of other phobic and anxiety problems. Obsessional disorders are a good example.

Obsessional–compulsive disorders

Obsessional–compulsive disorders are characterized by the dual components of obsessions and compulsions. Obsessions are recurring, repetitive thoughts, images or impulses which are experienced by the patient as intrusive, unwanted, and often abhorrent and senseless. They are often thoughts or images about doing harm or harm being done to other people. One woman, for example, was beset with the image of stabbing her daughter through the heart with a knife. Occasionally, meaningless, repetitive, phrases are experienced (e.g. 'Put jam on it'). The intrusiveness and the unpleasant content of the obsessions cause considerable distress and anxiety.

Compulsions are stereotyped, repetitive behaviour, often ritualistic, evoked by a strong, subjective urge which the patient finds hard to resist. Quite often the behaviour is designed to forestall possible harm (e.g. washing hands thoroughly to avoid contamination) and its performance tends to lead to feelings of relief and the reduction of tension. Obsessions tend to lead to compulsions, although not in all cases. The commonest obsessions are repetitive thoughts of violence, contamination, and doubt (e.g. wondering whether the house is securely locked). Compulsions included repeated hand-washing, counting, and checking.

Obsessional disorders are tackled on three fronts. Firstly, the emotional component of the problem is directly tackled by means of anxiety reduction methods. For example, a patient with obsessional anxieties about contamination by dirt may have his or her environment totally contaminated by the therapist in order to expose that person fully to obsessional stimuli and produce habituation of anxiety. Secondly, the behavioural components of the obsessional disorder, often expressed in terms of ritualistic behaviour designed to avoid or ward off anxiety, are directly tackled by a procedure known as 'response prevention'. As the name implies the patient is encouraged not to carry out ritualistic behaviour in order that full exposure to the anxiety cues is achieved. Finally, patients are taught to distract themselves from upsetting thoughts and ruminations and, if possible, to dismiss them as irrational and unwanted.

The treatment of obsessional patients by these procedures is not easy to carry out and is often facilitated by either admitting the patient to hospital and carrying out the treatment intensively with the help of other professional staff, as may be the case with the severer disorders, or carrying out the treatment in the patient's home environment, again on an intensive basis. Empirical research carried out both in England and in America has provided strong support for the effectiveness of a comprehensive behavioural approach of this sort. Rachman and Hodgson (1980) report a success rate of between 70 and 80 per cent for obsessional patients treated by this method and followed up for up to two years after the end of treatment.

THE BEHAVIOURAL TREATMENT OF ADDICTIONS

Addiction is a blanket term that is used to cover a variety of difficult problems including hard drug taking, dependency on tranquillizers and other prescribed medication, cigarette smoking, excessive consumption of alcohol, overeating, compulsive gambling, and even excessive sexuality. There is considerable controversy over the meaning of addiction; a widely held view is that it implies a state of *physical dependency*. This is usually inferred from the tendency of people to build up *tolerance* and therefore to require larger and larger doses of the substance, and from the report of *withdrawal symptoms*—for example the irritability, poor concentration, disturbed sleep, headaches, feeling of sickness, tremor, and a strong urge to smoke cigarettes that have been reported when cigarette smokers stop smoking. This is not the place to discuss the evidence for and against physical dependency; an excellent and informed discussion is provided by Orford (1985). A psychological model of addiction incorporates the fact that addictive substances have physical effects (e.g. the central depressant effects of alcohol; the stimulating effects of nicotine on arousal mechanisms in the brain), but places addictive behaviour in a psychological, social, and cultural context. For example, there are known social and cultural factors in the drinking of alcohol; in certain Muslim countries it is forbidden by law and against religious practice, whereas in most Western countries alcohol drinking is socially sanctioned and widely accepted. Any model of addiction must be a broad one that includes psychological, social, cultural, and biological factors.

A first step in the psychological treatment of addiction is to acquire a full understanding of its significance in the individual context. In discussing the contribution of psychology to problem drinking, Robertson, Hodgson, Orford, and McKenzie (1984) make the following sensible recommendations:

We believe that it may be more profitable for an understanding of drinking behaviour to search for individual factors in the process of acquiring, developing, and changing drinking patterns. In particular, we consider it may be helpful to view drinking in the context of other family, educational and occupational, and leisure time activities, rather than as an isolated behaviour. Like most social behaviours, drinking is linked with, or embedded within other behaviours, via a complex network of associations and discriminations. (p. 12)

These precepts are applicable to all forms of addictive behaviour. Any form of treatment should take into account the behaviour *in its context*. This will often mean that treatment is not restricted to the problem behaviour, but takes into account the causes and effects of the behaviour. Marital therapy, assertiveness training, psychosexual counselling, anxiety management, and other therapeutic approaches can be important in treatment of people with problems of addiction, depending upon the nature of the problem in the particular case.

Having emphasized the need for a comprehensive assessment, there is nevertheless a key characteristic of all addictions which has underpinned a psychological approach. That is, for all addictive behaviours the behaviour that leads to immediate, short-term reward (e.g. smoking a cigarette for the pleasure of it) conflicts with other behaviour whose immediate effect is not in itself rewarding but leads to long-term benefits (e.g. refraining from smoking leading to a healthier old age). The problem for addicts (and for all of us) is that immediate rewards are very powerful whereas the long-term benefits are diffuse and weak in their effects. How therefore can the long-term benefits be made more powerful and given effective control over immediate behaviour?

Behavioural self-control

The essence of behavioural self-control is the analysis of addiction in terms of conflicting behaviours at key choice points. Should I smoke the cigarette? Do I go to the pub for a drink? Should I eat the chocolate biscuit? In the myriad instances where choices of this sort occur, there are two types of behaviour involved:

(a) the response to be controlled (e.g. taking and eating the chocolate biscuit);
(b) the controlling response (e.g. 'No, I cannot eat that biscuit because I shall put on weight').

Behavioural self-control procedures are designed to help people strengthen their controlling responses to regulate the response to be controlled. Four strategies of self-control have been developed.

(i) Self-monitoring
In order to exercise self-control people must be aware that choices exist. Further, they must learn what behaviours are important in

ALCOHOL INTAKE RECORD

Date: 5th May, 1986   Name: John Smith

Please note down all alcoholic drinks that you have during the day. Give an estimate of the amount consumed (e.g. large whisky, pint of beer, schooner of sherry). In addition, note the *antecedents* of drinking, that is, the situation, events, feelings or thoughts which led to taking the drink, and the *consequents*, that is, the effects of the drink on your thoughts and feelings and your immediate environment. It is essential to be absolutely honest about your drinking pattern, as only by so doing will you be able to learn to control it.

Time	Alcoholic drinks	Where consumed	Antecedents—events etc. *before* drinking (see above)	Consequents—events etc. *after* drinking (see above)
A.M.				
11.00 to 11.30	2 large sherries	Home	Needed a pick-up before getting down to work	Felt more relaxed
P.M. 1.00 to 2.30	3 pints of bitter	Local pub	Wanted to work, but strong urge to drink and see friends	Fell asleep for couple of hours. Felt drowsy when woke up. Guilty as hell!
6.00	1 large sherry	Home	Another pick-up!	Felt better—more relaxed
EVENING				
7.15	1 large sherry	Home	Just before dinner	Had dinner & got down to some writing
9.30 11.00	2 pints of bitter 2 large whiskies	Local pub —again	Strong urge to drink. Work going badly	Enjoyed evening, but nagging guilt feeling. Went home & to bed

Fig. 2.1 Example of self-monitoring record

determining self-control. Self-monitoring consists of the systematic recording of relevant behaviour by means of diaries, record sheets, counters, and other assessment methods. An example of a self-monitoring record is given in Fig. 2.1. In this 'alcohol intake record', a record is provided not only of the amount of alcoholic drink consumed, but note is also made of thoughts and events that preceded and following drinking, i.e. the antecedents and consequences, giving some idea of drinking patterns.

Systematic recording is an important part of all self-control programmes. Not only does it provide an assessment of behaviour at significant choice points, it also provides a quantitative assessment of the problem itself. Self-monitoring can be therapeutic. Monitoring urges to smoke, for example has been shown to reduce cigarette smoking. However, in most cases, self-monitoring alone is insufficient to produce substantial or long term benefit.

(ii) Environmental planning

In Homer's account of the Odyssey Odysseus, desirous of hearing the song of the Sirens but unwilling to be lured for ever into their company, instructed his crew to tie him to the mast and gave them strict instructions not to heed his pleas to be released. They in their turn placed beeswax in their ears and rowed the ship successfully past the Sirens. This is a very early example of environmental planning, that is organizing and arranging ones environment in order to increase the likelihood of self-control in difficult or tempting circumstances. Strategies range from commonsense procedures such as not keeping cigarettes or alcoholic drinks at home to more drastic environmental changes, e.g. seeking a new circle of friends who do not drink or smoke. Planned environmental changes should be part of a person's desired normal lifestyle; it is of little benefit going to a health farm for two weeks only to return to a boozy and smoke-filled normal life.

(iii) Behavioural programming

Whereas environmental planning describes procedures used to change the environmental antecedents of a particular behaviour, behavioural programming describes procedures designed to change its consequences. A self-control programme for overweight people, for example, entails setting achievable weekly goals of weight loss (1 to 2 lb per week) and programming desired rewards when the goal is achieved. The reward may be a tangible one such as a valued or enjoyed activity or intangible such as self-praise. Another strategy consists of rehearsing and writing down the long-term benefits of weight loss and referring to these at times of temptation. Self-reward programmes have been shown to be moderately effective in the treatment of overweight individuals, at least in producing short-term benefit.

(iv) Maintenance of behaviour change

Embarking on a self-control programme can produce short-term gains but need not result in long-term benefit. The problem of relapse is particularly evident in the treatment of addictions. Cigarette smokers, for example, may successfully abstain from smoking at the end of a treatment programme, but only 30 per cent of them are likely to be abstinent a year later. Similarly high relapse rates are to be found in problem drinkers and over-eaters. What can be done to deal with the relapse problem?

Several strategies have been tried. Crisis preparation, for example, involves planning for and in some cases actually inducing relapse as part of the therapy programe in order to demonstrate and teach appropriate skills. Organizing necessary support from family and friends so that when formal treatment ends informal help continues. Booster sessions at various intervals up to a year or two years after treatment can be helpful. Working directly on attitudes and commitment in order to reinforce attitude change (e.g. from a smoker to a non-smoker). Nevertheless, the relapse problem persists as the most significant limitation of the behavioural or indeed any treatment of addictive disorders.

COGNITIVE THERAPY

In behaviour therapy particular emphasis is placed upon changing the patient's behaviour, for example getting a phobic patient to face up to his fears or teaching him to be more relaxed. Most behavioural treatments also pay attention to the patient's thinking processes since in so many instances these constitute a central part of the problem. Worrying thoughts, for example, are counteracted in behaviour therapy by encouraging more positive ways of thinking. Jean's panicky thoughts about catastrophe were countered by urging her to recognize that these were symptoms of anxiety and that she had learned ways of mastering anxious feelings.

Cognitive therapy consists of methods of treatment which are directed at the patient's cognitive or thinking processes. It is held that the emotional problems experienced by patients can be directly attributed to distortions in their thinking. These can take the form of the predominance of negative thoughts, thinking errors (e.g. over-generalization, polarized thinking) and irrational or maladaptive ideas and beliefs. In cognitive therapy patients are taught to recognize and counter their cognitive distortions and thereby reduce or manage their emotional distress. Like behaviour therapy, cognitive therapy is a practical, problem-solving form of treatment which has been particularly used in the treatment of depression and anxiety. The therapist takes an educational approach, although the value of developing a good therapeutic relationship is also stressed. The use of cognitive therapy in the treatment of depression is described in detail below.

Cognitive therapy for depression

Depression is characterized by persistent and pervasive feelings of hopelessness and low mood often accompanied by a number of somatic symptoms such as disturbed sleep, loss of energy, poor appetite, and psychomotor agitation or retardation. Depressed patients lose interest in normally pleasurable activities, find it difficult to concentrate or make decisions, and may experience intense feelings of guilt and self-reproach. Thoughts of death and suicide may be prominent. The experience of depression in mild or moderate forms is something many people have. Severe depression is experienced by a substantial number of people, perhaps as many as one in eight of the population.

Until recently antidepressant medication was the clear treatment of choice for depressed patients. Tricyclic drugs, the most commonly used antidepressants, have been shown to elevate mood and produce symptomatic improvement in a large proportion of depressed patients. For most doctors they remain the first choice in treatment. Medication, however, has several limitations. Not only can drugs produce toxic and side effects, but they can undermine the depressed patient's capacity to recover on their own. Any improvement may be attributed to medication rather that the patient's own resources. In this way medication can reinforce a patient's belief that he or she is hopeless and inhibit attempts to cope.

Cognitive therapy is a recently developed psychological treatment which aims to help depressed patients marshall their own resources to elevate mood, counteract depressive thinking, and to produce positive changes in their behaviour and environment (Beck, Rush, Shaw, and Emery 1979). It is practical and problem-solving, with the central aim of identifying and correcting the major distortions in thinking that are characteristic of depression.

Mrs Harris, for example, was severely depressed when referred for psychological help. She spent many hours of the day in bed and had great difficulty in getting simple tasks around the house done. She was frequently tearful and reproached herself for her inadequacy as a mother, housewife, offspring, and spouse. The first stage of therapy entailed asking her to keep a detailed record of her activities and from this selecting tasks that could be most easily mastered. She was seen twice a week at first and gradually, by means of structured planning and support, built up her activities. At the same time, she learned to attend to, monitor and eventually challenge negative thinking. For example, she frequently had the thought 'I am hopeless. I cannot do anything right'. In therapy the accuracy of this thought was questioned; she was asked to find and list things that she in fact had done correctly. The thought was seen as an example of depressive thinking rather than a realistic appraisal of herself. She was helped to find a way of countering the thought, firstly by distraction and then by direct challenge. She learned that she could in fact achieve many tasks provided they were specific and small scale. When Mrs Harris questioned the value of such achievement ('Anyone could do them. They are trivial'), therapy turned to a discussion of some of her basic assumptions and beliefs. It emerged that she had a adopted a very rigid and perfectionist set of standards, which had been instilled into her from early childhood. Until her treatment Mrs Harris had not articulated these standards and she was quite surprised at how extreme and rigid they were. It became clear to her that much of her depression was directly caused by her standards which, because of their extreme nature, made it very difficult for her to succeed at anything. As therapy progressed she began to experiment with alternative ways of seeing herself and the world. Her depressed mood began rapidly to lift.

Cognitive therapy is a fairly recently developed therapy. There is an increasing body of evidence to suggest that it is an effective method of treatment for depression. For example, in a controlled evaluation of cognitive therapy for depressed patients referred by general practitioners, Teasdale, Fennell, Hibbert, and Amies (1984) found that cognitive therapy resulted in a clinically and statistically significant improved rate of recovery compared to the customary treatment from their GPs. Other studies in Europe and America have supported the value of this therapeutic approach.

PSYCHODYNAMIC PSYCHOTHERAPY

Anthony Storr, a leading British psychotherapist, described psychotherapy as

the art of alleviating personal difficulties through the agency of words and a personal, professional relationship (Storr 1979 p. vii)

In all therapies, including behaviour and cognitive therapy, the relationship between therapist and patient is important since without a good relationship where there is an element of trust and respect there is unlikely to be the basis for meaningful change. In psychodynamic psychotherapy the therapist–patient relationship is the central core of the therapy and the main vehicle of change. The term 'psychodynamic' refers to the theoretical origins of this approach, in particular the ideas and practices of the psychoanalytic school. The focus in psychodynamic psychotherapy is not on producing symptomatic and behaviour change directly, but on establishing a therapeutic relationship in which the patient feels safe enough to reveal and explore emotionally charged and often upsetting material. This is a process of uncovering and of 'working through' with the therapist applying analytical skills to enable the patient to explore his intrapsychic world in a effective and productive way. There are many different 'schools' of psychodynamic psychotherapy which reflect theoretical differences and divisions in the psychoanalytic movement. However, it has been suggested that the common factors in psychodynamic psychotherapy probably outweigh the differences between schools. An example of a psychotherapy case is given to illustrate this approach.

A PSYCHOTHERAPY CASE

Jack is a 38-year-old teacher, married with three children. He was referred to a clinical psychologist who specialized in psychodynamic psychotherapy by his G P because of frequent bouts of depression. Jack was ill at ease when he arrived and initially quite reticent and defensive. He began by saying, 'I didn't really want to come here, you know. It was Sheila's idea. . . I don't want to waste your time.' He did not believe he had a 'problem' as such—just sometimes he got very unhappy. He did not know why. He was 'happily married' in a 'great job' with 'three lovely children'. As the interview progressed Jack relaxed and began to talk more freely about himself. He recounted some of the experiences of his childhood which had been quite harsh at times. His family had been poor. His father had been frequently ill and off work and there had been very little money around. He and his elder brother, Jim, had both done well at school, but, while Jim had gone on to University and eventually a successful job in engineering, Jack had left school at 16 against his parent's wishes. At first he had 'bummed around' taking various jobs before deciding upon teaching as a career. He entered a teaching training school where he had met Sheila. Shortly after he had qualified, they had got married and, after a couple of years in one school, he had got a job at his present school where he had been for the past 14 years.

Jack said that there had been times during his childhood when he had felt very unhappy, but once he began on his career as a teacher, he had felt fine, very happy. It was only in the last year or so that he had felt very depressed and he could not see why. He reiterated his statements about being really very happy with his family and in his work, but in a rather quiet and depressed tone of voice so that the therapist gained a strong feeling of deep unhappiness and misery. The assessment interview continued with the therapist asking Jack more about himself, his family and his current life. Jack's unhappiness became more obvious and at the end of the interview the therapist asked Jack whether he wished to embark on a course of psychotherapy explaining that this entailed weekly therapy sessions of 50 minutes lasting for up to a year. She said that she felt that Jack was indeed very unhappy and that psychotherapy was a way of exploring what the unhappiness was about and that sometimes this could be a painful and difficult process but in the end it could be of benefit. After a moment's hesitation, Jack agreed to 'give it a try'.

In an assessment interview such as this the therapist seeks to esbtablish some form of psychological contact which will serve as the basis of the psychotherapeutic relationship. She also seeks to understand what it is that is troubling the patient and perhaps already has some ideas about how to proceed. Jack's present unhappiness may well have an important relationship to his upbringing and the expectations of a bright young boy from a deprived background. But these are only tentative ideas. More will undoubtedly emerge as the therapy progresses. Jack too will have formed an impression of the therapist and have some thoughts about what therapy could offer. Sometimes these are unrealistic expectations and hopes which are modified during treatment. Like any other relationship a psychotherapeutic relationship entails a process of mutual adjustment and understanding.

It is not possible here to describe in detail the vicissitudes of Jack's therapy. Briefly, after a 'honeymoon period' of regular attendance, Jack became morose and withdrawn. He began missing sessions and arriving late. The therapist sought to explore what was happening in their relationship, thereby provoking considerable feelings of anger and hostility on Jack's part. A crisis point was reached when Jack might easily have terminated treatment. But the therapist worked hard to get through to Jack, accepting his anger without rebuff or recrimination and pushing Jack to examine why he should feel this way. Out of this emerged a picture of a younger brother who had felt neglected by his family and had harboured a deep resentment of his parents' apparent indifference to him in contrast to his elder brother. He had rebelled and left school and had eventually thrown himself into teaching partly perhaps as a way to provide others with the care and guidance he felt he had lacked. He had married a warm and openly affectionate woman who gave him the support and succour he felt he needed. He had immersed himself in bringing up his own family. However, lately when his depression had returned, he had a powerful conviction that he had really achieved nothing worthwhile in his life and that he was a charlatan, someone who did not deserve the attention and interest of others. In therapy he had become withdrawn and angry at the therapist's constant attention particularly as he had begun to develop warm and positive feelings towards her. His defence against such feelings was to withdraw, but when the therapist did not let him, he experienced powerful feelings of anger and hostility.

The experience of strong feelings towards the therapist, or transference as it is known in psychodynamic terms, is regarded by many as a vital part of the therapeutic process. Jack's feeling towards the therapist can be seen as reflections of feelings experienced at other times and towards others, parents perhaps. It is the therapist's job to recognize these feelings and with the patient to 'work through' them in therapy. The patient may then begin to learn something about himself and how his current feelings are expressions of other thoughts and experiences of which he may have been unconscious. In Jack's case the therapist's acceptance of his anger and the open way she talked about their relationship proved a turning point. He began to examine his past experiences, his childhood in particular, from a different perspective. He felt valued, almost for the first time, as a person in his own right. He saw how much he had striven hard either to meet the aspirations of his parents or to reject them. He ended therapy feeling an upsurge of morale and confidence and with the conviction that he had the capability to do well both at work and in his family.

A brief description such as this can only touch upon the complexities of a psychotherapeutic relationship. Patients vary as do the problems they present and the way they respond to treatment. Therapists too have different styles and theoretical orientations. The essential features that distinguish this approach from the behavioural and cognitive therapies described earlier lie in the focus on the therapist–patient relationship and on the analytic skills of the therapist in understanding and interpreting the feelings and problems of the patient. The practice of psychotherapy demands considerable personal skills from the therapist and the capacity to maintain a positive relationship with patients sometimes under difficult and trying conditions. Not all clinical psychologists feel equipped to offer this form of treatment and some are frankly antagonistic to it. Some schools of thought argue that those who practise psychotherapy should themselves have been in psychotherapy as an integral part of their training. Not all agree with this point of view. But certainly it is desirable that psychotherapists receive regular supervision from other experienced therapists.

THE ECLECTIC APPROACH

The differences between psychodynamic psychotherapy on the one hand and the cognitive–behavioural therapies on the other are not as definitive as might appear from the accounts of therapy given so far. Certainly there are real differences in theory, but theoretical differences relate only loosely to therapeutic practice. And some of the most obvious differences in practice can disappear as therapists of all persuasions converge towards an essentially similar pattern of treatment. One example is the trend towards brief psychotherapy amongst the psychodynamic therapists. Brief psychotherapy can be shorter in time than some of the cognitive–behavioural therapies, and although the approach is still essentially interpretive with an emphasis on the therapist–patient relationship, the treatment is problem-focused and time-limited. A patient receiving brief psychodynamic psychotherapy will be encouraged to select a specific problem in therapy to work on just as he or she will do so in cognitive–behavioural therapies. There may be differences in style and ways of working, but increasingly the similarities outweigh the differences. Many clinical psychologists now describe their therapeutic approach as 'eclectic'. By that they generally mean that they do not rigidly adhere to one treatment model, but are prepared to use a variety of models and techniques in helping a patient, i.e. they tailor the therapy very much to the individual needs. Susan's treatment is a good example of this form of 'eclecticism'.

The treatment of a student with an eating disorder

Susan is a 21-year-old student in the final year of a history degree. She had become obsessed with food to such an extent that she found it impossible to concentrate on anything else. Her work had 'gone' and she had stopped seeing most of her friends. The GP who referred her for psychological treatment diagnosed her problem as *bulimia nervosa*, an eating disorder characterized by episodes of binge-eating and self-induced vomiting or purgative abuse, a constant preoccupation with food and eating, and a morbid fear of fatness. Susan was not markedly underweight, but appeared pale and drawn. She admitted that she binged two or three times a week, eating huge quantities of food and then deliberately vomiting. At other times she ate very little and only a selection of carefully chosen 'good' foods which she believed were not fattening. Her mood was low and she felt unable to exercise any control over this part of her life.

A cognitive–behavioural treatment for *bulimia nervosa* has recently been described and evaluated (Fairburn 1985). It has three stages. Firstly, an intensive and supportive phase designed to disrupt the pattern of habitual overeating and vomiting. Susan was asked to keep detailed records of her food consumption and to identify meals in which she felt that she was in control and those in which she was not. She was advised to restrict her eating to three planned meals a day regardless of hunger. No attempt was made at this stage to check her vomiting or modify the type of food she was eating. The therapist gave Susan as much support as possible seeing her initially two or three times a week and provided her with corrective information about food, weight, and diet. As a result Susan gradually brought her eating more under control and the episodes of bingeing and vomiting were markedly reduced. Her mood lifted and she began to take up her work again.

In the second phase Susan was seen on a weekly basis and the focus shifted to the problems and stresses that had provoked the eating disorder. The therapist encouraged Susan to relax her rigid restrictions and try 'banned foods' as an experiment designed to demonstrate that this would not lead to a massive loss of control nor immediate weight gain. At this point Susan began to talk more generally about herself and in particular her parents. The psychologist detected ambivalent feelings in Susan about her family. She described her father in highly idealized terms, yet it also appeared that he was rarely at home and when he was he would shut himself away to work. Susan was often rather contemptuous about her mother's contribution to the family ('cook and housewife'). Yet it appeared that she was emotionally quite close to her. Susan also mentioned casually, in passing, an ex-boyfriend whom she had been very close to for most of her student life. These messages alerted the therapist to the role played by disturbed relationships in Susan's problems. Since the worst part of the eating disorder had been brought under reasonable control, the treatment focus could be shifted towards exploring Susan's feeling in relation to her family and her ex-boyfriend.

The final phase of Fairburn's approach focuses on the maintenance of change and preparation for possible relapse. In Susan's case, there was much less emphasis given to food as she regularly saw the psychologist over the next few months. Susan's trust for the therapist increased, she was able to admit for the first time how resentful and angry she felt towards her parents, her father in particular. The psychologist for her part was able to get Susan to see that such feelings were not abnormal and that Susan's worth as a person was not dependent on the approval of her parents or others. Susan's self-image had been narrowly restricted to her appearance, hence her excessive concern with food and eating. The treatment allowed her to see how other aspects of herself were valuable and important.

Susan's treatment illustrates how a practical cognitive—behavioural treatment can be successfully combined with a more psychodynamic approach. There was a clear need in the early stages of treatment for the therapist to provide practical help and emotional support. After that a variety of possibilities arose. A more specifically cognitive approach can be adopted in which the patient's beliefs and attitudes about food and eating are directly tackled. This could be very much a part of Fairburn's approach and for some patients this direct attack on their cognitions is of benefit. Alternatively, the patient's family could have been brought into treatment in the form of family therapy. The choice of strategy will depend very much on the type of patient and her problems as well as the particular experience and expertise of the therapist.

MARITAL OR COUPLE THERAPY

Most of the cases described so far have been examples of individual treatment where the therapeutic contact is between two individuals, patient and therapist. But, as the example of Catherine and Henry illustrated, sometimes patients can be seen in couples. In psychosexual counselling, it is generally desirable to see both partners, where that is possible, since the problem is expressed in terms of sexual relationship. Moreover the practical procedures that are part of sex therapy are obviously much more applicable to a couple than a single individual.

Marital therapy is another example where both partners are almost always seen for the same reasons as sex therapy. The relationship is the crucial factor and it is very difficult to work productively on a relationship when only one partner is present. In marital therapy, the psychologist's role is that of both facilitator and teacher. As a neutral outsider she or he can enable the couple to perceive and understand more clearly what the nature of their problems are, and by skilful guidance can hopefully help the couple resolve their difficulties and adopt a more productive way of relating to each other. Not all clinical psychologists will practise marital therapy, some preferring to refer patients to specialist organizations such as the Marriage Guidance Council in the UK. On the other hand, there has been a particular interest in applying behavioural and social learning theory to marital therapy and several practical psychological strategies have been devised (Jacobson and Margolin 1979). For example, where partners have a particular difficulty in communicating with each other, the psychologist can directly teach communication skills. This is done in relation to a practical problem in the marriage and can be expanded to include problem-solving skills in general. Another approach is to examine the ways in which the couple seek to influence each other's behaviour. In some instances couples may be encouraged to make explicit contracts with each other which are written down, specifying the behaviours that they would like to see and what contingencies would follow (contingency contracting). By making the rules specific and explicit, the couple can learn the important skills of reciprocity and positive reinforcement.

GROUP THERAPIES

Some people's psychological problems may best be dealt with in groups. This can be true when people share a common problem which requires a common treatment strategy. Agoraphobic patients, for example, with a fear of leaving the safety of their homes can be helped by means of a planned behavioural programme carried out in small groups of five to eight patients. The psychologist may set up a week's intensive treatment in which the group meets every day at the clinic and each day carries out a part of the behavioural programme, at first with the supervision of the psychologist and then on their own. Alternatively the group may meet weekly for a period of six weeks with homework tasks set in between. Behavioural groups such as these can be very effective, particularly when the group is cohesive and mutually supportive. It is easier for some patients to take risks when others are in the same boat.

For some patients a group is part of the problem. People who are shy, unassertive, nervous of others or who lack 'social skills' may benefit from a group treatment since it allows them to learn how to overcome their difficulties and interact more effectively with others. Social skills training groups, for example, are ones in which people are directly taught various social skills such as those used in holding conversations, making requests, forming friendships or dealing with people in authority. Another related approach is assertiveness training, in which anxious and inhibited patients are taught how to stand up for themselves more effectively and to be more open and expressive in their feelings towards others.

Social skills and assertiveness training groups vary in size from as little as four patients to as large as ten or twelve and often have two therapists. In most instances the period of training is deliberately circumscribed and a highly structured programme followed. The content of the training varies from focusing on small and specific aspects of social interaction, for example, eye contact in talking to other people or the use of gesture in conversation, to generalized and quite complex aspects of interpersonal relationships, for example, responding to criticism from other people, breaking into a social group at a party. Training consists usually of modelling or demonstration by the therapist or others of appropriate social behaviour, repeated practice in the form of role play in the group or individually with the therapist, feedback on how successful the practice was, further repeated practice, and homework assignments for the patients to carry out outside the treatment.

Some forms of group therapy are much less didactic. Group psychotherapy, for example, can involve two therapists and eight or more patients meeting weekly for as long as 18 months. The focus of the group is on interpersonal learning, but by means of shared experiences rather than specific teaching. Typically, the therapists do not 'lead' the group, but seek to guide it forwards, creating a constructive and helping atmosphere in which personal problems can be freely discussed. The group itself becomes an important and valued entity and is seen as the main vehicle of change (see Bloch and Crouch 1985). It may be that elements of both the skills training and the interpersonal learning groups can be combined to good effect. Practical role-playing exercises, for example, can often be a part of group psychotherapy, although their use is less for acquiring skills than providing personal feedback.

HOW EFFECTIVE ARE PSYCHOLOGICAL TREATMENTS?

This question is not an easy one to answer. Firstly, there are many forms of psychological treatment so that a general statement about their effectiveness is hard to make. In some quarters there is a widely held belief that all forms of psychotherapy are 'modestly effective' and no one treatment strategy is really superior to any other. But, optimistic as this verdict may be, it is undiscriminating and not very helpful. If all treatments are of equal validity, how does one decide which treatment to use? And is it plausible to maintain that *any* form of psychological treatment is of benefit? Surely some approaches are better than others.

A second difficulty in answering the question is the absence of good empirical knowledge about many treatments. Psychoanalysis, for example, the oldest form of psychological treatment, has had very little empirical research carried out into its effectiveness and undoubtedly a main reason for this lies in the enormous complexity of task. It is exceedingly difficult to translate the sophisticated theoretical terminology of psychoanalysis into practical data that can be scientifically measured and studied. The greater concreteness of behavioural and cognitive treatments has certainly helped researchers in designing and carrying out sound empirical research. It is easier to show that agoraphobic patients are able to go out more on their own after treatment than it is to show that their unconscious conflicts have been successfully resolved.

Thirdly, while people may show considerable improvement during treatment, it is sometimes difficult to distinguish the various factors that account for that improvement. The personality of the therapist, the personality of the client, the particular setting, the patient's desire to please the therapist, the reactivity of the measures used, the influence of extraneous variables, the passage of time, are all factors that can produce change. Research designs are becoming more sophisticated in the attempt to control for various factors, but it remains difficult to carry out complex outcome research successfully and very few research trials of a good methodological standard have been carried out. Therefore, many forms of psychological treatment remain of uncertain value. This does not mean that most treatments are ineffective, merely that there is insufficient knowledge to conclude definitely that a particular treatment works, a state of affairs that is not uncommon in other fields of clinical practice.

Clinical psychologists have shown a particular interest in treatment research and have often been in the forefront of designing and carrying out research studies. In most individual treatments careful attention is paid to monitoring and measuring change so that improvements can be objectively seen. Single-case experimental designs are increasingly used to evaluate changes more rigorously. These designs entail systematic data collection before treatment begins (baseline phase) and during the various phases of treatment (intervention phase). A number of strategies are used to test whether the changes seen are or are not due to the intervention. It has been argued that all therapists should be concerned to demonstrate that the treatment strategies used are effective by means of at the very least careful monitoring of progress during treatment.

SUMMARY

Clinical psychologists are specialists in psychological treatment and in particular have developed expertise in the short-term, pragmatic cognitive and behavioural methods. These methods are described and illustrated with reference to phobic anxiety and depressive disorders. Some clinical psychologists go on to acquire further specialist training which can take the form of a particular type of therapy (e.g. sex therapy, marital therapy) or a particular theoretical orientation and practical skills. The psychodynamic approach is described and illustrated with reference to a therapy case. Recently there has been a convergence of different schools of therapy and many clinical psychologists describe themselves as 'eclectic', preferring to use a variety of methods and tailor these to the individual case. Finally, the effectiveness of psychological treatments has been examined in various research studies. Although many psychotherapists are optimistic about the results of their therapies, methodological shortcomings combined with the difficulties involved in carrying out good quality treatment research mean that our knowledge about the effectiveness of psychological treatments is still only at a rudimentary stage.

REFERENCES

Beck, A. T., Rush, A. J., Shaw, B. F. and Emery, G. (1979). *Cognitive therapy for depression*. The Guilford Press, New York.

Bloch, S. and Crouch, E. (1985). *Therapeutic factors in group psychotherapy*. Oxford University Press, Oxford.

Fairburn, C. (1985). Cognitive behavioural treatment for bulimia. In *Handbook of psychotherapy for anorexia nervosa and bulimia* (ed. D. M. Garner and P. E. Garfinkel). The Guilford Press, New York.

Hawton, K. (1985). *Sex therapy. A practical guide*. Oxford Medical Publications, Oxford.

Jacobson, N. S. and Margolin, G. M. (1979). *Marital therapy : strategies based on social learning and behaviour exchange principles*. Brunner/Mazel, New York.

Mathews, A., Gelder, M. G. and Johnston, D. W. (1981). *Agoraphobia. Nature and treatment*. Tavistock, London.

Orford, J. (1985). *Excessive appetites : a psychological view of addictions*. Wiley, New York.

Rachman, S. and Hodgson, R. J. (1980). *Obsessions and compulsions*. Prentice-Hall, Englewood Cliffs, N J.

Robertson, I., Hodgson, R., Orford J. and Mackenzie, R. (1984). *Psychology and problem drinking*. The British Psychological Society, Division of Clinical Psychology.

Storr, A (1979). *The art of psychotherapy*. Heinemann, London.

Teasdale, J. D., Fennell, M. J. V., Hibbert, G. A. and Amies, P. L. (1984). Cognitive therapy for major depressive disorder in primary care. *Brit. J. Psychiat.* **144**, 400–406.

FURTHER READING

Bloch, S., ed. (1986). *Introduction to psychotherapies* (2nd edn). Oxford Medical Publications, Oxford.

Oatley, K. (1984). *Selves in relation. An introduction to psychotherapy and groups*. (New Essential Psychology Series). Methuen, London.

Rowe, D. (1983). *Depression. The way out of your prison*. Routledge and Kegan Paul, London.

3

Psychological work in institutions
John Hall

Most people, whether currently seeing a clinical psychologist or not, spend most of their lives in their own homes. A small but important proportion of the population spend a significant amount of time in some form of institution, while an even smaller proportion live virtually their entire life in an institution. This chapter is concerned mainly with those people with major psychological difficulties who live in some sort of institution. Many of the dilemmas discussed in this chapter are applicable to those with other chronic handicaps who also spend long periods of time in institutional care.

WHAT IS AN INSTITUTION?

An institution is a living place where there are separate groups of staff, and inmates/residents/patients, and where the living conditions of the resident group are primarily determined by the staff group. Western European societies have traditionally provided a number of such institutions, most notably prisons, hospitals, and accommodation for the poor and 'needy'. The period since the Second World War has seen the emergence of an anti-institution attitude, with a consequent reduction in the size of institutions for the mentally ill and for children, if not for offenders. Pungent criticism of institutional care by sociologists, and the indictment of official committee of enquiry reports at some psychiatric hospitals, have together combined to produce a situation where the need for institutional care has to be argued anew.

A psychologist should, of course, be asking, 'Why institutions anyway?' If the present institutions did *not* exist, would it be necessary to invent them? This chapter discusses the contribution of psychologists to institutions that currently exist, though that very contribution leads many psychologists to think that institutions, where the client need justifies institutional provision, should be as need-specific as possible. Providing an institutional solution to the needs of a patient when other solutions, maybe those open to 'normal' people, have not been explored, may serve to further remove them from normal services of support and service. Adopting this approach would no doubt lead to a new type of institutional provision, such as the hospital–hostels for younger chronic patients that are now being developed. By implication, such provision would also be in smaller units than at present, and very different total numbers of institutional places might be required.

Erving Goffmann (1961) is probably the best known critic of institutional care. He coined the phrase 'total institution' which he defined as 'a place of residence and work where a large number of like-situated individuals, cut off from the wider society for an appreciable period of time, together lead an enclosed formally administered round of life'. Goffmann considered that *the* central feature of institutional life is a breakdown of barriers between three spheres of life: sleep, work, and play. This definition emphasizes a number of characteristics of the total institution, such as one organizational system embracing all aspects of the resident life and the homogeneity of the population of residents of any one institution. The total institution is at one end of a continuum, the other end of which is 'normal' self-determined life in domestic surroundings, with work and leisure carried out in different places.

What this definition makes clear is that institutional care is defined by a pattern of life, as much as by other features of the institution. Thus many people with severe psychological difficulties live in group homes run by charitable bodies, in hostels provided by public social welfare or social services departments, in sheltered housing with resident workers, and in night shelters for the homeless as well as in psychiatric hospitals. Whatever the label attached to these institutions, some of the practices encountered in Goffman's total institutions *may* be encountered there. Handicapped people have traditionally been disadvantaged and indeed exploited (as in the public showing of lunatics in the old Bedlam Hospital in England), and some of the most handicapped people require a specially structured environment to enable them to acquire and maintain the skills they lack. This does not suggest they require institutional care, in the passive meaning of that word, but perhaps they do require a special place for living that cannot readily be provided in ordinary unstaffed domestic housing.

The discussion so far has concentrated, at least implicitly, on institutions for living. Goffmann's definition included reference to places of work: ordinary people usually go to work at a place other than their home, and those who work at home typically enjoy more autonomy in their pattern of work than those who are employed outside their home. A characteristic of many psychiatric institutions is that day activities are provided on the same site as the living facilities, and that the same group of staff supervise the residents in both settings, so the range of social relationships in which they are engaged is thereby narrowed. Providing day activities away from residential facilities then broadens the range of social relationships, quite apart from the extra social contact that results.

WHY DO PEOPLE LIVE IN INSTITUTIONS?

The answer to this question will be examined with respect to psychiatric hospitals—the type of institution that includes the largest single institutions still operating in Britain, but also smaller hospitals with possibly only a dozen or so long-stay residents. There is little doubt that the initial enthusiasm for asylum care in the nineteenth century was for genuinely humanitarian reasons, and the very title asylum implied the recognition of the need for a safe place to protect the incapacitated. In the run-down of large psychiatric hospitals that has been going on since the mid-1950s, surveys suggest the specifically psychiatric nature of handicaps is often unclear in a substantial minority of the most chronic cases, although the application of modern diagnostic criteria retrospectively to these patients is admittedly fraught with theoretical difficulties

However, the continuing accumulation of 'new chronic' patients suggests that even with the most vigorous pharmacological and social care, a small proportion of patients cannot be satisfactorily left unsupported. The most frequent disorder found is chronic schizophrenia, and it is significant that with increasing lengths of stay, the proportion of patients who are so diagnosed increases to well above 50 per cent. Chronic schizophrenia thus forms the most serious psychiatric condition to continue to be found in psychiatric institutions. Other major diagnostic groups are chronic affective disorder—chronic depression or mania—and chronic personality and neurotic disorders. As these people become older, they are likely to have physical problems and even among younger patients physical needs should not be overlooked. Thus most people who have lived continously for any length of time—say 1 or 2 years or more—in a psychiatric institution will have had access to psychotherapy, social case-work skills, and other treatments, and in a sense are the 'failures' of acute psychiatric and psychological help.

Another reason why people may be living in a psychiatric institution is lack of an alternative place for them to go. There are several clinical groups, such as young adults with serious head injury, mildly mentally handicapped people with behaviour problems, and people with some progressive physical conditions, such as Huntington's Chorea, which are small in number but whose members present considerable problems of community or family tolerance. The ability of a family to cope with these difficulties is strained by the constant vigilance required or sometimes by aggressive attacks, so that people who are strictly speaking not psychiatrically ill may be cared for on a long-term basis on a psychiatric hospital ward. Their needs are not primarily psychiatric, but are for a stable planned regime which will facilitate new learning, maintain existing skills, and accommodate disturbed and disruptive behaviour: this does not necessarily mean a hospital regime.

THE PROBLEMS TO BE FACED

A major concern in this chapter has been the environment, or setting, of the patient, as well as the patient himself. A psychological analysis of the problems of the institutionalized patient should therefore take account of the problems posed by the institution, and of the problems posed by the patient.

Problems of the institution

The problems of the institution may be considered under two broad headings, the physical, and the social.

The physical problems of some of the larger older institutions are considerable. They are remote both from the neighbouring community, so reducing the chance of patients using local shops, libraries, etc., and the community of origin of the patients, so that relatives face a time-consuming and expensive journey when and if they visit. The wards are large and barrack-like making it difficult to provide much privacy. Some of the more modern units have the virtue of being smaller and more flexible in use, but may be designed on the same 'race-track' layout as a general hospital ward, not particularly suitable for psychiatric use. At a more micro-environmental level, storage space needs to be arranged so that recreational materials can be used readily, not just put in an inaccessible cupboard at the end of the ward. Chairs need to be arranged to encourage communication, not to line ward walls

The social problems of the institution originate from two main sources: the staff, and the rules of the institution. Dr Albert Kushlick has suggested a notation for the role of different staff groups, based essentially on the amount of time that members of each staff group are in direct contact (DC) with the patients. Ward nurses, and residential social workers are by his notation 'DC 12 hours'—they are in contact with the patient for all their waking life. Psychological studies of nurse–patient interaction indicate that the least well-trained direct-care staff spend more time interacting with patients than the more well-trained and senior staff, at least in part because of the ward-level administrative duties, which take them away from the patients. Together these points mean that in many settings the staff who have the greatest potential to modify the patients' behaviour, psychologically speaking, are the least well-trained. This is not to deny the real interest shown in their patients by many such ward level nurses, but to acknowledge their special needs, and to recognize the consequences of continued low staffing levels and sometimes poor morale. These staff may lack a coherent view of what rehabilitation is all about, may form a cohesive social group resistant to changes which threaten their status quo, and need both relevant training and continuing guidance and encouragement to give of their best, so that very careful design of both training courses and monitoring is required.

The rules of the institution form the other determinant of the institutional environment. One approach to assess the effect of these rules is to examine the 'restrictiveness' of a ward or unit, noting the amount of restriction on tobacco use, access of visitors, the time when lights have to be out, etc. (see Wykes 1982 for an example of psychological measures of restrictiveness). Some of these regulations are purely local to an individual hospital, while others have their origins in the practices of individual professions or of national guidance, but many tend to lead to a lack of individualized care.

Problems of the patient

The problems posed by the patient are the conventional focus for treatment in institutions, but they cannot be understood in isolation from the setting in which they occur. Psychologically, the problems of these patients are not defined primarily by their diagnosis. Thirty years ago the diagnosis of chronic schizophrenia may have carried with it a stereotypic view of the chronic patient. Paradoxically perhaps the reduction in in-patient numbers over the last 30 years has meant that the extremely heterogenous nature of the group is now clear. People with a chronic psychiatric disability form an extremely varied group by any standards. Quite apart from the primary problems arising from their psychiatric condition, chronic patients may have disabilities of other origins. They frequently have other pre-morbid handicaps, such as lower intellectual ability or poorer work records before they ever became ill. They also may have secondary handicaps arising from the way in which their families view and respond to them. Indeed the strictly psychiatric disabilities which remain may often not be the major focus of treatment for an individual.

From the point of view of an experimental psychologist, most chronic patients do have some common attributes. Many are slow, the slowness showing not only in experimental tasks, but in speech—meaning that enough time needs to be given for them to reply to questions—as well as in rate of output in jobs they do. Many may lack concentration, so they are relatively easily distracted from what they are doing, and easily influenced by peripheral stimulation. The more handicapped patients may have very low levels of motivation, as indicated by their poor response to those normal encouragements of praise, money, or tobacco, leading in the extreme to 'anhedonia'—the total absence of any apparent pleasure-seeking tendencies.

From the point of view of a clinical psychologist, the most obvious problem of these patients is lack of skill or motivation in a range of normal social behaviour. Some of these skills are related to looking after themselves—a lack of attention to personal hygiene, a lack of willingness to cook even simple meals for themselves. Other skills are related to getting on with other people—an unwillingness to initiate conversations with other people, a lack of persistence in some social game or activity, a lack of eye-contact with other people. It is these deficits of behaviour which comprise the overwhelming management problem of these patients.

By contrast, fewer patients show examples of bizarre or odd behaviour. Some patients may be seen as 'potentially' violent or aggressive, but are so controlled in one way or another that years may pass without a single violent episode. Yet undoubtedly some of them may behave in a very odd manner, such as the drum-majorette twirling of fingers and hands seen in some patients, and the peculiar forms of dress and self-adornment, such as the tin- and enamel-badge bedecked patient sometimes seen. Delusional ideas and hallucinatory experiences give conversations with some of these patients a profoundly unreal flavour. Even though such deviant and symptomatic behaviour is usually less frequent than behavioural deficits, it has a particular capacity to antagonize family and neighbours.

Last of all, it is important to acknowledge the need for medical care for many of these patients. Many of them are receiving maintenance medication, either of oral phenothiazine drugs, or of depot injections of neuroleptic drugs, which ensure that medication can be reliably administered without the individual patient needing to remember a complex tablet-taking regime. For some patients in regular contact with their families, correct medication may be very important in preventing relapse and it may be important for other patients. Second, chronic patients may need medical attention for ordinary physical ailments, especially since some of them may not spontaneously respond to pain and discomfort in their bodies, and thus physical problems may be well advanced before they are detected. Providing physical aids and prostheses, such as dentures and spectacles, can overcome some problems, but only if patients understand their value and are trained to make use of them.

The work of the clinical psychologist with institutionalised patients

The generic phrase 'rehabilitation' is often used to describe the range of activities undertaken to care for and treat chronic patients. However, one term is really inadequate to describe the range of procedures that have to be carried out with the extremely heterogeneous group of patients found in most institutional settings. The most handicapped group of patients may lack basic self-care skills, may be heavily dependent on care staff, and will most probably continue to spend most of their lives in a highly sheltered environment. Such a patient might be a 67-year-old woman who has been in hospital for the past 23 years. Admitted after her parents died, she never married or carried out a full-time job, and is not able to dress herself without help. She does not concentrate on games or other recreational activities, and positively avoids conversation with other residents or staff unless coerced to do so.

An intermediate group of patients may be able to use a wide range of community facilities, such as local shops, and can usefully be encouraged to use even more facilities, with suitable help. A group of 'new long-stay' or 'high contact' patients may still be in close contact with their families and may be seeking work, even though they have intermittent episodes of acute symptoms. An example of such a patient would be a 31-year-old man who failed to complete a college course of higher education, and who then drifted into casual hotel work. He can still keep such a job for a few weeks when demand for such work is higher over the summer, but has periodic psychotic episodes which gradually have become longer and longer. He then comes into hospital when his landlord realizes he cannot cope in his lodgings, despite the well-meaning support of his married sister who lives nearby. Hospitals vary in the extent to which old long-stay patients have left hospital, and in the range of hostel and group-home accommodation—and perhaps housing provided by voluntary Housing Association—associated with them. The task of the clinical psychologist will vary considerably, according to the mix of patients and the range of settings in which they live.

For many professional staff, the care of acutely ill people offers more professional gratification than the care of people with more chronic conditions. With the less severely ill, progress is usually more rapid; it is certainly easier to see the relationship between the use of particular treatments and specific benefit; and usually acute patients tend to be more articulate and verbal, so they are more rewarding to help. Whatever is meant by rehabilitation, it is important to define goals of work with chronic patients, and for all the staff involved to adjust to longer time-scales and slower rates of expected improvement. For example, some care staff remember past peccadilloes of the chronic patients they are working with, but find it hard to say what three things they would like a patient to be able to achieve over the next three months.

One psychological contribution to this field is the development of overall goals of services to handicapped people. Perhaps the concept of 'normalization', applied particularly with respect to mentally handicapped people, is the best known example of an overall service concept. This initially simple idea has been developed so that it carries with it the notion of availability of choice in different areas of living, the use of socially valued means of help with problems to counteract stigma, and the corollary of having to face reasonable risks. However, a number of other overall or superordinate objects of services have been suggested for work with chronic patients, which bear examination.

One such concept is the 'least restrictive environment'. Hospitals, according to this model, are the most restrictive type of environment because they cater for peoples' total needs over a 24-h period. Even quite disabled people do not necessarily need total care in all areas of their life for 24 h, and to that extent more of the person's life may be controlled in hospital than is necessary. By contrast, the services should seek to provide the least restrictive environment possible for an individual, based on an assessment of his continuing abilities and disabilities offering the 'minimum therapeutic dose' of assistance needed for each area of disability. A similar notion is that of the 'least segregated environment', suggested in a major policy document produced by MIND (1983), Britain's biggest voluntary body concerned with mental health. Segregation implies reduced contact with the neighbouring community, whether family, friends, or facilities such as shops and pubs. Segregation would then be reduced not only by the siting of an environment near main centres of population, but also by ensuring, in detail, that the environment was near a post office and a bus stop, and that members of the outside community really did come into the environment.

A rather different objective is that of 'personalization'. The concept of institutional neurosis views loss of personal events and personal possessions as one of seven contributory factors to this type of neurosis. The appropriate corrective action would accordingly be to restore personal events such as birthdays, and personal possessions, such as little trinkets and photographs, next to where the person sleeps. Personalization is also one component of 'resident—

orientated' care, as opposed to the depersonalization seen in 'institutionally orientated' care.

A particular contribution which clinical psychologists can make is to offer some sort of conceptual clarification to their colleagues. Overall objectives like those outlined can be very helpful as a way of bringing cohesion to what could otherwise be a rag-bag of low-level subordinate goals, such as 'encouraging conversation' or 'going to the shops more'. An overall objective, accepted by all staff concerned, can help to develop a detailed programme of targets and a set of evaluation measures which are mutually consistent, and which can then provide an overall framework of treatment for staff and residents alike. More fundamentally, a psychologist may have to address the paradox of 'treating' chronic patients who some staff may see as untreatable. Is there still a need for a concept of asylum? A psychologist working closely with direct care staff is bound to encounter these issues, and can help them to think through the issues of handicap and disability, as well as issues of treatment.

Assessing and understanding chronic psychiatric disability

The first practical task of the psychologist may well be to contribute to an understanding of the range of needs that a 'rehabilitation' service may try to meet. This may lead to a distinctive type of assessment procedure, a large-scale survey of the residents of a hospital or clients in contact with a service which has no parallel in work with more acute patients.

It is common for there to be relatively little information in long-stay patients' case notes, and what information there is often fails to indicate clearly the current problems of the patient, and how much he or she has changed over recent weeks or months. A detailed knowledge of the history of a patient, by contrast, can give an idea of past interests—to be hopefully re-awakened—and possibly of those circumstances that the patient has found particularly stressful. A systematic survey can then identify gross characteristics of the patients in standard form, including details of the patient's current behaviour in addition to other relevant information, such as the patient's current income—this may determine what activities he can afford—and degree of contact with relatives.

A large-scale survey of this sort may easily cover 200 or 300 patients in 10 or 15 wards, so the organizational aspects of a survey may require careful attention by a psychologist. A frequent consequence of such a survey is that patients are regrouped, so that any one ward contains patients more similar to each other than previously. This certainly assumes that staff are agreed about the main patient attributes—such as absence of physical and verbal aggression or level of self care—which determine the groupings and also requires some statistical sophistication, often supplied by a psychologist, to carry out such a grouping. Views differ on how to regroup, or indeed whether to regroup at all. One approach is to produce wards, or groups of patients as homogeneous as possible in their behaviour. This approach applied to the most handicapped or most over-active patients may produce a group of patients which would place unacceptable demands upon ward staff. If some patients have grown old together and show some evidence of friendship with each other, perhaps they should not be regrouped for the sake of homogeneity alone? Inevitably a psychologist involved in this type of exercise will need to be able to manipulate large numbers of variables, but also to retain some clinical sense of the needs of individuals while doing so, such as producing groups of patients that the staff can cope with.

After such a general survey or regrouping, the assessment task of the psychologist becomes more refined and detailed. Now the task is to identify those attributes of the patients that are relevant to their future care. This may involve lookng at some general area of functioning, such as the patient's ability to care for his own personal needs, and separately to assess skills in washing, dressing, shaving, sanitary care, cleaning teeth, toiletting, feeding, etc. Abilities may need to be defined at several different levels of handicap, so some sort of rating technique may be required to produce a change-sensitive measure of each individual skill.

There is evidence that identifying specific therapeutic goals precisely, and communicating these goals clearly to both direct care staff and to the patients themselves, is therapeutic. From a psychologist's point of view, this means that only a limited number of goals can be presented—so that staff and patients alike are not overwhelmed by too many goals—and the goals must be presented in a straightforward way.

Just as important as the initial specification of the goal is the regular checking or monitoring of the target that has been set, to see if change is indeed occurring. An interesting contribution to the way in which psychologists can help to evaluate change over a long period of time is the comparative study of Woods and Cullen (1983). They compared four studies, carried out with mentally handicapped and chronically mentally ill people, where behavioural data had been carefully collected over many months—up to five years for some patients. A summary table of the results (see Table 3.1) shows how little relation there was between what improvement had occurred, and what improvement care staff *thought* had occurred. This illustrates the difficulty of maintaining staff behaviour over the very long periods of time inevitably involved with patients in institutions, and the possibility of complex relationships between staff and resident behaviour.

The focus of most assessment methods is the behaviour of the patient, both past and present, and looking at the remaining assets, as well as the deficits (or negative handicaps) and the deviations (or positively odd behaviour) of the patient. However, it may be important to assess the physical environment of the patient, as that environment may be setting limits to the patients' behaviour. Alternatively, it may be helpful to assess the social environment of the patients, typically the pattern of interaction of staff with the patients. All these assessment methods should be capable of being repeated from time to time to review patients, especially for those inoffensive and thus unnoticed patients who often compose the majority of the residents of a ward.

A peculiar difficulty in working with chronic patients is their reticence in expressing their own wishes in a way that is consistent. Often such patients may have difficulty in understanding questions, may be inarticulate in their replies, or may be easily influenced in their

Table 3.1 Effects of four behavioural programmes on residents and staff

Study	Resident behaviour	Staff perception	Staff behaviour
1. Toileting	Gradual improvement	No improvement	Sustained
2. Toileting	Gradual deterioration	No improvement	Sustained
3. Room management	Rapid improvement	Definite improvement	Not sustained
4. Token economy	Gradual improvement and maintained at stable level	Little or no improvement	Sustained

answers, so it is difficult to have confidence that you really have found out what *they* want. This can lead to ethical difficulties, since such patients, unlike many residents of mental handicap hospitals, have no relative or next-of-kin to whom you can turn when difficult decisions have to be made. This suggests more psychological attention should be paid to finding out how best to communicate with such patients.

For all of these assessment decisions—categorizing, target-setting, or monitoring—there is a range of procedures available. In general, tests are not now widely used, and self-completion questionnaires are rarely used for more chronic patients, for the reasons just discussed. The two most frequently used types of assessment are ratings—either of ward behaviour or of interview behaviour—or behavioural assessment procedures.

Ratings require an observer to record, in a standard way, his *opinion* of the relative strength of a particular attribute. Ratings of ward behaviour are usually completed by nurses, often on the basis of a few days observation, and typically are high on general relevance. Conversely, ratings of interview behaviour may be more reliable, but may not be closely related to what the patient does outside the interview. Careful design of the ratings, and careful training of raters, can overcome these problems, as shown in the example.

Rating chronic psychiatric patients

Many scales have been developed to assess chronic patients, some based on interviews with the patients themselves, some based on direct observation of the patients. A useful assessment instrument in this sort of setting should meet a number of criteria, including: (a) the possibility of its use in different types of setting, in particular in both hospital and community settings; (b) inclusion of items that differentiate between those patients who may be able to live independently, and those probably requiring some continuing degree of supervision; (c) the possibility of detecting change in behaviour, even when change is limited in extent and occurs over a period of months.

With these aims in mind Baker and Hall (1983) have developed over a period of eight years a new behaviour rating scale, REHAB, for use by direct care staff. There are a number of important features in this scale. The content of the items was chosen from research studies, to include items of problem behaviour that occurred most frequently, items considered by key staff groups to be most important, and those shown to be sensitive to treatment change. The individual items were designed to cover the full range of disability that can be shown with this client group, so that in the event a wide range of scores resulted, showing a good spread of scores. The whole scale was also worded and set out so that it could be easily read and understood by direct-care staff, such a nursing assistants, who may not have a high level of formal education. The scale was factor-analysed, in such a way that the factors that emerged were robust over the whole range of patients who were studied, so that the factors made practical sense both for the most handicapped and least handicapped patient. The scale was developed on nearly 1 000 different patients, mostly from the three different centres of Aberdeen, Cardiff, and Leeds, so the scale does not simply reflect conditions in one locality or hospital.

Some of the detailed investigations necessary to design properly a scale like this are of interest. It is obviously important that any standard instrument is used in a standard way, so a clear description is given of how to train raters, and copies of a special user's guide are issued with the scale. Most handicapped patients, irrespective of diagnosis, show two main types of behaviour problem. On the one hand they show deficits, or lack, of behaviour—they don't talk much, or they move slowly, for example. This type of behaviour may be assessed using a linear–graphic type of item, as shown below:

Item 8: 'How well did the patient get on with others on the ward or unit?'

Very poor relationship with other patients Solitary and withdrawn	Got on with some patients	Got on well with other patients

On the other hand they show deviant, or bizarre behaviour — typically infrequent and unpredictable behaviour, such as shouting. This requires a different sort of item, mainly assessing the frequency with which such behaviour occurs, as shown.

Item 1. Incontinence		
Incontinent more than once a week	Incontinent once a week	Never incontinent

Another important feature of such scales is that they can be used in regular monitoring of the progress of chronic patients. It is very difficult to keep in mind the characteristics of patients over many months without some sort of systematic record: assessing acute patients is relatively easy by comparison, because change is so marked and rapid.

Behavioural assessment procedures usually involve some timing or counting of events as they happen, with immediate recording using either a time measure or direct count of number of events, or use of a simple coding system to categorize events. There is currently a lot of psychological interest in the extent to which staff communicate with patients, and the extent to which patients keep their attention on therapeutic tasks. 'Time-sampling' is a frequently used behavioural assessment procedure in such 'staff–patient interaction' or 'engagement' studies. Time-sampling, in such a study, involves selecting a suitable system for observing each patient in turn, so for example, every 20 s a patient would be observed for 5 s exactly, and at the end of that 5 s period the patient's behaviour would be coded, using a set of behavioural categories. Adequate time must always be allowed for the appropriate category or categories to be selected and recorded, so the observer can then pick out the next patient in plenty of time, without being hurried. Using this schedule, a group of nine patients could be observed once in 3 min, or three times each in 9 min. Although there can be a problem of 'reactivity', which is the way in which a patient behaves differently because he knows he is being observed, an observer can be passive and non-responsive to patients, thus minimizing this problem. Since the rate of behavioural change with chronic patients is usually slow, it is possible to observe quite large groups of patients at a time, a task impossible with, for example, behaviourally disturbed children.

Psychological assessment has often been seen as the exclusive preserve of the psychologist. In long-term care settings, by contrast, the psychologist is very much concerned to work with other groups so that the assessment which *they* necessarily must make can be better understood and used. The psychologist is also concerned to work with others to clarify the goals of assessment, so that assessment decisions can be made as effectively as possible.

Psychological interventions with chronic patients

Historically, the treatment of chronic patients in institutions has been dominated by so-called 'social' models of treatment, and work-related approaches to treatment. Going back to Pinel and Tuke in the eighteenth and nineteenth centuries, 'moral' treatment approaches were the most influential, and indeed represented an often heroic attempt to combat exploitation and devaluing of the chronic patient. The place of work was central in most hospital regimes, culminating in the Industrial Therapy movement of the 1930s and 1960s.

The Second World War led to the development of more structured ideas of social treatment, particularly associated with the Therapeutic Community movement. This movement was strongly influenced by the work and ideas of Maxwell Jones, and therapeutic communities, whether hospital-wide or simply involving one ward, became quite common. The next major innovation, led by clinical psychologists, was the introduction of token economy programmes, based on an operant conditioning model and following the innovative work of Ayllon and Azrin. Although therapeutic community concepts and token economy concepts have been viewed as antithetical, a close examination of working practices in the two types of regime often shows surprising similarities. More recently other essentially psychological techniques of intervention have been used, such as social skills training, and problem-solving techniques. It is perhaps a paradox that just as the numbers of long-term patients in psychiatric hospitals continue to fall, albeit more slowly than before, more psychological interest is being shown in how to treat such patients. The range of approaches and procedures available can be illustrated by briefly considering three of the main techniques or approaches.

The milieu approach

All wards necessarily have some sort of milieu or atmosphere, but it may not be specifically recognized as a major tool in rehabilitation. Milieu approaches can be categorized under three main headings. Milieu Therapy is the general concept of the milieu as a mode of treatment, including theory and practice; a therapeutic milieu is a particular setting positively designed for the practice of social therapy, to produce desired change in those who enter it, and thus refers to a range of settings, such as hostels and workshops; a therapeutic community is a specific type of therapeutic milieu. The therapeutic community concept has been further subdivided into the general therapeutic community approach, and the therapeutic community 'proper'. This provides an essentially hierarchical classification, but an examination of therapeutic communities highlights some of the main features of this approach.

A fundamental feature of the milieu approach is its treatment of authority, so that authority on a ward is not exercised hierarchically, but diffused through the staff. Authority is often invested, at least partially, in regular ward meetings, which focus on immediate events and identify publicly the contribution of individual community members to those events. Responsibility is seen as being passed back to the patient for most areas of his life, including caring for himself and his immediate personal space, so no special efforts are made to spruce up patients on the ward so they look 'nice'. Reality confrontation may be an important part of small groups within the ward, and the detailed analysis of events that thus occurs makes it difficult for conventional barriers of confidentiality to be maintained.

The contribution of a psychologist in this sort of milieu is likely to be similar to the contribution of members of other professions, for a large proportion of the time. The specific professional skills of the psychologist—and of the occupational therapist—may be called upon, but both will be asked to contribute to group meetings, and perhaps to lead staff feedback groups after main group meetings. Involvement in this sort of regime may both help a psychologist to develop group therapy skills, which might then be useful in, say, an addiction unit, and offer an opportunity to contribute other psychological skills, such as evaluating the effectiveness of the ward.

The token economy approach

Rewards have traditionally been given by hospitals to chronic patients, for example cigarettes doled out by ward and domestic staff. Such essentially casual systems of payment may conflict with the way in which any other money the patient has is distributed, and are not usually related to the main presenting problems of the patient. By contrast the token economy approach (see Kazdin 1982) introduced on a wide scale the use of planned targets and systematic reinforcements to the large mental hospitals in the early 1970s.

The central physical feature of a token economy is some physically durable object, such as coloured plastic disc, or punched card, which has a distinct numerical value attached to it, and which acts as currency within the programme. The exact form of the token is essentially unimportant. However, a secondary benefit of token economy procedures is that an element of choice is restored to the patients: the patient has to choose how to spend his tokens, whereas before he made no choices in his day-to-day life. In a similar way, tokens can reintroduce the idea of cash values to a patient. Very often such patients may spend *all* the money they have in an extravaganza of tobacco early in the morning, and thereafter make no further use of money. Now, they are repeatedly confronted with token—economic decisions, which can be encouraged by using educational money as plastic money. A psychologist who is running a token economy, or other group behavioural programme, will have a number of different tasks to perform. Individual and group targets will have to be set; a careful system of charting introduced; care staff will have to be given specific training in how to dispense tokens; and some quite complex individual programmes will probably have to be carried out on a one-to-one basis. Setting up a regime of this sort can certainly take half a psychologist's time for six months, but only with that level of investment of time can the foundations be laid for a realistic programme that will carry on for some time.

The social skills approach

A third treatment approach is that known generically as Social Skills Training (SST). A number of treatment packages have been described (Spence and Shepherd, 1983), many concentrating on the improvement of behavioural skills. The main feature of this approach is the use of modelling (the demonstration of the relevant skills), rehearsal (repeated practice by the patient in a 'safe' setting), and feedback (detailed comment and criticism both by the therapist and by the use of audio and video-tape recordings).

This approach lends itself to group work, as it is usually fairly easy to find small groups of chronic patients with similar deficits in the area of social functioning. The psychologist's contribution to such a programme would involve a number of different components. The patients would need to be selected, and common goals identified.

Probably other trainers would be needed, so nurses and other staff would have to be prepared for the task. The psychologist and others would have to contribute to the initial modelling of the deficient skills, so a certain degree of acting talent, and willingness to make a bit of a fool of yourself, might then be desirable professional qualities! As in all rehabilitative treatments, steps need to be taken to ensure that the results of the treatment generalize, or spread, to other novel situations. Thus one of the distinctive features of SST is the amount of therapeutic training that may take place actually in the supermarket, or at the bus-stop, or at the bar of the local coffee-shop or pub!

The place of work

As already discussed, work therapies have historically been an important way of structuring the daily activity of chronic patients. More recently, work as a form of therapy has become less common as a consequence of widespread unemployment severely reducing the availability of work to those suffering from major psychiatric handicaps. For similar reasons the range of work available within hospitals has also contracted, often to offering only simple packaging and assembly work. At the same time, the role of work in offering a range of structured social relationships, and in requiring the individual to meet a range of expectations in the areas of skill, work-rate, timekeeping, has become apparent.

This means that the role of the psychologist in contributing to the design of work regimes for people living in institutions is a complex one. Unless work is to be merely the performance of simple repetitive tasks, patients should be offered tasks which are within their competence and interest, but which also stretch them. Imaginative voluntary schemes have set up retail outlets and craft workshops where patients can be involved in a complete process of production and selling, where patients can be fitted into the right slot for them. The system of hospital reward payments and social security benefits in Britain is so complicated that considerable attention needs to be paid to incentive schemes for them to work. A number of countries have sheltered workshops, which may offer an offsite day activity for people who still have homes in hospital. Thus in Australia such workshops are operated by voluntary bodies with a gradually reducing state subsidy both for capital and staff costs, and with an incentive reward for every person who returns to outside employment.

Planning a ward rehabilitation programme

Whatever the theoretical background to a ward regime, a psychologist is likely to have a number of skills to contribute to planning and running the programme. The rehabilitation of the individual is obviously important (and is well illustrated in the appendix to Shepherd 1984), but ward rehabilitation programmes require an additional ability to plan a system of care.

A typical ward might consist of a 30-bedded mixed-sex ward, with two separate large dormitories and five single sleeping rooms. There is a large day room with easy chairs and television, one small side room, and a spacious ward corridor (doubling as a dining area) leading to the main hospital corridor, off which open a few office rooms. There are 27 patients on the ward, 16 women and 11 men, aged from 28 to 76, though 14 patients are aged over 60. All but five patients have been continuously in hospital for at least 8 years—one for 43 years—but two of the patients have been in hospital for less than a year, both previously having several years experience of 'revolving door' admissions to the hospital.

The routine on the ward revolves around meal times and drug rounds. While eight patients go off the ward for a couple of hours each morning and afternoon, most patients do not have a regular therapeutic activity, apart from a large group meeting four times a week and an assigned job on the ward. The number of staff on duty at any one time ranges between three and seven, and while one or two of these staff will always be qualified staff permanently assigned to the ward, other staff may be drafted in to 'cover' from other wards, or may be mostly nursing aides or student nurses.

A psychologist becoming involved with this ward could start off with any one of a number of preparatory activities—first making sure she has the time to follow through all that will be involved. The literature on the psychologist's role as a 'change agent' will alert her to the need to promote group cohesion and group commitment to change amongst the ward and off-ward staff involved. Visiting two or three other active rehabilitation units, and calling in two or three credible experts will enable staff to see that change is possible. A short but relevant staff training programme will both help staff to

formulate objectives, and begin to think of detailed procedures—
such as a regular ward-based activity regime they could introduce.

Assuming the original patients remain on the ward—and maybe
one or two will be too old, or too mentally or physically handicapped
—the assets and problems of each patient will need to be assessed.
This may lead to the formation of three or four groups, each with
relatively similar problems and each with an assigned trained staff
member, which will have their own group programme. Resources of
staff and equipment may well be limited, so it may be better to
provide half an hour of structured activity each day—such as going
through local papers to identify times of buses and films—rather
than dilute the same amount of real learning over two hours. Doing
regular assigned jobs can be helpful, as long as each ward resident
does a job at the right level of difficulty, changes job at least every
month or so, and perhaps always does the job with a companion or
buddy. Success at these therapeutic tasks may then lead to a patient
moving to, say, a pre-discharge hostel and another programme
aimed at his new abilities and needs.

Stitching together a programme in this way indicates the amount
of overall planning and co-ordination required. Figure 3.1 indicates
how this co-ordination can be viewed as an overall system, requiring psychological contributions to assessment and monitoring (the

Fig. 3.1

psychologist as psychometrician), promotion of group working among both staff and patients (the psychologist as group facilitator and therapist), fitting both staff and patients to the activities to which they are best suited (the psychologist as occupational adviser), and the design of individual therapeutic programmes (the psychologist as expert therapist). Obviously this co-ordination cannot be carried out by a lone clinical psychologist, but the scope for psychological contribution to this type of development is enormous.

CHAPTER SUMMARY

Psychologists have a number of specific contributions to make to the care of patients in institutions. Most institutional residents have major chronic difficulties. Those difficulties can be conceptualised in psychological ways that help to frame treatment objectives, and may even lead to re-evaluating the type of institution in which that treatment should occur. Those difficulties need to be understood specifically and individually, and carefully chosen and applied psychological instruments can add to that understanding. Some of those difficulties can be overcome, if only partly and slowly. A major area of concern is the relative lack of evaluation of the effectiveness of the treatment available in institutional settings. Specific treatments have been evaluated, but the same attention has not been paid to the overall funtioning of the institution. For example, there has been relatively little examination of the effectiveness of the major discharge policy adopted in Britain and most other European countries. Braun, Kochansky, Shapiro, Greenberg, Gudeman, Johnson, and Shore (1981) give a detailed analysis of attempts at de-institutionalization in the USA and Europe: there is little factual evidence to support a complete abolition of institutional care. This does not mean that large, isolated, minimally resourced institutions should continue. It does mean that some small, accessible, adequately resourced institutions will continue to be needed, and that a wealth of psychological, sociological, and psychiatric guidance now exists to give no excuse for not providing a facilitating, appropriate, and caring regime.

REFERENCES

Baker, R. D. and Hall, J. N. (1983). REHAB: *rehabilitation evaluation. Hall and Baker.* Vine Publishing, Aberdeen.

Braun, P., Kochansky, G., Shapiro, R., Greenberg, S., Gudeman, J. E., Johnson, S. and Shore, M. F. (1981). Overview: deinstitutionalisation of psychiatric patients, a critical review of outcome studies. *Am. J. Psychiat.* **138**, 736–49.

Goffman, E (1961). *Asylums: essays on the social situations of mental patients and other inmates.* Anchor Books, New York.

Kazdin, A. E. (1982). The Token Economy: a decade later. *J. Appl. Behav. Anal.* **15**, 431–45.

MIND (1983). *Common concern.* Mind, London.

Shepherd, G. (1984). See 'Further reading'.

Spence, S. and Shepherd, G. (1983). *Developments in social skills training.* Academic Press, London.

Woods, P. A. and Cullen, C. N. (1983). Determinants of staff behaviour in long-term care. *Behav. Psychother.* **11**, 4–18.

Wykes, T. (1982). A hostel-ward for 'new' long-stay patients: an evaluative study of a 'ward in a house'. *Psychological medicine monograph* Suppl. 2. Cambridge University Press, Cambridge.

FURTHER READING

Jones, K. and Fowles, A. J. (1984). *Ideas on Institutions.* Routledge and Kegan Paul, London.

Shepherd, G. (1984). *Institutional care and rehabilitation.* Longman, London.

Watts, F. N. and Bennett, D. H. (1983). *Theory and practice of psychiatric rehabilitation.* Wiley, Chichester.

4

Working with children and young people

Dorothy Fielding

It has been estimated that of a total of 1 600 clinical psychologists working in the National Health Service some 240 work full-time with children and adolescents. Clinical psychologists are therefore currently providing a sizeable service in the field of child and adolescent health.

Traditionally child clinical psychology services developed alongside those of child psychiatry. In those early days particular emphasis was given to the assessment role of the psychologist within the multidisciplinary team. Clinical psychologists would be asked to contribute to the work of the team by providing intellectual and educational assessments and making any comments about the child's personality or general adjustment that might aid in management.

In recent years, however, there have been substantial changes in the context in which child clinical psychologists work. A number of factors have contributed to these changes. In the first instance, reorganization of clinical psychology services into health district departments have given a wide range of professional workers access to psychological services. Secondly, legislative changes regarding the education and care of children, and the publication of a number of influential government reports have emphasised the advice-giving consultative and policy making roles of clinical psychologists. Finally advances in research and clinical practice have widened the range of expertise of clinical psychologists thus changing psychologists' perception of their own role. The following chapter reviews these developments in clinical practice by describing the settings in which child clinical psychologists now work and the contributions which they make to the health care of children and young people.

THE CHANGING HEALTH NEEDS OF CHILDREN AND YOUNG PEOPLE AND THE ROLE OF CHILD CLINICAL PSYCHOLOGISTS

Any discussion of services for children must take into account the changing patterns of health and disease amongst the child population. There is no doubt that over the last 50 years there have been dramatic improvements in the health of children and young people. Many of the crippling infectious diseases prevalent in the early part of this century have been eliminated and there have been impressive reductions in the mortality rate of young infants. Increased survival has been accompanied by improved growth. Children are taller and heavier than they were a generation ago. However, the factors that have brought about reduction in infant mortality and morbidity have also resulted in the saving of life of more low birthweight babies, and babies with inherited diseases and congenital conditions. More children therefore survive with chronic and handicapping conditions. With the declining importance of infectious diseases, chronic disorders (malformations, chronic illness, physical and mental handicaps) have become a major focus and concern for health care provision. These disorders call for a different approach on the part of professional staff working with them. For example, nursing staff may be involved in the treatment of these children's conditions over long periods of time. They may need to encourage them to participate in unpleasant medical procedures with distressing side effects. They may be required to counsel very sick and dying children and their families. It has become increasingly clear that families and staff who care for chronically sick or severely handicapped youngsters are subject to considerable stresses. Increasingly paediatricians, nursing staff, and social workers are calling for psychological help with these difficult health problems of children.

Interview transcript—Psychological problems of a family with a chronically sick child

Alan is a fifteen-year-old boy who has been on dialysis since the age of 8½ years. He has now obtained a transplant. His illness commenced not long after his birth and he has a long medical history including many hospital admissions. He lives at home with his mother, father and sister Sandra. The family has few social supports and much of the responsibility for bringing up the family has fallen upon Alan's mother as Alan's father's job has often taken him away from home. Alan's father and mother have disagreed about ways of treating their sick son. Alan's father has tried to take a more strict approach and Alan's mother a more lenient approach. The following transcript of an interview with mother and father illustrates some of the psychological problems arising in families who care for chronically sick youngsters.

These include marital problems and problems with their daughter (speech delays, complaints of pain, demanding behaviour). Finally, Alan's mother describes how near she has come towards harming her daughter.

Marital problems

Father: There was a period of time when we could have split up due to the pressures of this. I think there was one time that Irene thought that she couldn't rely on me to a certain extent.

Interviewer: In what way—

Mother: Bill at first would carry on and lead his life sort of thing. To me it should be—well if he was going to drink at least we should know where he was going.

Father: I disagree—on most occasions Irene—there was one or two occassions when I did slip up.

Interviewer: He'd leave it mostly to you and that upset you.

Mother: At times you get to a point when you feel it's all on you.

Father: There's ways in which Irene carries on, if I was that sort of person, I could get upset—you know I'm a man, but in our house there's two. In our house everything is done for Alan we don't have a social life—an active social life. I'd like to take Irene out. She'd say 'How about Alan'. It wasn't making the situation any better molly-coddling him.

Interviewer: Do you agree?

Mother: (nods) Got to the stage where Alan felt you shouldn't go out. No, he's got to learn—else he'll grow up thinking that you've got to do what he wants.

Interviewer: So, he was right. You've come round to that now.

Mother: I'll go out now, but I'll worry inside.

Reaction of other children in family

Interviewer: How did the situation affect Sandra?

Mother: You tend to feel guilty. Because Sandra was 18 months when Alan first went on the machine. So you either had to bring her with you so she had to spend a lot of time here (in the hospital) or you'd have to leave her.

Interviewer: Why did you feel guilty?

Mother: Because the time I'd been able to spend with Alan when he was little playing games and things—you couldn't do that with Sandie. We say she's old-headed.

Interviewer: (to father) What does Sandie say to you?

Father: She says, 'I don't like this house, everybody hates me'.

Interviewer: How do you cope with that?

Father: To be honest I say don't be bloody ridiculous. Then I'll leave her for 20 minutes and then fuss her.

Interviewer: Has it made her react in any other way? Has she thrown up any problems?

Mother: Her speech. (Sandie was late to talk and needed to visit a speech therapist.) You give her material things—but most important is time and affection—she doesn't get that.

Interviewer: Does she understand this?

Mother: She demands financial things. If you can't give them to her she says—well Alan doesn't have to wait, then if Alan wants a roast dinner she'll say, 'I don't want that'. She'll rebel. Then she'd complain of pain and things.

Stress on parents

Father: At one time Irene's nerves went all to pieces.

Interviewer: (to mother) How did it affect you?

Mother: I thought that if I hit her then I really couldn't stop myself. I really would hurt her. I went to see the doctor about it but I was too embarrassed to tell him. It seemed as if everything was on top of me. He said you must know what's at the bottom of this—but I couldn't say. He gave me some tablets—I threw them away, they didn't do me any good.

Improved standards of medical and nursing care and the development of new and effective treatments have obviously made considerable impact on the health of children. However, the decline of infectious diseases, already commented upon, has relied equally upon the development of better standards of living, for example reduction in overcrowding, improved diet, and smaller families. The epidemic diseases of today (for example, lung cancer, heart disease) are associated with particular styles of life (diet, smoking, lack of exercise). Many of these habits are built up in childhood and early adolescence and it is increasingly recognized that future improvements in child health (and ultimately adult health) may depend as much upon changes in behaviour as upon changes in the technical aspects of medical practice. This has far-reaching implications for the role of psychologists within the health service. Increasingly child clinical psychologists are being asked to contribute to educational and preventative aspects of child health services.

One of the major concerns in child health is the large number of children with emotional or behavioural difficulties. One estimate suggests that in the course of one year some 5 to 10 per cent of children present with problems of sufficient severity to handicap them in everyday life. Ten years ago the report of the Committee on Child Health Services (Court 1976) noted the important role that clinical psychologists play in the assessment and treatment of these disorders. Whilst clinical psychologists are often involved in the direct treatment of such problems in community and hospital settings, many psychologists have found that they can work equally or even more effectively by passing on some of their skills to other professionals such as teachers, health visitors, occupational therapists, or social workers. Much of their time is then spent working in a consultative role for these professions.

The health needs of youngsters are often intimately linked with the social and environmental circumstances in which they live. In the last 20 years there have been dramatic changes within society. The breakdown of the extended family and the rising divorce rate have led to an increasing number of single parents bringing up children in unsupported and isolated circumstances. Even where families are intact, young mothers may find themselves in neighbourhoods with few friends and little support. The high incidence of depression in the mothers of pre-school children is well documented. Under such circumstances normal childhood difficulties (for example, feeding, sleeping, and toileting problems) may loom large. Of the group of professional workers who are available for consultation by the parents of pre-school children, clinical psychologists, by virtue of their special training and expertise, are particularly able to give advice concerning the management of these frequently occurring childhood emotional and behavioural problems.

In extreme circumstances some parents may become locked into cycles of excessive punishment. Occasionally injury to the child results. Whilst the true prevalence of such violence is unknown, it has been conservatively estimated that in Britain some 8 000 children each year suffer 'non-accidental injuries'. These reported cases obviously represent only a fraction of those who are maltreated. In recent years clinical psychologists working in health settings have begun to provide assistance to social service departments both in assessment and management of these problems of child abuse.

The rising unemployment figures have meant that many families suffer considerable financial hardship, with several family members out of work. The relationship between such social and economic changes and psychological well-being is neither simple nor clear cut. However, some out of work youngsters with time on their hands will find themselves in the hands of the police as a result of petty crimes and excessive alcohol or drug use. In some parts of the country drug abuse and drug dependence amongst young people has reached epidemic proportions, causing health authorities to act swiftly in the setting up of new drug dependency facilities. Psychologists working within adolescent health services are becoming increasingly involved in the in-patient and community care of youngsters with drug and alcohol dependency problems.

WORK SETTINGS OF CHILD CLINICAL PSYCHOLOGISTS

The preceding section has reviewed some of the health needs of children and young people and hinted at the settings in which psychologists work. Generally speaking children and young people do not seek help themselves—instead they are referred by adults who are close to them or who come into contact with them through their work. Whilst in some cases youngsters are referred by parents, in many instances it is other professional workers, for example teachers, paediatricians, school medical officers, health visitors, and social workers, who recognize that they are in need of psychological help. Children are therefore referred to clinical psychologists

Table 4.1 Settings in which child clinical psychologists work and examples of their work

Setting	Example
(a) *Health*	
(i) Community	
Child welfare clinics	Liaison/consultation with health visitors
Health centres	
GP practices	Parents groups for behavioural, sleeping, feeding problems of under-fives
(ii) Hospital	
Ante-natal clinics	Counselling of mothers with suspected handicapped child
	Counselling of adolescents deciding about termination of pregnancy
Intensive care neonatal units	Counselling for staff and parents
Paediatric assessment clinics	Assessment and remediation of development delays
Paediatric hospital wards	Preparation of parents/children for hospitalization
	Counselling of parents/staff dealing with terminally ill children
Casualty wards	Crisis counselling for adolescents who have taken overdoses
Psychiatric in-patient and out-patient units	Assessment and treatment with families of children showing emotional and behavioural problems
	Consultation/training of psychiatric child care staff (in psychological procedures)
(b) *Social services*	
(i) Local authority nurseries	Advice to nursery nurses concerning problems of child abuse
	Assessment of development delays
(ii) Community homes	Consultation with staff concerning management of difficult behaviour problems
	Counselling foster parents
(c) *Voluntary organizations*	Drop-in clinics for adolescents with drug taking or alcohol problems (e.g. Samaritans, Adoption Societies, Brook Advisory Centres, Grapevine etc.)

through the wide network of health, education, and social services. Table 4.1 describes some of the settings in which clinical psychologists work, giving some examples of the kinds of work that they do. Obviously not all child clinical psychologists are involved in all of these activities. The type of service provided within a district health authority will depend upon the availability of expertise of clinical psychologists who specialize in working with children. However the table reflects the range of activities that many clinical psychologists are engaged in.

ORGANIZATIONAL ASPECTS OF CHILD CLINICAL PSYCHOLOGY SERVICE

Historical accident and unevenness of health care provisions have led to a situation where some health districts are well-endowed with child clinical psychologists whilst others have few or even no clinical psychologists working exclusively with children. Nationally there is therefore a great variation in the type of child clinical psychology services provided at district level and in the representation of child clinical psychologists in relevant health service committees such as health care planning teams or joint care planning teams. However where psychological facilities are operating at a reasonable level there will be a well-experienced child clinical psychologist organizing psychological services for children within a health district, and a team of other child clinical psychologists providing sessions to the community, hospital and social, and other services (Table 4.1). Child clinical psychologists will have representation on health care planning and joint care planning committees for child and adolescent services. In addition they will be called on to contribute to special working groups to set up specialist health projects within a health region or district (for example community adolescent services, drug dependency clinics). An essential part of the role of the clinical psychologists is collaboration with other professional workers in policy and planning of services for children.

Clinical psychologists are not the only group of psychologists working with children. All Local Educational Authorities (LEAs) employ educational psychologists who provide a school psychological service. There are some 1 300 educational psychologists working within LEAs in the UK. They act as advisers to LEAs and particularly to schools. Whilst both groups of psychologists have distinctive contributions to make to the health and educational needs of children, there is also a degree of overlap both in terms of clients and in terms of services provided. For this reason close collaboration between the two disciplines is frequently required. This is achieved either by the establishment of close personal contacts between individual professional workers or by local advisory groups on psychological services for children on which both educational and clinical psychologists are represented.

SOME GENERAL ISSUES CONCERNING WORK WITH CHILDREN AND YOUNG PEOPLE

Before proceeding to a more detailed description of the ways in which clinical psychologists work with children and young people it is important to consider some general issues concerning the context in which childhood problems occur. These issues have implications for both assessment and treatment. Furthermore they may determine whether intervention is made at all in some cases.

Social context of problem behaviour

It is generally adults who refer children to psychological services. For this reason it is often worthwhile considering why a particular child is referred at a certain point in time. Why did this mother come to the GP at this time for help with her three-year-old son's temper tantrums? Why did the ward sister refer this particular eight-year-old who is fearful when blood samples are being taken? Why did this member of the child care staff feel that this fifteen-year-old was particularly difficult to handle? Of course, it may be that these problems were so severe that they caused special concern. However, this is clearly not always the case. Studies which have compared mothers attending clinics for help with a particular child's problem with mothers who are not attending a clinic yet have children with the same problem, have shown the 'clinic mothers' to be more anxious. Furthermore it appears that schools in quite similar areas with pupils from quite similar socio-economic backgrounds may have very different referring rates to educational psychology services. These simple examples illustrate the importance of the social context in which the childhood difficulty occurs, since this may determine whether help is sought at all. Moreover, the examples given above suggest that particular 'systems', be they families or institutions, play a part in creating and maintaining difficult psychological problems in children.

Developmental context

Development during childhood and adolescence is often rapid and sometimes uneven. Such change has implications for both assessment and treatment. Firstly, the significance of certain childhood problems may vary depending upon the age of the child. Table 4.2 displays a number of childhood behaviours which may cause parents, doctors, and other professional workers to seek psychological help. Surveys of the general population reveal that many of these problem behaviours occur quite frequently amongst a normal

Table 4.2 Common childhood problems for which psychological help may be sought

Somatic complaints (e.g. headaches, stomach-ache etc.)
Fears and phobias
Obsessions
Temper tantrums
Fighting
Lying
Bullying
Destructive behaviour
Stealing
Distractibility
Over-activity
Poor concentration
Language delay
Reading retardation
Bedwetting
Soiling
Tics
Thumb sucking, nail biting
Over eating
Under eating
Sleep disturbance
School refusal
Autism
Childhood schizophrenia

sample of children. Some behavioural problems are more frequent at certain ages. For example, bedwetting is so common amongst three-year-olds as to be considered normal. It is much less common in seven-year-olds, the age at which many paediatricians begin to consider children for treatment. Temper tantrums are very common in pre-school children but much less common in eight-and nine-year-olds. Such findings illustrate the importance of taking the age of the child into account when considering psychological intervention.

The fact that developmental change may be rapid during various stages in childhood also carries implications for the stability of assessment information over time. For example, assessment of behaviour at one age (particularly at younger age levels) may not be predictive of behaviour at a later age. Moreover epidemiological studies which have followed normal groups of children over time indicate that many childhood problems are short-lived. Decisions concerning the mode and timing of the treatment intervention must be viewed in the light of existing knowledge concerning the natural remission rate of such problems.

Continuous influences on childhood development

Increasingly, research investigations of childhood development are emphasizing the importance of *continuous* influences on a child's development. Infants and children are remarkably adaptable. For example, adverse environmental conditions resulting from separation from parents, and institutional care in infancy and early childhood do not inevitably produce severe long-term effects. If the child is later placed in the long-term care of a family that is warm and supportive, the effects of early deprivation may be considerably reduced. However, and equally important, children brought up in extremely deprived circumstances may be influenced little by remedial programmes that are brief and take little account of the later impoverished environment at home or at school. It is these and similar findings that have directed many clinical psychologists towards working directly with families and particularly parents rather than working individually with the distressed child or young person. In the case of children in care or children in a residential hospital unit many psychologists will work through the child care or nursing staff who are with the child for much of the day. The aim is to produce maximal, long-term changes in the children's environment that will enable them to make healthy future adjustments.

WAYS OF WORKING

Orientation

A range of factors may influence the style of work of a clinical psychologist, for example the availability of residential facilities, the existence of community teams, the number of child clinical psychologists in a district health authority, or the people who make up the multi-disciplinary team. However, also important is the training and theoretical orientation of the clinical psychologist concerned. During their training clinical psychologists will be exposed to a variety of psychological approaches, for example dynamic psychotherapy, family therapy, and behaviour therapy. Their later clinical work will be influenced by the theoretical model they adopt following training. Not all of these approaches to child problems are equally effective with all client groups. Moreover some therapeutic procedures are under-researched in terms of their effectiveness.

In the following sections emphasis is placed upon those ways of working that have been subjected to empirical investigation. Problems of the child are viewed in a developmental and family context and an emphasis placed on those strategies that encourage children and their families to develop problem-solving skills.

Assessment and formulation

When a child is referred for specialized help assessment is obviously the first step that needs to be taken. The process of assessment involves the psychologist and co-workers in a number of tasks. The first of these involves *identification and specification of the problem* for which help is being sought. At first glance this might appear to be a simple task. However in any group, be it school, family, marriage, child care establishment, or hospital ward, each member may well have a different perception of the problem. For example, in a family a mother may regard her difficult to manage son as suffering from a form of 'hyperactivity', which should be treated by management of his diet, whilst his father may believe that his son is disobedient, in need of strict discipline and that his wife is too lenient with him. Since such factors may well influence the parents' handling of the problem and their reaction to future interventions, it is important that the psychologist obtain information from all those directly concerned with the child. Also, it is not uncommon for child care workers, teachers, and parents to focus on the problem as if it resides solely in the child and is unaffected by their response to it. Accordingly, assessment of the problem is broadly conceived so that the focus is not solely on the child referred for treatment. In some cases where, for example, parental or staff expectations concerning the child are unrealistic, this may become the focus of intervention rather than the behaviour of the child concerned.

A second task of assessment involves *identification of factors influencing the occurrence of the problem*. This includes not only a detailed enquiry about early development, social and educational details, and a history of the current complaint, but also a thorough investigation of circumstances affecting the occurrence of the problem in the present. For example, it is necessary to consider the range of situations in which problems may occur (e.g. home, school, playground etc.) Surveys of the child population show that childhood problems are often situation-specific, so that problems may occur at home but not at school and vice versa. It is also important to note parents' or teachers' or care staff's current ways of handling the child's difficulties. Enquiries into this area may elicit factors which may be encouraging the persistence of the problematic behaviour. Finally, assessment will also include *detailed analysis of the potential of the child and significant others* for coping with the problem. Parents often come to the clinic focusing upon the negative aspects of their child's behaviour and in doing so they may overlook important positive things that the child does. A recognition of these aspects of the child may raise their own self-esteem as parents and encourage their later participation in treatment.

For the clinical psychologist, assessment is therefore seen as an attempt to answer a series of interlinked questions about the child and family (school, child care establishment, or hospital ward). What is the child doing or not doing that is considered problematic? What is the frequency/intensity of the problem behaviour? How does this child compare with other children of the same age group? Where does the problem occur, with whom, and when? What events usually precede the problem behaviour and what follow it? What factors in early development may have contributed to the problem? What does the child or adolescent do that is not considered to be problematic?

Accordingly a range of variables (physical, biological, social, and

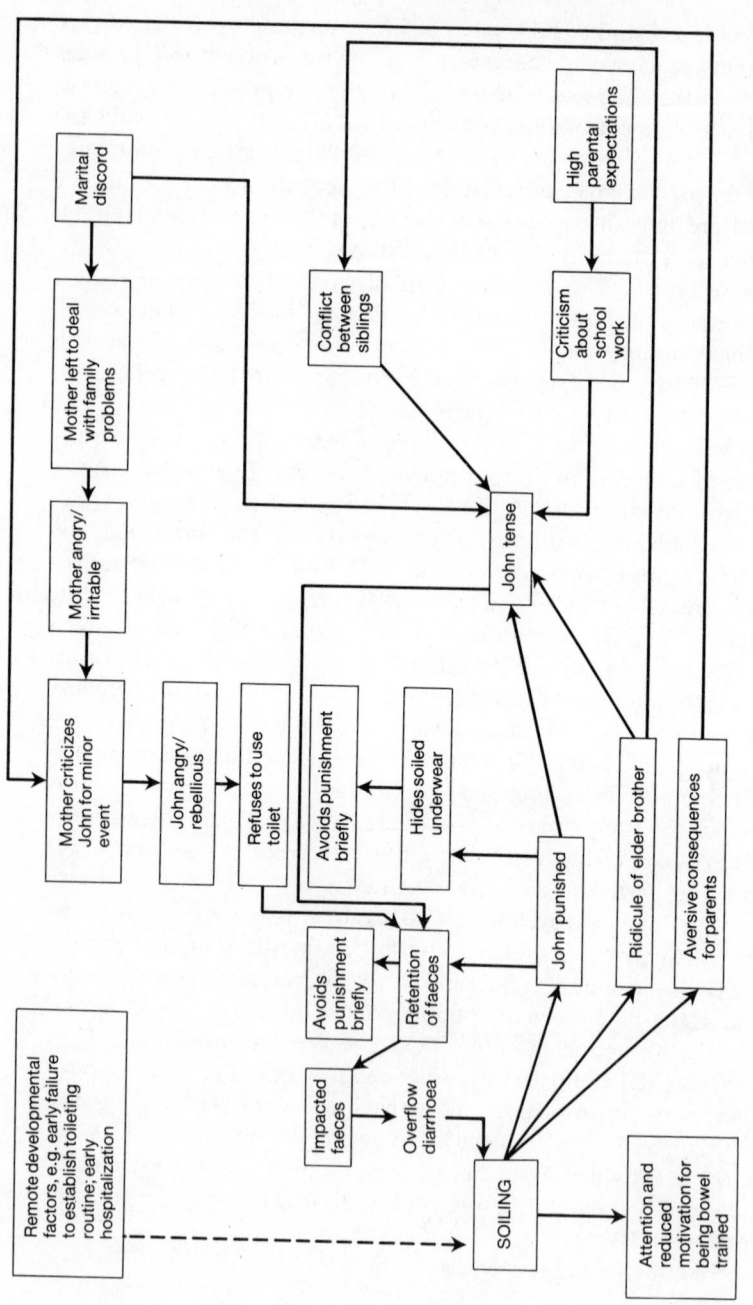

Fig. 4.1 Psychological formulation of events surrounding encopresis for a nine-year-old boy.

environmental) are considered in relationship to the child's problem. No prior assumptions are made about the relative importance of these variables. Instead their importance is determined by a careful analysis, based on a detailed observation and measurement. Such assessment may include the use of systematic interviews (with family, child, or parents alone) structured rating scales or behavioural checklists (given to parents, child or teachers/care staff) behavioural diaries (kept by the child or significant adult) or standardized psychometric tests, (intelligence test, reading test etc.). In addition, detailed and systematic direct observation of the child's behaviour, the behaviour of other children (siblings/classmates), or significant adults (parents, teachers, ward staff) may be carried out.

Details obtained from the assessment allow the psychologist to prepare a detailed formulation of the problems. This formulation is basically a series of hypotheses capable of explaining:

(a) the development of the problem;
(b) the persistence of the problem and the likely response to a particular treatment intervention.

An example of one such clinical formulation for a nine-year-old encopretic child is shown in Figure 4.1.

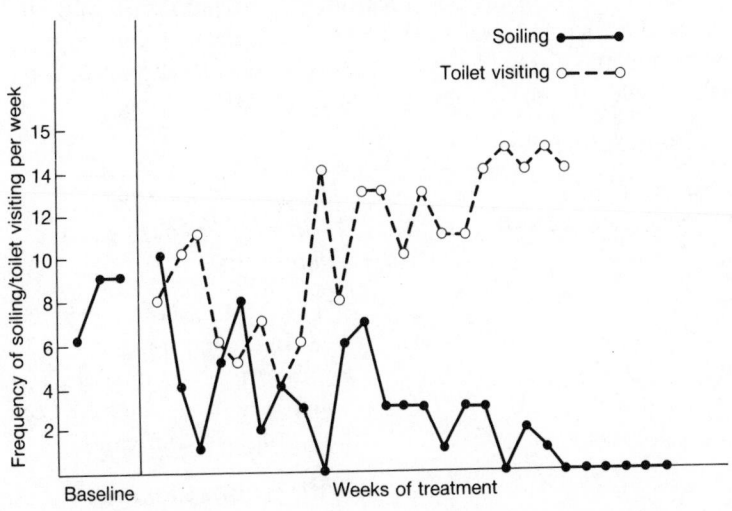

Fig. 4.2 Therapeutic progress of a nine-year-old encopretic boy

Treatment of a nine-year-old boy with soiling problems

Brief description of problem

John lives in the family home with his mother, father, brother Paul (aged 12), and sister Karen (aged 3). John has never been able to control his bowel motions and the longest time he has removed free from soiling is a period of one week. He was referred to a clinical psychology department by a consultant paediatrician.

Assessment

Family interview;
Daily records of soiling and toilet visiting;
Daily diary of other activities;
(including ratings of tension 1–10);
ABC form of soiling.

Formulation of the problem

Detailed questioning of family members and examination of assessment records revealed a number of contributing factors (see Fig. 4.1). John received little praise or affection from his parents. Instead, most of the interaction between John and his parents took the form of arguments or criticism regarding his behaviour and in particular his soiling. Questioning of John's mother revealed a number of dissatisfactions regarding her relationship with her husband, which appeared to exacerbate her critical reaction to John. Both Paul and Karen received more praise and affection than John, which added to the conflict between John and his siblings.

Treatment programme

Treatment goals	Therapeutic procedure
1. *Encourage daily toilet visits*	*Written instructions given to John:*
	'Take Senokot before going to bed. In the morning have warm drink. 30 min later go to toilet. Tell mum you have been and complete your chart'
	Written instructions to parents:

'Praise John for visiting toilet. Help him to put a sticker on his chart if he has used the toilet and give extra praise.'

2. *Discourage retention of faeces and hiding of soiled underwear*

Give explanation using diagrams to parents and John how retained faeces can lead to overflow diarrhoea, which cannot be controlled.

Instructions to parents:

'Eradicate all criticism and punishment concerning soiling. Expect soiling at early stages of treatment.'

3. *Encourage effective communication/problem-solving regarding toileting*

Analogy of footballer in training used. John (like a footballer) has to complete programme (training) with parents (footballer coach) so that his muscles will be strong.

4. *Increase parental child management skills*

Discussion of management of all children in family using examples from daily diary. Prevent 'scapegoating' of John.

5. *Increase communication between parents*

Encourage effective communication between parents regarding inequitable distribution of domestic chores.

6. *Monitoring of treatment*

Daily records of toileting, soiling, and other behavioural problems to examine treatment effectiveness (see Figure 4.2).

The treatment of this young boy and his family was carried out by Mrs A. Devon while working with the author.

Selecting treatment goals and planning treatment intervention

Once the problems have been precisely defined, the psychologist and others (parents, teachers, nursing staff, and the child, if old enough) make arrangements upon what course of action is to be followed. Although the child or adolescent has presented as a focus for treatment, the treatment goals may not include direct changes in the child's behaviour. For example in the case of a mother seeking help for treatment of her three-year-old's essentially normal 'bed-wetting problem', possible goals for treatment could be a lowering of mother's expectations and anxiety. Treatment might then involve explanation of what bladder control skills are considered normal for a child of this age, practical advice on how to encourage dry beds once they have occurred (lifting, praise, star charts etc.), and explanation of what treatments are available if the problem persists. In the case of chronically ill children referred because of their excessive anxiety when undergoing painful hospital treatment, goals of intervention might be the construction of new methods of preparing children for hospital treatment. (e.g. using specially constructed videos and explanatory leaflets geared to the child's level of intellectual development). Choice of treatment goals takes into account a wide range of variables including:

(a) age and developmental stage of the child;
(b) frequency, intensity and duration of the 'problem behaviour';
(c) potential value for the child of developing new behavioural skills;
(d) likelihood of successful results following an intervention;
(e) important aspects of child's environment which may require change (for example behaviours of siblings, or significant adults).

Once treatment goals have been clarified decisions can be made concerning implementation of treatment. Intervention may be made at a number of different levels. At one level the psychologist may work directly with the child or adolescent singly or in a group. At a second level, the psychologist may decide to work primarily with the adults who are responsible for the child (parents, teachers, child care staff). This may involve the psychologist working with individual parents (teachers or hospital/child care staff) who are experiencing difficulties in dealing with particular childhood problems or with groups of adults.

Finally, the psychologist may decide to operate at a third level, that is with the institution or system (school, hospital, ward, or unit) making child referrals. This level may involve the psychologist working with the staff of the institution on policy and planning issues.

Each level of working carries with it particular advantages. For example, working directly with children and adolescents avoids some of the difficulties of working with unco-operative adults who

Table 4.3 Examples of ways of working at different levels of therapeutic intervention

Level	Example
(a) *Working directly with children and adolescents*	
(i) Individual work	Counselling/behaviour programmes for adolescents with sexual difficulties, cognitive therapy for adolescents with low self esteem/negative thoughts
(ii) Group work	Social skills groups for adolescents—decision-making groups for adolescents in residential unit/community home—'coping with illness' groups for chronically sick youngsters
(b) *Working with parents/ teachers/child care staff (triadic model)*	
(i) Individual	Behavioural programme to be carried out by parents of a youngster with 'temper tantrums'
(ii) Group	Training group for local authority nursery staff dealing with pre-school children with language delays—group for parents with enuretic children using 'dry-bed programme'
(c) *Working with systems*	Planning treatment environments in conjunction with senior clinical staff on oncology ward dealing with children and adolescents—working with staff groups in community homes to discuss structure of unit, deployment of staff etc.

are responsible for the youngster. Furthermore, individual therapy might be the most appropriate way of helping some young people, for example an adolescent who is not happy to discuss certain problems with his parents, or a youngster whose difficulties are relatively inaccessible to others (e.g. negative thoughts, low self-esteem).

However, in certain circumstances a particular level may incur certain disadvantages. For example, when the child's home or school environment is maintaining the child's difficulties only limited change may be possible with individual therapy. In such a case it may be more appropriate and productive to work directly with adults responsible for the child. Some examples of different ways of working are given in Table 4.3.

At whatever level the psychologist chooses to work, an essential part of any intervention is an appraisal of its effects. A clear specification of treatment goals allows successive measurements to be made throughout treatment in order to monitor the effectiveness of the intervention. In the case of the nine-year-old encopretic boy described earlier, records of toilet visiting and soiled garments kept by the child and parents during treatment allowed them to examine the effects of their efforts (see Fig. 4.2). In the case of a new ward programme to prepare chronically ill children for painful treatment procedures a comparison of anxiety levels (measured on self-report and observer-rated anxiety scales) of all children entering treatment over a specified time period both before and after the implementation of the new regime allowed its effectiveness to be ascertained. The following sections give some further illustration of the kinds of treatment interventions made by clinical psychologists in health care settings.

Helping children acquire skills

A frequent goal of many psychological interventions is to enable children and adolescents to improve existing skills or acquire new skills. For example, the psychologist may begin work with nursery staff to increase a pre-school child's language ability. The mother of a mentally handicapped child may be encouraged to teach her child to dress and feed himself correctly. The staffing in a community home may be helped to set up a group to teach adolescents interview skills, or a psychologist may work with nursing staff to construct a training programme to teach parents and haemophiliac youngsters skills which will enable them to take an active part in the management of their illness. Psychologists involved in such training schemes draw upon their knowledge of psychological theory and their understanding of clinical research, which has established the effectiveness of such treatment interventions. Such research emphasizes that skills should be broken down into *simple well-defined steps* and that strategies such as *modelling, rehearsal*, and *corrective feedback and positive reinforcement* are important in establishing skills. Table 4.4. shows some of the basic steps employed in a training scheme to teach

Table 4.4 Sample items from a behavioural assessment instrument used in factor replacement therapy

Reconstitution behaviours
1. Wash hands
6. Double-ended needle—snap open
10. Insert needle end into sterile water bottle
14. Insert exposed needle into concentrate bottle
15. Add sterile water to concentrate
20. Sterile technique used throughout
Syringe preparation behaviours
2. Attach filter needle to syringe
7. Insert filter needle attached to syringe into concentrate bottle
9. Withdraw concentrate into syringe
11. Remove air bubbles
13. Twist filter needle off syringe
20. Sterile technique used throughout
Infusion behaviours
4. Scalp vein needle—bend wing ends
6. Place tourniquet on hand or arm for venipuncture
7. Select venipuncture site
8. Swab skin surface with alcohol
12. Pierce needle through skin
13. Insert needle into vein
14. Secure needle in vein
15. Tape needle to skin
16. Release tourniquet
20. Attach scalp vein tubing to syringe
22. Inject concentrate slowly
27. Remove needle from skin
28. Apply pressure over venipuncture site
29. Place Band-Aid over venipuncture site
36. Sterile technique used throughout

Source: Reprinted with permission from Varni (1983).

haemophiliac youngsters and their parents to carry out factor replacement therapy in the home (Varni 1983).

In this training programme, nursing staff were trained to build up skills gradually. First, youngsters and parents observed nurses carrying out (modelling) the first component of the skill: mixing the plasma concentrate. Parents and child then practised this part of the procedure themselves (rehearsal). Nurses prompted where extra help was needed and offered praise (positive reinforcement) where performance had reached the required level. Once this component of the skill was learnt parents and children moved onto the two other components of the skill: preparing of the syringe and carrying out the injection. The final stage of injecting the concentrate was first practised on a dummy arm and then on an adult volunteer. Finally all aspects of the skill were combined.

Obviously, factor replacement therapy requires strict adherence to all procedures so that sterility is maintained and infection, damage to the veins, and spread of hepatitis to family members are avoided. Effectiveness of the new training regime was ascertained by comparing the adherence rates of parents trained under the scheme with parents who had been trained prior to the introduction of the new training method. At follow-up parents trained by new methods were found to adhere to 97 per cent of the component parts of the regime, whilst parents trained by the old methods showed only 65 per cent adherence. Similar training methods have been used to encourage asthmatic children to use inhalation equipment properly, to train children and parents to carry out home haemodialysis, and to teach diabetic children how to carry out their insulin injections correctly (Fielding 1985).

The skills taught above are obviously specialist skills not normally required by parents or youngsters. However, many children, because of depriving life circumstances, lack some of the crucial skills to cope with life in a satisfactory manner.

Some adolescents who are unable to cope withdraw from social contacts and become socially isolated. Others become depressed and some make suicide attempts. Surveys of suicide rates in the general population show that highest rates of attempted suicide occur in the age range 15–20 years. This provides a major problem for health care provision. In contrast, some youngsters may respond to stress and frustration with violent and aggressive behaviour. Recent research suggests that many adolescent institutionalized offenders are deficient in terms of complex interpersonal skills and basic social skills when compared with youngsters of the same age and social background who have no criminal record (Spence and Marzillier 1981).

Clinical psychologists working in different settings have approached these skill deficits in young people by instituting skills training programmes. They have been carried out in the context of youth clubs, in health centres, and in a local authority community home (Spence and Marzillier 1981). Youngsters have been trained in a range of skills including basic conversational skills, dating skills, interview skills, and skills of communication within the family.

On the whole good short-term improvements have been achieved by such programmes. However longer term effects have proved more difficult to achieve and research continues in order to establish methods of improving generalization of these procedures.

Helping children overcome fears

Fears and anxieties are common during childhood and frequently disappear over time. However in certain cases they persist in providing serious disruptions in a young person's life. For example, it has been estimated that some 17 children per 1000 show serious phobic reactions to school and that 16 per cent of school-age children exhibit serious fear and avoidance reaction to dental treatment. Non-attendance at school can obviously give rise to other important problems such as educational underattainment and difficulties in peer relationships, whilst avoidance of dental treatment may have long-term implications for dental health.

In selecting an individualized treatment for a fearful or anxious child the psychologist will want to carry out a detailed analysis of the problem (Barrios, Hartmann, and Shigetomi 1981). This will include a detailed description of the child's physiological, cognitive, and motor responses, as in the care of a child showing marked anxiety during a blood test. Physiological responses may include raised heart rate and respiration rate, while the child's cognitive response may include catastrophic and sometimes erroneous thoughts. In addition, the psychologist will want to examine the sorts of situations that elicit these responses and also the responses of other important adults in the situation. Depending on the initial analysis of the problem, treatment may involve explanation and reassurance, observation of a model participating in the feared situation, gradual exposure to the feared situation, praise and rewards for the child's efforts, or instruction to relevant adults in the appropriate way to react to fearful behaviour. In addition children may be taught various relaxation and self-instructional skills to enable them to manage stressful situations.

In the case of an eleven-year-old boy suffering from panic and anxiety attacks at school, a combination of procedures was used following assessment of his problems (Ballard and Yule 1981). The boy's anxieties revolved around the belief that his mother might be killed in a car crash whilst he was at school. The school had previously dealt with his panics by allowing him to telephone home to check that his mother was there, while his mother was forced to remain at home during school hours. Treatment involved training the boy in relaxation skills and gradual exposure to situations where he was separated from his mother whilst she took her car for increasingly long journeys. Rapid progress in treatment was maintained over 10 weeks of treatment and anxiety attacks had disappeared by the end of treatment. No problems were shown at 3-month and 15-month follow-ups.

Fears and anxieties may frequently arise in the context of medical treatment. For example, children may become distressed and fearful when admitted into hospital for surgical procedures. Furthermore, it may be necessary for children with certain chronic illnesses to undergo painful and distressing medical procedures. Patients with childhood cancer, for example, may be required to undergo painful diagnostic tests such as bone marrow aspiration and lumbar punctures. The anxiety and distress produced in anticipation of aversive medical procedures may be so severe that children exhibit symptoms such as nausea, vomiting, insomnia, nightmares prior to the procedures (Katz 1984). Recent psychological research has suggested that preparation procedures carried out before hospitalization and surgery can do much to reduce parental and child anxiety. Preparation may involve observation of a film of a child going into hospital, or home visits may be made by a paediatric nurse. Families may be shown visual aids that simulate hospital procedures, and they may be given specially constructed educational pamphlets to explain how and when these procedures will be carried out. In addition children may be directly taught ways of coping with anxiety and pain. For example, the child may be taught relaxation or self-hypnotic procedures. Alternatively, distraction through play may be used. Psychologists working with children undergoing painful treatments have placed reliance on the child's ability to use imagery. For example, whilst relaxing and imagining a 'story book' scene children may be taught to imagine 'magic potions' or 'dimmer switches', which will enable them to reduce pain and increase relaxation. In addition specific therapeutic suggestions may be made to reinterpret the context of pain and anxiety. For example, during hydrotherapy for severe burns a child imagines he is swimming to his friends to save them from drowning.

These psychological strategies to alleviate pain and anxiety in sick children are at an early stage of development. However when viewed against some of the problems of medical management of pain (e.g. increasing dependence on large doses of analgesics) they must be seen as a worthy area for further investigation (Fielding 1985; Katz 1984).

Encouraging self-control and managing aggressive behaviour

Surveys indicate that from one third to one half of children referred to psychologists from parents, teachers, and social workers are concerned with child and adolescent behaviour problems such as aggressiveness towards others (hitting, kicking, fighting) physical destructiveness, disobedience, and to a lesser extent problems such as stealing or firesetting. Developmental studies show that many children exhibit some of these behaviours at some time in their life and that these problems are likely to decline with age. Follow-up studies of children with *severe* conduct problems show that if these problems go untreated they frequently persist into adult life.

Aggressive behaviour may occur in the context of the family, the hospital ward, the school, or the community home. Clinical psychologists may therefore be approached by a range of professional workers for help with such problems.

Examination of the families of aggressive children often show distinct patterns of interactions. Observations show that many members of the family may be involved in coercive and aggressive behaviour. Moreover the perpetual conflict, anger, negative attitudes lead to low self-esteem, anger and helplessness in mothers of these problem children. It is within this context that child abuse may occur.

Such patterns of interaction with families have led psychologists to develop programmes of intervention which include parent training as an important component (Herbert 1978; Smith and Rachman 1984). Such programmes typically employ an initial intensive assessment phase involving all members of the family. Parent–child interactions in the home are observed and information obtained concerning the frequency of pro-social and coercive behaviour of the child. An analysis is made of important events leading up to and following disruptive behaviour.

In addition a study of the child's strengths and competencies is made. Parents are taught to define, track, and record aggressive and pro-social behaviour and they may be required to attend a parent training group on child management skills. Modelling and role-playing are the principal methods used and sessions may consist of two-hourly weekly meetings over a period of 8–12 weeks. Training sessions may also be conducted in the home, with parenting skills modelled by therapists. Such training programmes have brought promising short-term results. Of 117 families referred to the Leicester Child Treatment Research Unit some 61 per cent were considered to have 'satisfactorily improved', 21 per cent 'moderately improved' and 18 per cent showed 'no change'. Using more specific outcome measures some American psychologists have shown significant decreases in aversive behaviour when measured during naturalistic observations. In these studies, decrease in symptom frequencies were also reported by parents.

Not all families treated require the same level of therapeutic work. In one therapy programme approximately one third of families responded to quite simple interventions. However a further third required help resolving marital conflict, and dealing with depression and additional problems in the family. Accordingly therapeutic time with each family ranged from 6h to 133h. Whilst complete follow-up data appears to be difficult to achieve, a number of studies now suggest that, in certain families at least, effects may be long lasting.

Aggressive behaviour may also cause difficulties outside the family. Similar methods to those described above have also been adopted in such settings as a residential children's home. Herbert (1978) describes the treatment of a 12-year-old boy who had multiple problems including aggressive outbursts, encopresis, and social isolation within such a setting. An additional important feature of this programme was individual training in social and self-control skills including the use of relaxation to deal with anger and frustration.

Finally, in some residential settings the whole unit may be run along behavioural lines. Reid (1981) has described the setting up of a treatment regime for adolescents who cannot be contained within a normal community home system. In Glenthorne Youth Treatment Centre (YTC) the clinical psychologists act mainly in an advisory capacity, while the front-line therapists are group workers coming from the teaching, nursing, and child care professions. The main goal of treatment is to establish through reinforcement, modelling, and instruction, behavioural competence in social, educational, vocational, and self-care skills. In addition, attempts are made to modify those disruptive behaviours that have often brought youngsters to the centre in the first instance.

Initially, all young people entering the YTC are admitted into the assessment unit, which is run as a points economy system. Here young people earn points for achieving specified goals. Accordingly, this unit allows a detailed assessment to be made of the youngsters' level of functioning. From here allocation is made either to one of the secure units or to an open unit or hostel. As the youngster progresses to lessening degrees of security, fewer prompts are given by staff and more reliance is given to naturally occurring contingencies (e.g. verbal approval, self-control). In addition, youngsters are able to spend increasing amounts of time outside the centre and practise developing skills in the 'real world'. Great emphasis is placed on the flexible design of individual programmes, direct observation, and detailed monitoring of achievement goals by staff. Although this centre is in its early stages of development the treatment approach which emphasizes the acquisition of positive problem solving skills appears to be extremely promising.

Promoting health-related behaviours

An earlier section of this chapter alluded to the shift in emphasis in child health care provision from acute to chronic diseases. Moreover it was noted that many of the risk factors associated with major chronic diseases in adults (e.g. cardiovascular disease and cancer) had their origin in health-related behaviours such as dietary habits, exercise, and smoking. Such behaviours are frequently learned during childhood and adolescence. For example, the adoption of smoking habits typically occurs during adolescence. It has been estimated that one third of all adolescents smoke. Furthermore adolescents are more likely to smoke if one or more of their parents or older siblings smoke. An additional influence is the smoking habits of their friends and social contacts.

In recent years health care professionals have become increasingly interested in preventative aspects of health care. Prevention may be developed at three levels. *Primary prevention* refers to efforts designed to prevent the occurrence of a disease, while *secondary prevention* refers to early detection and treatment of the disease to prevent increased morbidity and mortality. Finally, *tertiary prevention* refers to rehabilitative efforts to prevent further morbidity, which may be associated with chronic disease and disability. This section comments upon the contribution of clinical psychologists to these three levels of preventative care.

Present levels of staffing in child clinical psychology services prevent a major contribution to the first level of primary prevention. However, given the growing problems of addictive behaviour amongst young people and the difficulties in providing adequate and effective treatment provision, preventative aspects of health care may assume much greater importance with child clinical psychology services in the future. The main impetus for *primary* prevention programmes for adolescents has come from the USA. Research has noted that although numerous health programmes have been instituted in schools, these have traditionally sought to promote behaviour change by emphasizing the harmful long-term effects of excessive smoking and drinking. Such studies, while frequently demonstrating changes in the knowledge and attitudes of young people, have shown little effect upon behaviour. Much more effective are those programmes which have encouraged adolescents to develop coping skills to resist social pressures to drink and smoke. For example, one such large-scale study selected popular high school youngsters to carry out a health programme within a school. These 'peer leaders' were specially trained to teach other people to recognize social influences (advertisements, television, friends) which might encourage young people to smoke. In addition they helped youngsters to practice ways of resisting such pressures. For example, a peer leader might encourage another youngster to rehearse different ways of responding to friends who called them 'chicken' for not accepting a cigarette (e.g. 'I would be more of a chicken if I smoked just to impress you'). Early results of such skill training programmes have produced promising results as follow-up.

Clinical psychology services may also contribute to preventative medicine in their treatment of youngsters with severe eating disorders and alcohol or drug-related problems. Treatment may take place in a variety of settings, including paediatric out-patient clinics health centres, psychiatric out-patient (Fairburn 1985) and residential settings (Garfinkel, Garner, and Kennedy, 1985).

Finally, some clinical psychologists are begining to examine methods of assisting paediatricians and nursing staff dealing with difficult chronic conditions of childhood and adolescence. Recent research suggests that psychological distress is a common feature of the families of chronically sick youngsters (Fielding 1985). Moreover additional problems such as high rates of non-adherence to diet, exercise, and medical regimes, of crucial importance for health and survival, are frequently found. Clinical psychologists working with chronically sick youngsters are begining to assess the effectiveness of therapeutic interventions to improve treatment adherence.

In the identification of important antecedents and consequences related to various health-related behaviours, behaviour using self or parental monitoring is seen as an important first step. Where non-compliance is related to the aversiveness of the therapeutic regime, anxiety and pain management procedures described earlier may be appropriate. Where misunderstanding or lack of comprehension or recall is the issue, then care can be taken to provide preparatory verbal and written information that is specifically categorized and dispensed carefully over time.

Alternatively if treatment results in major disruption in the child or family's life-style then additional strategies such as self-reinforcement, parental reinforcement, or contingency contracts may be used. In studies where such methods have been adopted there have been some promising results. For example, peer-group reinforcement has been found to be useful in groups of boys with haemophilia undergoing therapeutic exercise. Similar strategies have improved dietary adherence for youngsters on renal dialysis and regulation of urine glucose levels in diabetic children.

CONCLUDING COMMENT

The foregoing discussion has outlined some of the contributions that clinical psychologists are making to the health care of children and young people. In view of the many changes in this field, this chapter has given as much weight to these new developments as to those areas which have typically provided the routine day-to-day work of many child clinical psychology departments. In many parts of the country demand for child clinical psychology services far outstrips the current provision. In the present economic circumstances the vast increase in child clinical psychologists needed to meet these demands in unlikely. The future challenge for the practising child clinical psychologist is to find ways of applying important new clinical and research developments for the benefit of children and their parents, without detriment to current services. In this task the closest collaboration between psychologists and other child care professionals is essential.

REFERENCES

Ballard, M. and Yule, W. (1981). A case of separation anxiety treated by in vivo systematic desensitisation. *Behav. Psychother.* **9**, 105–10.

Barrios, B., Hartmann, D., and Shigetomi, C. (1981). Fears and anxieties in children. In *Behavioural assessment of childhood disorders* (ed. E. Mash and L.Terdal). The Guilford Press, New York.

Court, S.D.M. (1976). *Fit for the future: report of the Committee on Child Health Services.* HMSO, London.

Fairburn, C. (1985). Cognitive–behavioural treatment for bulimia. In *Handbook of psychotherapy for anorexia nervosa and bulimia* (ed. D. Garner and P. Garfinkel). The Guilford Press, New York.

Fielding, D. (1985). Chronic illness in children. In *New developments in clinical psychology* (ed. F. Watts). BPS/Wiley, Leicester.

Garfinkel, P., Garner, D., and Kennedy, S. (1985). Special problems of in-patient management. In *Handbook of psychotherapy for anorexia nervosa and bulimia* (ed. D. Garner and P. Garfinkel). The Guilford Press, New York.

Katz, E. (1984). Psychological aspects of cancer in children, adolescents, and their families. *Clin. Psychol. Rev.* **4**, 525–542.

Herbert, M. (1978). *Conduct disorders of childhood and adolescence. A behavioural approach to assessment and treatment.* Wiley, Chichester.

Reid, I. (1981). The development and maintenance of a behavioural regime in a secure treatment centre. In *Development in the study of criminal behaviour. Volume I: the prevention and control of offenders* (ed. M.P. Feldman). Wiley, London.

Sergis-Deavenport, E. and Varni, J.W. (1983). Behavioural assessement and management of adherence to factor replacement therapy in hemophilia. *J. Pediat. Psychol.* **8**, 367–77.

Spence, S. H. and Marzillier, J. S. (1981). Social skills training with adolescent male offenders—II short term, long term and generalised effects. *Behav. Res. Ther.* **19**, 349–68.

Smith, J. E. and Rachman, S. J. (1984). Non-accidental injury to children —II. A controlled evaluation of a behavioural management programme. *Behav. Res. Ther.* **22**, 349–83.

Varni, J. W. (1983). *Clinical behavioural pediatrics.* Pergamon Press, New York.

FURTHER READING

Fielding, D. (1983). Adolescent services. In *The practice of clinical psychology in Great Britain* (ed. A. Liddell). Wiley, Chichester.

Herbert, M. (1974). *Emotional problems of development in children.* Academic Press, London.

Yule, W. (1983). Child health. In *The practice of clinical psychology in Great Britain* (ed. A. Liddell). Wiley, Chichester.

5

Working with mentally handicapped people

Laurence Tennant and Chris Cullen

WHAT IS MENTAL HANDICAP?

People who have difficulty in learning from early in their lives are often referred to as mentally handicapped. This simple statement requires some elaboration before we can get a clear picture of the situation. Most of us have some difficulty in learning some things, but a mentally handicapped person finds it difficult or even impossible to acquire important skills. These might even include self-care skills such as washing, dressing or feeding oneself, and if this were the case, then the person might be described as severely mentally handicapped. They would be described as profoundly mentally handicapped if they could not communicate at all with those around them and if they had very little awareness of the world around them. Mildly mentally handicapped people can be expected to learn to care for themselves in many respects, but will have problems with more advanced skills such as handling money, using public transport and other local amenities, reading, writing and so on.

It is relevant to consider why a person has difficulty in learning. A small child cannot handle money and would have difficulty learning to do so before other relevant skills are acquired. Such a child would not, though, be referred to as mentally handicapped. So there must be some reference to the person having failed to learn things that others of his or her own age can do. Some people fail to demonstrate normal behaviour because they have suffered an injury that prevents them from doing so. Here the issues become contentious, and it is more difficult to be certain. If a perfectly normal person has a road traffic accident that leaves them incapable of speech, incontinent and immobile, should they be called mentally handicapped? Probably not, although methods of helping them might well be those used with mentally handicapped people. If a child is born with cerebral palsy, a disorder of the central nervous system that may make it very difficult to acquire some basic skills such as walking or self-feeding, should that child be described as mentally handicapped? No, because he or she is almost certainly failing only because of a physical handicap. In fact, it has only recently been realized that there are many people who have been labelled as mentally handicapped who have physical handicaps which have prevented them from acquiring normal behaviour. Deafness is a good example. It has been estimated that there are significant numbers of people cared for in mental handicap services whose main problem has been that they did not develop normally because they were deaf or hard of hearing.

No mention has been made so far of *intelligence*. This is not because it is irrelevant, but to focus attention on a person's behaviour as one of the most important factors in deciding whether mental handicap services are relevant. There are some people who score poorly on intelligence tests but who are totally independent and could not sensibly be called mentally handicapped. There are those who score within the normal range on intelligence tests yet whose skill level is such that they can be helped by mental handicap services. Level of intelligence is only a rough guide.

The needs of clients

People with mental handicap need the same range of services, including general health care, as any other section of the population. Beyond this, some may need specialist medical care. From a psychological perspective the major special needs are for:

—help with learning difficulties;
—a range of facilities, such as residential and day care settings which will encourage as normal a life as possible.

People will have varying requirements for facilities and training at different stages in their lives.

Mental handicap is often identified at birth or in the first few years of life. It is possible to recognize certain handicapping conditions as the unborn child develops in the womb, but they account for only a small proportion of cases; more often the specific cause is unknown. The identification of a handicap is the point at which the psychological needs can first be addressed for the individual, and more importantly for the parents and other family members. Families adjusting to this situation will clearly require counselling and support in dealing with their own emotional reactions. They will later need advice and training in child management in relation to handicap, and such support and specialist advice should continue at some level throughout the child's pre-school period.

Educational facilities for children with special needs, while imperfect, have progressed considerably in recent years. Special schools are often able to admit children at a very early age and good schools have working links with the families they serve. Self-care, communication, and pre-academic skills are likely to be central to the educational and social care planning undertaken in the schools and within the community. The focus then is upon applying specialist knowledge of teaching methods to helping both child and family.

The implications of the 1981 Education Act are that special schools will be phased out and that mentally handicapped children will be taught in normal schools, with special help where necessary. It has still to be seen how successful this will be.

When a child is clearly benefitting from being at school, education in Britain is often extended to the age of 19. Further specialized day training is offered within Adult Training Centres or Social Education Centres managed by Local Authorities, and some mentally handicapped people have opportunities at Colleges of Further Education. However, the quality of day services for mentally handicapped adults in Britain varies considerably throughout the country, a point made in the important House of Commons Social Services Committee report on community care (House of Commons 1985). Some areas have a reasonable network of day facilities, including special-care units for profoundly handicapped people, sheltered workshops for less severely handicapped people, and recreational facilities supported by Community Mental Handicap Teams. Other areas, unfortunately, have poor and inadequate services.

The other kind of facility which may be required by handicapped people and their families is residential care. In the early years the emotional and practical demands upon a family can be great and a child with a handicap requires a disproportionate amount of parental time and effort. Families may require a relief care facility to give them chance to relax or give time to other members of the family. This kind of support may be offered in a number of ways including the use of foster families, hostels, or group homes. Many professionals feel that it is particularly important that families are encouraged to use these facilities as the child grows older, both for the immediate relief they offer and because they afford an opportunity for parents to view their growing child in a normal way. Most non-handicapped children leave home at some time and live away from their parents, and the use of short-term care not only provides relief but also enables families to prepare for the eventual separation of parent and child at the point at which this seems natural. Of course, the achievement of this objective requires appropriate facilities such as group homes and hostels, and this is an area in which an immediate growth in community resources must take place if a real alternative to hospital care is to be achieved.

In summary, the developmental needs of a person with mental handicap are similar in pattern to those of any other individual, but differ in both time scale (they change more slowly) and the extent of independence (they may require a more elaborate supporting environment than the average person). From the psychologist's point of view the individuals and their families are susceptible to the same range of needs as any family. In addition they may require special help, counselling, or training in relation to the learning difficulties experienced by the handicapped person and in relation to the emotional pressures which may result directly or indirectly from the handicap. In practical terms, the points at which a clinical psychologist may help depend upon the nature of local services and may range from a direct role in the teaching of a handicapped person to a role in the planning and management of facilities.

The clinical psychologist's role

A clinical psychologist working in a mental handicap setting is almost always working in an actively multi-disciplinary environment. This will include Local Authority professionals such as teachers, social workers, and care staff; health professionals such as doctors, nurses, and health visitors; administrators and planners; and, most importantly, parents. Each discipline has its own definable contribution, although there is some overlap in the activity of the clinically oriented groups such as social workers, community nurses, and some clinical psychologists. This is particularly so in the

area of general counselling and recently in the teaching of behavioural training techniques. The exact contribution of each clinician
tends to be determined by a combination of professional training,
some statutory responsibilities, and local need.

There are two related but separate aspects of the psychologist's
role. First is the application of the findings of researchers which are
related to problems in mental handicap. This could be a particular
teaching procedure, such as errorless discrimination learning (see
below) or it might be the implementation of a service delivery plan.
For example, the move to community care has come about *partly* as
a result of research showing that institutional care leads to identified
disadvantages for mentally handicapped people. Clinical psychologists have been prominent in bringing this information to the
attention of service planners.

The second aspect of the psychologist's role is the application to
everyday clinical practice of a systematic or scientific approach. Like
the more academic researcher, the work of the clinical psychologist
is guided by a framework which helps in the formulation and
treatment of problems. This psychological analysis has the following
characteristics:

1. Assessment—the process of gathering information about a
person;
2. Interpretation—relating the observations to a broader theoretical
framework;
3. Intervention—putting into practice a treatment plan which
follows from the interpretation;
4. Evaluation—monitoring change and, where necessary reformu-
lating the initial interpretation.

Assessment and interpretation

The initial exercise is to find out enough about the person and the
problem to enable a treatment plan to be drawn up. The key issue is
that the assessment ought to lead to some action. It is feasible that
the purpose of an assessment is simply to say whether or not a person
is mentally handicapped. This is essentially a screening function, and
it might here be appropriate to use a test which compares the person
with others of his or her own age. Such tests are called norm-
referenced tests, and include the familiar intelligence and personality
tests. While these procedures have a wide acceptance in society, their
use by clinical psychologists working in mental handicap has

decreased steadily during the past two decades. The main reason (although there are others) is that the results do not help particularly in determining a plan of action. It is of little *practical* use to know that a person has an I Q of 57 or a Developmental Age of 2½ years, except in placing him or her on a scale, perhaps for the purpose of deciding which class he or she goes in.

The alternative to norm-referenced assessments is to measure how much of a skill someone has. This allows a training procedure related to that measure to be devised. Most of the assessment now carried out in mental handicap settings is of this sort. There is a wide range of such assessments available, and some of them are related to norm-referenced tests because they allow a computation of developmental age so that a comparison with other mentally handicapped (and non-handicapped) people can be made. Some of the most popular functional assessments in current use are the Progress Assessment Charts, the PIP Development Charts, the Adaptive Behaviour Scale, the Behaviour Assessment Battery, and the Everyday Living Skills Inventory.

All of these allow the assessment of important skills. The items are usually ordered in increasing difficulty. The same broad skill areas are covered in each (for example self-care, communication, educational achievement, and socialization). Sometimes the items are linked together forming a chain leading to a final goal. For example, 'visual fixation' precedes 'visual tracking' in the Behaviour Assessment Battery. Some of the assessments allow a measure of how much help a person must have—what type of prompt—before they can complete a task. This kind of information is very useful in designing treatment plans, since it helps to know what the minimum help has to be in order to get the person to succeed at the task.

For a complete assessment it is important not only to have a picture of what the client can do—referred to as *assets*—but also what behaviours the person has which are in *excess*. For example, a mentally handicapped child might giggle and run away whenever she is asked a question. This would not be noted on a typical assessment scale, but could be very important in understanding the child and subsequently helping her. A different kind of assessment procedure would be undertaken, one aimed at finding out something about the causes of the behaviour. Someone in regular contact with the child, perhaps the mother, would be asked to keep a careful record of the following:

1. Antecedents—under what circumstances does the child run away? From which people? What locations? What kind of questions?

2. Behaviours—exactly what form does the behaviour have? Does she run far away, or does she simply run out of reach? Does she look to see what reaction she is getting?

3. Consequences—what happens when she runs away? Does anyone chase her or remonstrate with her? Does it result in the question being asked again?

4. Alternatives—what would it have been more appropriate for her to have done under those circumstances?

After a few days of collecting observations the following picture emerges. She runs away when she is not familar with the person asking the question *or* when she is unlikely to know the answer. The usual effect is that she receives attention by being followed—in fact, she does not go far and seems to be waiting to be followed. She also manages to avoid answering the question, since it is usually not asked again.

This kind of exercise involves an assessment of the situation and an interpretation of possible causes. It leads to a programme which concentrates on the child's *deficits*, i.e. things she cannot (or does not) do. For example, she should be taught to say 'I don't know' if she cannot answer a question; she needs to learn ways of getting to know people with whom she is unfamiliar; and she needs to be taught to ask questions herself.

To summarize, an assessment should tell us about:

1. Assets—those skills or patterns of behaviour in an individual's repertoire which are acceptable or useful and strong;

2. Deficits—those skills or patterns of behaviour which are absent or weak and thought to be desirable or necessary;

3. Excesses—those patterns of behaviour which are strong, and unacceptable or disadvantageous to an individual.

There is subtlety in this which may not be apparent. These ways of describing behaviour are culturally relative: what may be acceptable in one setting and can be described as an asset may not be in another setting, and may be thought of as an excess. We can still wryly recall the occasion when a case conference at a mental handicap hospital was called to discuss the public disrobing problem of a young lady (surely an excess) when we understood that she could not undress herself (a deficit) and we were trying to teach her to do so!

Another subtlety is that what may at first be considered an excess can be turned into an asset. Fleming (1984) reports the case of a mentally handicapped man who had a history of ejecting clothes through a ward window and hiding them behind lockers. These were not his own clothes but those other residents had left lying around. Rather than simply dealing with this as a problem to be removed, Fleming construed the situation in a different way. The man had a *useful* skill; he could recognize unattached and disordered items of clothing, collect them and transport them, with the effect of tidying the environment. The intervention, which depended on an imaginative assessment and interpretation of the situation, was to ask the man to collect any loose items of clothing and to take them to a large cupboard. This took place six times each day, and he received praise from staff for completion of the task. There was decline in the number of items of clothing which were ejected through the window and six weeks after the intervention ended, when staff were no longer asking him to take items to the cupboard, the man was reported to be independently collecting items and taking them to the cupboard.

Assessment and interpretation, therefore, is not a mechanical exercise. It requires clinical judgment and experience. It is important to consider the *functions* which are to be served. Three such functions might be:

(a) helping in the formulation of objectives for care plans;
(b) producing data which would allow progress to be evaluated;
(c) discovering the critical functional relationships between key behaviours and the environment—the causes of behaviours.

These often require different methods. As noted above, formalized rating scales may help the clinician to describe current skills and should lead to an outline plan for further investigation. However, more detailed observation and recording of activity will usually be required prior to the instigation of a training procedure in order to clarify the nature of the skills to be taught and to provide a baseline against which progress may be measured. This latter is particularly important in mental handicap since change is often slow and can, therefore, be missed.

Observation and Assessment of a young man at an Adult Training Centre John came to the attention of the local community mental handicap service when his family moved into the locality. An initial contact through the Adult Training Centre was followed by a visit from one of the members of the Community Mental Handicap Team, in this case the clinical psychologist. As part of a general information-gathering exercise the psychologist reviewed a number of issues with the family using a rating scale as a way of structuring the interview. The psychologist arrived at an outline picture of the family; the views of significant individuals concerning John's needs and also some idea of John's own view of his needs. It appeared that John was quite proficient in self-care, and in general life-skills in association with home, and the psychologist was satisfied that opportunities for new learning at home were occurring. However, the parents indicated their concern (which supported a view offered by the Adult Training Centre manager) that their son was finding difficulty in communicating with his peers. Staff at the Training Centre had mentioned that on a small number of occasions John had been involved in a minor fracas and were concerned that this should not develop into a major problem—they said that John was having problems in 'settling in'.

Information gained from the parents suggested that there was not a general social skills deficit. John coped well at his previous Training Centre and has a number of well established friendships. John himself seemed to be aware of a problem but unable to give a clear account of it. The next step was to ask staff at the Centre to undertake some simple recording of incidents including basic behaviour–environment interactions. They were asked to complete an observation sheet with the following headings:

What did John do?

What happened immediately before the incident?

What happened after the incident?

At the same time a key member of staff was asked to record on a sampling basis the general interactive social behaviour shown by John during his working day.

When the observations were reviewed, two key factors emerged. Firstly, the incidents were often preceded by an interaction with a particular trainee at a time when John was required to share his tools with this person. The disagreement between them led to John shouting, which was quickly followed by an intervention from a member of staff who resolved the situation. John's behaviour in this environment appeared to have been prompted by circumstances with which he was not familiar, nor was he effective in resolving the situation. It was noted in the more general observations that there were often times (usually at the change points in the daily timetable) when John found himself alone, perhaps because he had not yet learned what the next required activity was.

As a consequence of these observations of frequency of behaviour and its environmental links, the staff arrived at the view that John and his co-trainee required special attention at the point at which they needed to share tools and, secondly, that just before each change point on the timetable a member of staff should ensure that either they or a trainee explain to John the next activity. Recording continued and showed a rapidly declining frequency of incidents.

A simple problem perhaps, but allowing John to continue to 'settle in' without definite action may have strengthened the anti-social pattern. The initial interview provided background information which continued to be useful and required regular updating. The specific observations identified deficits. John was not learning 'what followed what' in the timetable, but probably to wait to be taken to the next activity. The solution was to give him specific assistance which could be gradually faded out as he became more able.

The observations also helped interpretation of the causes of behaviour—note the links between John's complaint and the behaviour of staff. Finally, the observations allowed some evaluation. The interpretation was essentially the formation of an hypothesis and the intervention was in this sense experimental—the declining frequency gives confidence that the initial interpretation was accurate.

Supportive contact would continue with a family such as this, allowing regular reviews of target areas for progress and perhaps some help in bringing about change. The focus of intervention may be at any time very specific, as in this case, or more broad and long-term. For example, we might encourage the family to allow John gradually more frequent opportunities to stay away from them, taking holidays with his new friends, perhaps occasionally using a hostel or even preparing for a place in a group home. This kind of intervention would be directed both at John—allowing him to develop more independent behaviours—and at the family, in adjusting to this change. This family counselling would be very similar to that undertaken in other specialities and emphasizes the range of clinical activity undertaken by clinical psychologists in mental handicap.

INTERVENTION

It is impossible to cover all the ways of changing behaviour which are available to the psychologist. Instead, we will discuss some of the basic principles and concepts which must be taken into account when designing an intervention.

First, it must be decided whether the aim is to remove an excess or to remedy a deficit. Is the problem one of too much behaviour or not enough? This question is not as easy to answer as it first appears, because there is a complementarity between behavioural excesses and deficits. For example, if a person is engaging in a self-destructive activity, such as self-hitting, that might be construed as an excess behaviour to be removed, *or* as a behavioural deficit. Perhaps the person does not have any alternative way of occupying himself, or gaining attention, of dealing with frustration, and so on.

As a general rule, it is probably better to 'translate' a problem of excess behaviour into one of behavioural deficit if at all possible. Not only are there ethical issues invariably associated with removing behaviour, but it is also difficult to achieve. So, if the problem can safely be ignored, it is advisable to do so and to concentrate instead on building skills which will eventually displace it. If a handicapped child continually waves her fingers in front of her eyes, she could be taught to do something more productive with her hands.

Sometimes, though thankfully only occasionally, an excess behaviour cannot be ignored, either because it interferes with attempts to teach new, adaptive repertoires, or because it is damaging the person or others. Examples might be self-mutilation and aggressive behaviour. Here there is probably little alternative but to implement procedures which are specifically aimed at reducing or removing behaviour. Often these procedures have an aversive element to them, and there are serious ethical considerations which have to be taken into account. The decision to use such procedures *must* involve all those who have a reason to be involved, including the client or representative, and the likely long-term benefits to the individual must be weighed against the short-term discomfort. In 1982 the Association for the Advancement of Behaviour Therapy published a report on the treatment of self-injurious behaviour (A.A.B.T., 1982). This was compiled by a 'task force' of some of the most eminent psychologists working in this field in the United States. Their recommendations included that there be a proper analysis of the causes of the behaviour and of the factors maintaining it before the institution of special procedures to remove it. They reviewed the viable 'suppressive' procedures, and the reader is referred to this source for a description and review of the literature. They also, though, pointed out the necessity of teaching alternative behaviours which will result in a more rewarding lifestyle, and it is to this which we now turn.

There is an increasingly complex technology of teaching which is available to help mentally handicapped people. Some of the more recent advances rely on sophisticated computer technology, but all have common characteristics. The first of these is to break the behaviour down into small steps which can be tackled independently. How many components will depend on the current skill level of the person, since not everyone starts at the same point. Consider the (apparently) simple act of putting on a pair of shoes. Identifiable components include recognizing that there is a right and a left, putting the shoes on without laces and tongue getting stuck in the shoe, and tying the laces. Each of these is then capable of being broken down into its own constituents. Tying laces, for example, includes taking one end in each hand, crossing the separate ends and putting one end over and through to form a knot (this involves changing hands!), forming one loop, and then crossing the loose end over the loop, round it and pulling through to form the double bow—don't pull all of it or you finish with a single bow! We have no doubt that the literate person reading this who was unable to tie shoe laces would be unlikely to be able to learn from this description. What this shows, of course, is the complexity of tasks which most of us take for granted.

Having broken the task down into teachable components, each can then be taught separately—but in what order? Clearly, it does not make sense to start in the middle. Surprisingly, it is often best to start at the end, using a procedure known as *backward chaining* (because the elements are gradually linked together, starting from the last one). So, the handicapped person would be taught first to pull the two bows tight, everything else having been done by the trainer. She or he would be taught this by manual guidance and verbal encouragement, called by psychologists *physical* and *verbal prompts*. Upon completion of this small step, the person would be given a reward. It might be that the reward would be something tangible such as a sweet or a hug, but more appropriate on this occasion would be the opportunity to go somewhere interesting, in the same way as any other person would once they had fastened their shoe laces.

Once the step of pulling the two bows tight has been mastered, the person is ready to move on to the preceding component: pushing the loose end through to form the second bow. Having done this, probably with some prompting at first, she or he can then *independently* pull the bows tight, hence completing the task. Two components have been mastered, the third from the end would be tackled, and so on. In this way, many basic skills can be taught.

We have referred to the help or prompting which is given. As the person learns, this help has to be gradually removed. Skilful *fading* of prompts can lead to learning which is totally errorless. If we are teaching a child to recognize which shoe to put on which foot, for example, we might paint two halves of a cat on the toes of the shoes, and teach the child that the picture of the cat is only complete with the shoes on the correct feet. Fairly soon, this visible cue will lead to the child always putting the shoes on the correct feet. Then, by putting on a layer of polish, the picture can be made less distinct and, over time, it is faded out completely by further layers. Other cues, such as the shape of the shoe and the 'feel' on the feet become the ones which are important, as they are for competent dressers.

A certain degree of ingenuity is called for when things seem to go wrong with fading procedures. Some time ago we were involved in teaching a discrimination between simple words such as TOILET, DANGER, EXIT and so on. Based on errorless learning principles, the procedure was as follows. The 'target' word that was being taught was presented to a mentally handicapped child, with the alternatives from which it was to be chosen completely obliterated by several layers of tissue paper. On the instruction 'point to the word which says . . .' there was only one visible word for the child to point to. When this was being done reliably, with the word in any position relative to the other cards with obliterated words, a layer of tissue was removed from each of these alternatives, so that they were slightly more visible. The child was still expected to point to the target word. Then another layer of tissue was removed, the procedure repeated, and so on. Eventually, all the alternative words were fully visible through a single layer of tissue, with the child still correctly pointing to the target word.

When the final layer of tissue was removed, to our surprise the child no longer pointed to the target word but pointed to any word on a completely chance basis. After some consideration, we realized that the child had acquired a strategy which we had not foreseen. He always pointed to the card without tissue and, for most of the time, in fact right up until the final trial, that strategy served very well, and he was always correct and was rewarded. Only when there was no tissue paper present anywhere did his strategy fail. The answer? To start again, this time having the target card covered by a single layer of tissue, although still easily visible. It was not possible for the clue to success to be the absence of tissue paper. This time, the fading was successful, and the child was ultimately able to point to the correct word in the presence of a number of alternatives, even when none of them had a covering of tissue paper.

The term for the important concept involved here is *stimulus control*. Its importance cannot be overstated, although there is insufficient space to discuss the topic in detail here. Faulty stimulus control is the cause of many problems faced by psychologists in mental handicap settings. The person who urinates in public rather than in a toilet is under the control only of bladder cues rather than bladder cues plus various social cues. The person who echoes phrases meaninglessly does so because the verbal repertoire is not under the control of appropriate situational cues. The person who wanders aimlessly is not susceptible to normal social cues. The list is almost endless. The task for the psychologist is to devise ways of bringing behaviour under appropriate stimulus control.

CHANGING SYSTEMS OF CARE

So far we have described aspects of the psychologist's role that involve face-to-face contact with clients. However, there are other considerations which have influenced how psychologists work. One of these is that there are far too few psychologists to carry out all the one-to-one teaching required and much of the work can be carried out by appropriately trained direct care staff or parents. This has led in recent years to a burgeoning of staff training workshops and home-teaching systems. Essentially, psychologists are operating through others, the people who are in most contact with the handi-capped person.

Staff training has been the subject of evaluative research, but unfortunately, the outcome is not particularly encouraging. Most authors who review the field of staff training have found that, while it is possible to achieve short-term changes in staff skills and atti-tudes, they are rarely found to last and staff do not usually change their practices back in the workplace. So, their mentally handi-capped clients do not benefit from the new procedures which the staff have learnt. Of in-service training for staff—usually conducted by psychologists—Ziarnik and Bernstein (1982) write:

It is our contention that the effectiveness of staff training has yet to be demonstrated because it is often incorrectly applied. That is, the asumption underlying the decision to provide staff training is that staff cannot perform the needed skills. That assumption is not always correct. Poor performance may be related to a variety of factors, only one of which is skill deficiency.

This is an interesting comment because it indicates that the failure of staff training to result in lasting changes in staff behaviour may be due to other factors. It is a consideration of these other factors which has led to some psychologists moving away from face-to-face client teaching and from staff training. Often it is the very setting in which a mentally handicapped person lives which is the main cause of the problem.

A middle-aged woman who had been newly admitted to a hospital ward was referred to the psychology department. The woman had spent much of her life in institutions, was active and relatively able in self-care. Nursing staff requested help with persistent behavioural difficulties, the most evident of which was a tendency to strip off her clothes. As part of an assessment of the situation, interactions between the woman and ward staff were observed. This was done by having staff watch the woman for short periods of time during the day, choosing time samples so that a representative picture of the whole day would eventually be formed. Table 5.1 shows the propor-tion of sample observations for each of three interaction categories.

An intervention was then designed which had two major components:

1. An attempt to increase adaptive behaviour through brief periods of individual training planned to occur on a regular basis involving

Table 5.1 Percentage of different types of interaction

Type of interaction	Percentage of total observations
Unattended	63.4
Engaged with staff in connection with problem behaviours	33.3
Engaged with staff in connection with acceptable behaviours	3.3

ward staff as far as ward commitments would allow.

2. A management procedure designed to affect the disrobing problem directly incorporating a procedure where she was removed briefly from the ward, contingent on disrobing. This is referred to as time-out.

Both aspects of the programme were monitored by nursing staff with the support of clinical psychologists. The frequency of the use of time-out declined from an initial average of 14 incidents per day to approximately one per day by the 45th day of the procedure.

Less helpful was that, while the number of training sessions initially increased, a gradual decline took place between days 25 and 45. The frequency of training appeared to follow the frequency of problem behaviours. After day 45 both frequency of problem behaviours and that of training sessions rose again.

It seems as though pressures on staff in some way contributed to this phenomenon. The resident may initially have been seen as extremely difficult and time-consuming for staff. A consequence of the programme was a reduction in problem behaviour and consequent demand on staff time. Hence relative to other residents this woman became less of a problem and less often a subject of discussions between ward staff and senior managers. Other residents became more of a priority. The effect for the woman, as the problem reduced in frequency, was a reduction in the overall level of contact with staff. So, the frequency of problem behaviour then increased as she returned to ways of behaving which had been successful in gaining staff attention. It seems likely that, in general terms, managers are most concerned about resident behaviours which injure others or damage property . Consequently, ward staff work hard to reduce these behaviours and are forced into an orientation which produces cycles of behaviour problems. The task for the clinical psychologist is to reverse the tendency for staff to be most affected by behaviour problems and achieve a switch of emphasis to the need for and maintenance of developmental gains. In this instance contacts between staff and the resident were almost invariably prompted by the behaviour problem. A procedure was designed which could effectively operate on this, but the institutional system worked against long-term maintenance.

If it is the whole system which is at fault, the solution is to change it. Clinical psychologists are currently involved in two different ways of trying to achieve this.

Influenced largely by Wolfensberger and his colleagues from the United States, many psychologists have turned to *normalization* as a means of solving the problems of mentally handicapped people. The basis of the approach is that it is largely the way in which society as a whole treats mentally handicapped people which is at the heart of the matter. The community has refused to accept mentally handicapped people as equal members with equal rights and privileges, and has devalued them by either consigning them to segregated settings or by refusing them access to normal facilities and services. Change all that, and many of the problems will disappear. The argument is *not* that mentally handicapped people will somehow become 'normal' (in the sense of suddenly acquiring new repertoires) but that they will become 'equal' and will then be able to acquire new repertoires in a more supportive and conducive environment.

This is not the place to enter into a lengthy description of this topic. Suffice it to say that, for its proponents, normalization is a cohesive and comprehensive approach to service planning and design, with a sophisticated way of evaluating the effects of a service for mentally handicapped people (Flynn and Nitsch 1980; Wolfensberger and Glenn 1975). There are those, though, who see normalization as a collection of slogans and statements, some of which are contradictory, and few of which are based on evidence that mentally handicapped people would benefit from the changes suggested (Rose–Ackerman 1982).

For those psychologists who see the need for a more pragmatic approach to the problem of mental handicap services and who prefer to leave the business of changing society to others, the field of *organizational behaviour management* has become attractive. Here again the emphasis is on the whole system rather than the individual mentally handicapped person. The essence of the approach is that the contingencies under which care staff operate have to be changed by appropriate management strategies if the care staff are to engage in more appropriate client-related activities. These strategies have included giving instructions (both general and specific) and providing models for staff to copy. Special consequences such as written or verbal feedback from supervisors, monetary rewards, and the public posting of the results of care programmes have all been tried. The results of organizational behaviour management programmes have been variable, with most success seeming to come with procedures that incorporate more than one strategy. Ivancic, Reid, Iwata, Faw, and Page (1981), for example, combined a brief programme of in-service training (consisting mainly of direct instructions, modelling by trainers, and practice by the staff) with a system of prompting (i.e. publicly posted instructions, vocal instructions, and further modelling). They also included a feedback procedure, consisting of praise from supervisors and the public posting of results. All this resulted in an improvement in the staff's use of language training activities with multi-handicapped children during institutional care routines.

Excursions into staff training and systems change are partly a result of realizing that a clinical psychologist, or indeed any member of staff, cannot expect to make such change by working with individual mentally handicapped clients. There have been other ways of tackling the problem. One is to work with groups of mentally handicapped people. A distinction must be made between procedures which are aimed at dealing with mentally handicapped people *in* a group, for reasons of economy of staff time, and procedures for helping mentally handicapped people to work *as* a group, the aim being to encourage co-operative social behaviour. An example of the former is *room management*, which has become popular in Britain in recent years. This involves two elements. One staff member is designated as a room manager. It is their job to move around the group, praising clients who are busy with some activity, ensuring that everyone has access to materials, briefly prompting people who are not busy, and changing activities for those who have finished. A second staff member is designated an individual helper, and their job is to spend a short (pre-determined) time with each person in turn doing individual training. The individual helper is also the person who answers the telephone, takes people to the toilet, deals with emergencies such as fits, and so on. The initial studies on room management indicated that two staff could thus work with up to fifteen mentally handicapped people, and that the results in terms of levels of group engagement were very good.

Unfortunately, the results tend to last only a few months and, where they last considerably longer it is found that the clients are perhaps busy but not learning very much. They may be still engaged on the same table-top tasks they were given many months previously. Research on working with mentally handicapped people *as* a group is still at an early stage, although there are some promising avenues to be explored. Cullen (1985) has reviewed work with mentally handicapped adults in groups.

The area of home teaching has been shown to have particular promise as a way of maximizing the efforts of psychologists. In Britain since the mid-1970s there has been an increase in the number of home teaching systems based on the Portage approach. A recent estimate is that there are around 60 such services operating, mainly in the densely populated areas of the country. This is paradoxical because the value of home teaching systems has been claimed to be for rural areas, where distances make it even more difficult for psychologists to have significant impact with a number of clients.

The defining characteristics of a Portage system are:

1. A home teacher visits a family and assesses the mentally handicapped person. This home teacher, using teaching guidelines, shows the parents how to help their child to achieve a specific target. Visits are made regularly to monitor progress, set new targets, solve problems which arise, and so on. The home teacher may be someone already in contact with the family, perhaps a health visitor, or may be recruited specifically for the job. They will be given a basic training, lasting around one week.

2. Data on the child's progress are taken regularly to the supervisor, who is usually a psychologist. It is the psychologist who trains the home teacher, and who advises on problems which the home teacher cannot solve.

3. A management team, which is multi-disciplinary, meets regularly to consider issues such as funding, work-loads of the home teachers, recruitment, etc.

Portage-type systems can be effective in disseminating a psychological influence. It is obviously a more useful way of using a scarce resource, but, as in all such systems, there is a price to be paid. The system itself has to be maintained, and so attention has to be given to those factors which are likely to threaten it. We touched on this issue above in our discusssion of organizational behaviour management. In opting for a system which seems to make life easier for the psychologist by easing the burden of too many direct client contacts it seems that the problem has simply been changed into one of how to motivate home-teachers, monitor their work, secure funding for the system, and so on. Also, whenever a psychological approach is disseminated it is likely to be diluted, and some of the subtleties may be lost. As we mentioned above when talking about stimulus control, it is likely to be just such subtleties that are important when helping handicapped people. The benefits of Portage home teaching systems are currently outweighing any disadvantages, so it is likely that their use will continue.

CONCLUSION

The picture of clinical psychology in mental handicap services we have presented is one of some diversity, ranging from direct work with mentally handicapped clients to systems change and planning.

Overriding all is the simple fact that mentally handicapped people are people, although they may sometimes have special needs which are satisfied in different ways, depending on their age and the nature of the services in their local commmunity. The first characteristic of a psychological contribution is an analysis of the situation of the mentally handicapped person. This is accomplished by a variety of means but leads to an intervention, which is an experiment in the sense of being susceptible to continual modification in the light of changes for the handicapped person. The interventions may be simple or complex, but they should be flexible.

In an attempt to help wider groups of clients, many psychologists have moved to work at a macro-level, designing and influencing systems. The knowledge base is not so secure here, and some activities—such as staff training and room management—are yielding disappointing results. But, so long as psychologists work at the macro-level with the same experimental rigour as they do at the micro-level, there is cause for optimism. It should be the central concern of psychologists that whatever is done for mentally handicapped people is done with good reasons. The history of services show that there is rarely a shortage of good intentions, but one of the roles for the psychologist should be to provide evidence to show which of the available options are likely to lead to the most benefit for clients. This should apply as much to service systems as to individual therapy.

REFERENCES

Association for Advancement of Behaviour Therapy (1982). The treatment of self-injurious behaviour (Report of Task Force, Chairperson J.E. Favell). *Behav. Ther.* **13**, 529–54.

Cullen, C. (1985). Working with groups of mentally handicapped adults. In *New developments in clinical psychology* (ed. F.N. Watts). The British Psychological Society, Leicester.

Fleming, I. (1984). The constructional approach to 'problem behaviour' in an institutionalized setting. *Behav. Psychother.* **12**, 349–55.

Flynn, R.J. and Nitsch, K.E. (1980). *Normalisation, social integration and community services.* University Park Press, Baltimore,ML.

House of Commons (1985). *Second report from the Social Services Committee: community care with special reference to adult mentally ill and mentally handicapped people.* HMSO, London.

Ivancic, M.T. Reid, D.H., Iwata, B.A., Faw, G.D., and Page, T.J. (1981). Evaluating a supervision program for developing and maintaining therapeutic staff–resident interactions during institutional care routines. *J. Appl. Behav. Anal.* **14**, 95–107.

Rose-Ackerman, S. (1982). Mental retardation and society: the ethics and politics of normalisation. *Ethics*, **93**, 81–101.

Wolfensberger, A. and Glenn, L. (1975). *Program analysis of service systems: a methlod for the quantitative evaluation of human sciences.* National Institute of Mental Retardation, Toronto.

Ziarnik, J.P. and Bernstein, G.S. (1982). A critical examination of the effect of in-service training of staff performance. *Mental Retardation* **20**, 109–14.

FURTHER READING

Clarke, A.M. and Clarke, A.D.B. (1986). *Mental deficiency: the changing outlook* (4th edn). Methuen, London.

Hogg, J. and Mittler, P.J. (in press). *Issues in staff training in mental handicap.* Croom Helm, London.

Mittler, P.J. (1979). *People not patients.* Methuen, London.

Vargas, J.S. (1977). *Behavioural psychology for teachers.* Harper and Row, New York.

6

Working with physically handicapped people
Barbara Wilson and Diana Staples

INTRODUCTION

The patients

Physical handicap may result from neurological dysfunction or from musculo-skeletal disorders. In the former group the handicap follows impairment in the central nervous system rather than from damage to the limbs themselves. This is sometimes difficult for patients to understand, and it is often the case that a person with hemiplegia following a stroke will believe that the affected limbs are actually damaged rather than appreciating that damage to that part of the brain which *controls* those limbs is causing them to malfunction. When the handicap results from a musculo-skeletal disorder then obviously the problems encountered in manoeuvering are directly caused by some dysfunction of the muscles, bones, or peripheral nerves.

It is possible for a patient to have both kinds of impairment. For example, a head injured patient may have a physical problem resulting from severe brain stem injury together with problems following directly from damage to one or more limbs. The patient's condition could be even further complicated by contractures or myositis ossificans (bony growths) which are sometimes caused by inappropriate treatment.

A further example of neurological and musculo-skeletal problems occurring together would be seen in a patient with cerebral vascular disease necessitating amputation of a limb. However, most people with physical handicap will have either neurological *or* musculo-skeletal disorders. Some common causes of physical handicap can be seen in Table 6.1

137

Table 6.1 Types and causes of physical handicap

Type	Some common causes
Neurological dysfunction	Severe head injury
	Cerebral vascular accident (stroke)
	Degenerative diseases, e.g. multiple sclerosis, Parkinson's disease
	Cerebral and spinal tumours
	Trauma to spinal cord
	Infections, e.g. encephalitis
	Poisoning, e.g. carbon monoxide
Musculo-skeletal disorders	Rheumatoid arthritis
	Osteoarthritis
	Amputations
	Peripheral vascular disease
	Muscular dystrophy
	Congenital abnormalities

The settings

Clinical psychologists may be found in neurology and neurosurgical departments, in rehabilitation centres, and in orthopaedic and paediatric departments. Occasionally they are attached to Social Services departments such as those for the young chronic sick, and sometimes they work in young disabled units run by the Health Service. Not all of these departments will have the benefit of the services of a clinical psychologist. In some centres there is no contact at all with a psychologist; in others psychologists may be asked to see the occasional patient for assessment or treatment; others will have a regular part-time psychologist, and still others a full-time clinical psychologist.

The role of clinical psychologists working with physically handicapped people

There are several ways in which clinical psychologists can work with people who have physical handicaps. Firstly, they can assist patients in managing their disease or condition by providing information about (i) the disease itself, (ii) ways of pacing activities, (iii) the use of drugs, (iv) ways of combatting deleterious effects of modern living whilst promoting healthy activities. Secondly, they can work alongside other therapists in teaching the use of aids, orthoses, and alternative methods of carrying out activities connected with daily living. Thirdly, psychologists can get involved in sexual counselling. Fourthly, vocational and educational guidance can be given by psychologists. Fifthly, anxiety and pain can be diminished by the application of management programmes, and psychological treatment may be available for dealing with depression.

When cognitive or behaviour problems accompany the physical handicap psychologists may well be called upon to reduce or remediate some of these. Finally, psychologists may spend part of their working lives attempting to modify the attitudes of various sections of society towards people with physical handicap.

ASSESSMENT

Assessments are carried out in order to answer questions. These questions should be related to each patient's needs and rehabilitation programme, and the psychologist must therefore be flexible in developing assessment and rehabilitation procedures. While the physically handicapped individual is usually the focus of assessment, the physical and social *environment* may also need to be assessed and possibly changed in order to maximize learning and independence. Sometimes assessment is needed for administrative purposes in order to implement planning changes and staff levels.

There are several types of assessment procedure from which clinical psychologists can choose when they seek to match a particular form of assessment to a particular question. Standardized tests are the most widely known tool of psychological measurement: there are tests to measure overall intellectual function as well as specific tests to measure congnitive functions such as attention, perception, language, reasoning, problem-solving, memory, and learning.

Other forms of assessment involve direct or indirect observation of the patient in the natural setting of home or work, in a hospital or rehabilitation centre, or in simulated situations such as a mock office. Behavioural assessment involves analysis of the relationship between the patient's behaviour, its antecedents, and consequences. The antecedents and consequences may then be altered to produce behavioural change in the desired direction. Rating scales are also used in order that the patient, relatives or staff may make *judgments* about specific observable behaviours and about inner states and feelings.

Assessment techniques need to have the technical features of all good measuring devices: they need to be valid, which means they must measure what they state they measure; they need to be reliable, which means they must measure the same thing on different occasions or when used by different observers; they need to be generalizable, and sensitive to change.

Neuropsychological assessment

Neuropsychology is the study of the relationship between the brain and behaviour. A neuropsychological assessment will examine abilities such as memory, language, perception, attention, reasoning, and planning. For patients with neuropsychological damage a neuropsychological assessment can be particularly helpful in pinpointing specific problem areas that will require treatment. Sometimes it is also necessary to carry out a neuropsychological assessment of a patient with a musculo-skeletal disorder in order to obtain information about cognitive functioning. Such information may be used in several ways. One of the most frequent reasons for carrying out a neuropsychological assessment is to estimate a patient's level of general intellectual ability. This is often obtained by the administration of an intelligence test such as the Wechsler Adult Intelligence Scale, which consists of 11 sub-tests. Each sub-test measures a different aspect of intelligence. Some tests are primarily concerned with language skills and others with visuo-spatial skills. Because several of the tests have to be completed within a certain period of time, patients with motor problems are sometimes at a disadvantage and may score poorly, due to their impaired manipulative skills rather than any deficiencies in intelligence. However, with sensible interpretation of the scores and due recognition of the disadvantages experienced by such patients the test can supply important information.

In addition to assessing current levels of functioning it is often necessary to estimate premorbid intellectual ability, particularly for patients with neurological damage. If a head-injured patient, for example, scores in the average range on an intelligence test it will not be clear whether this represents any deterioration in intellectual skills. It is often possible to get some idea of what a patient's functioning was like before the injury by studying school records or assessment of professional qualifications where these are available. In cases where there are no qualifications or records the usual procedure is to estimate premorbid levels by comparing performance on tests known to be sensitive to brain damage with performance on tests known to be fairly resistant to brain damage. For instance, performance on some visuo-spatial tests is vulnerable to many kinds of cerebral disorder, whereas knowledge of the meaning of words is fairly resistant to brain damage unless the language area of the brain itself is involved. This type of estimation obviously has to be cautiously interpreted.

Another reason for carrying out a neuropsychological assessment is to determine which cognitive abilities are intact or relatively intact, and which are impaired. Thus a picture will be built up of a patient's intellectual strengths and weaknesses. This may be particularly important information when designing a treatment programme. If, for example, memory deficit is associated with widespread intellectual deterioration then amelioration procedures will be different from a case where no other cognitive impairment is present.

Sometimes psychologists are asked to determine whether a problem is due to an organic or an emotional cause. Some psychiatrists mistakenly believe, for example, that left hemiplegic stroke patients (with right hemisphere damage) are depressed because they fail to show facial expression and look emotionally flat. However, problems with emotional expression are frequent after right cerebral damage, and are associated with other problems—particularly visuo-spatial ones—and with denial of or indifference to their physical and cognitive difficulties.

Psychologists may be asked to carry out an assessment in an attempt to find out which part of the brain is damaged. Frontal lobe damage will result in certain kinds of deficits, temporal lobe damage will produce others, and parietal lobe damage yet others. Such localization has to be performed cautiously as other factors may be involved (for example, intracranial pressure may make specific diagnosis difficult). Localization of damage is a less common reason of assessment today because greater use is made of CT scans than formerly (although some kinds of neurological deficit, such as anoxia, cannot be detected by CT scans).

Assessments are also carried out in order to obtain a baseline against which to measure future recovery or deterioration. Again, caution must be exercised as there may be a practice effect which leads to better performance on a test simply because the patient has performed the test on an earlier occasion. If alternative versions of the test are given to reduce the practice effect then the tester needs to know the comparability of the two forms of the test in order to avoid differences in levels of difficulty. Using neuropsychological tests as baselines has limitations because the tests are frequently insensitive to the measurement of improvement. It is often better to use a behavioural assessment (described below), which can be made more sensitive to small but real changes.

Neuropsychological assessments can answer certain questions well. For example they can tell us whether a person's score on a test is in the impaired range, how a person compares with others of the same age in the general population, and whether a pattern of results is typical of a particular syndrome. However, there are other questions which neuropsychological assessment cannot answer so well. For example, we know little about the relationship between performance on tests and performance in everyday life. We do not know what treatment to offer as a result of a neuropsychological assessment; neither do we know how patients are responding to any treatment while it is in progress. In order to answer these and similar questions it will be necessary to use other procedures, such as behavioural assessment.

Behavioural assessment

As mentioned earlier, behavioural assessment involves an analysis of the relationship between the antecedents and consequences of the behaviour under consideration. Rather than focusing on whatever caused the problem and the internal state of the patient, the main interest is in current factors in the treatment setting that can be used to alter behaviour. Physical and social determinants of behaviour must also be recognized, as these may place limitations on treatment. Gross anatomical damage or physiological malfunctioning will limit improvement in motor skills. On the other hand, observers should not be *too* ready to accept these limitations because functioning can sometimes be changed under special conditions. For example, it has been possible to improve short-sightedness with specially designed treatment programmes (Collins and Gil 1983).

One of the characteristics of behavioural assessment is that it has a direct relationship with treatment, unlike neuropsychological assessment, described above. If the behavioural assessment has correctly identified those factors which elicit and maintain behaviour, then those factors can be manipulated so that the behaviour itself will change: such change is the goal of treatment. Thus any distinction between assessment and treatment would become artificial and in practice the two are indistinguishable.

In order to measure behaviour it is first of all necessary to define exactly what one is going to measure. It is not possible to observe and record everything the patient says or does. If the observer decides to measure pain behaviour or aggression then it is important to be specific about what constitutes pain or aggression as far as the particular patient is concerned. Recording the number of times the patient complains about pain, or swears at staff, will perhaps be appropriate, but it might be necessary to achieve even greater specificity. For example, the therapist may need to decide whether a groan on the part of a patient represents a complaint, or whether the expletive, 'Damn you!' amounts to swearing. The answers to such questions will depend on specific circumstances, but everyone involved in the assessment and recording will need to know what to include and what to exclude. It is also essential that the behaviours in question should be observable or rateable, and clearly and unambiguously defined.

Behavioural assessment will establish the extent of the problem prior to treatment, and it will also indicate whether observing the behaviour actually *changes* the behaviour. (As can happen, for example, when a person whose eating habits are being observed and recorded actually eats less because they know they are being observed.) Another difficulty can arise if assessment and treatment are introduced together, because it will be impossible to know whether any changes result from the assessment, the treatment, or both. In order to know whether the treatment itself has changed the behaviour, the behaviour during treatment must be compared with the baseline level so that progress can be monitored. It is also important to observe and record the events or situation that precede and follow the behaviour in which we are interested because it is usually these factors that are manipulated in a behavioural treatment programme. If, for example, a physiotherapist frequently lets a patient who complains of physiotherapy have a short rest (thus rewarding inappropriate behaviour) we need to know how often this occurs before changing the situation. We might then persuade the physiotherapist to allow the patient a short rest when a certain exercise has been *completed* (thus rewarding appropriate behaviour).

The main tool of behavioural assessment is direct observation of the patient in a natural or simulated situation. The most useful methods of sampling and recording this behaviour and the relevant stimuli involve counting and/or timing: the observer counts the number of times the response occurs during a given period. Indirect measures could involve counting the products of behaviour such as number of footprints on a chalky surface in a gymnasium, the number of articles completed in the workshop, or the number of soiled incontinence pads use in a day. Timing methods such as interval recording, time sampling, and duration recording are all methods of measuring which behaviours occur during a given observational period or specific times. They may also be used to measure the length of time a behaviour occurs.

The instruments used for recording include simple hand-held counters, wrist counters, stop watches and specially prepared recording sheets on which tally marks are made. It is also possible to use automated measurement and recording devices which are operated directly by the patient's own movements. Some subtle behaviour changes can only be detected when special instruments are used. An increasing number of devices for automatically measuring behavioural deficits have recently been constructed. Voice-operated relays have been used to measure changes in voice loudness. Instruments have been developed for automatically recording changes in muscle tension, posture, position of the head, dribbling, sphincter pressure, and urine flow.

Other devices that are not operated directly by the target behaviour have been developed to simplify the mechanics of data collection. For example, timing signals may be recorded on tape so that observers may observe without having to glance repeatedly at a stop watch. Audio-visual tape recordings allow behavioural episodes to be preserved for rescoring at a later date, and electrical counters have been developed so observers may obtain frequency counts. These instruments can save time and effort, yield data on extremely subtle events, and lead to greater inter-observer agreement.

Factors influencing behaviour may include place, time of day, the patient's own position, the behaviour of other people around the patient, and what are termed 'mutually exclusive' and 'concomitant' behaviours. Several instruments have been developed to record this kind of information, one such being Lieberman's Behaviour Observation Instrument, which enables a trained observer to observe and record four of these dimensions with a group of patients. For example, the 'mutually exclusive' dimension is composed of five behaviours: running, walking, standing, sitting, and lying. Obviously, only one of these can be coded during the observation interval. 'Concomitant behaviour' may include anything which has been previously clearly defined, such as talking, grimacing, crying, eating, reading, smoking, or laughing.

Other categories can be devised. For instance, therapist or family behaviour could be coded in such categories as instructing the patient, correcting the patient, praising the patient, instructing other patients, and engaging in non-treatment behaviours such as looking out of the window, writing notes, or talking on the telephone. Information obtained this way is not only useful for developing treatment programmes but it is also useful in training staff and families to learn the skills to help their patients and relatives.

ASSESSMENT OF MEMORY FUNCTIONING IN A YOUNG MAN FOLLOWING A SEVERE HEAD INJURY

Mark was a young man who sustained a severe head injury at the age of 25 years and was unconscious for several weeks. During the months following his accident he made a partial recovery but he remained physically and intellectually handicapped. On leaving hospital he went to a rehabilitation centre where he was referred to the clinical psychology department for help with his memory problems. Before any treatment could be implemented it was necessary to carry out a full assessment of his memory functioning. Both neuropsychological and behavioural methods were employed to obtain information on the strengths and weaknesses of Mark's memory.

(a) Neuropsychological measures

One of the first tests administered to Mark was Digit Span. In this task Mark had to repeat numbers read out by the psychologist. He was able to repeat back seven digits before making mistakes. This represents an average score and indicated that Mark's immediate memory was normal. Many people, including those with extremely severe memory difficuties, have a normal immediate memory span.

Mark was then asked to listen carefully to a short story and then repeat back as much as he could remember. The story was about six lines long and contained 23 sections or ideas. Mark only managed to recall four sections accurately, a poor score for someone of his age and overall ability. Half an hour later and without any warning Mark was asked to recall the story again. This time he remembered none of it, and in fact he did not remember having been told a story at all. Most people would be able to remember nearly as much after half an hour as they had when first asked to recall the story.

Several other neuropsychological memory tests were administered to Mark. These assessed his immediate and delayed visual memory, his ability to recognize faces and words after a short delay, and his ability to learn new information. On all of these tasks Mark was very seriously impaired. Finally, he was given several tests of remote memory which tested his ability to remember events, faces, personalities, and incidents that had been parts of his experience prior to the accident. When people have been unconscious it is common for them to have retrograde amnesia, that is loss of memory for experiences that happened *before* the onset of coma. In addition to retrograde amnesia, Mark had anterograde amnesia which extended back some seven or eight years. Thus, he thought he was 18 years old and worked at a job he had held some eight years earlier. He did not remember changes of address during the eight-year gap, he did not know the current year or current Prime Minister, and was quite unaware of recent happenings in the news.

(b) Behavioural measures

The tests mentioned above provided considerable information on Mark's memory. However, they did not throw much light on how Mark's memory problems affected his everyday life. In order to do this, several behavioural assessment techniques were employed. The psychologist observed Mark in different settings, including physiotherapy, occupational therapy, the ward, and in a memory group session that Mark attended. Some major problems became evident during these observations. Firstly, Mark was frequently lost, he could not remember his way from one department to another and had to be helped or rescued by members of staff or other patients. Secondly, he could not remember either the names or the faces of anybody working at the centre. Thirdly, he failed to refer to his time-table or his notebook to find out where he was meant to be.

In addition to direct observation, Mark's parents were inter-viewed and asked to describe what they considered to be Mark's main problems. They were also given a rating scale to complete which compared Mark's memory before and after the accident. This rating scale was adapted from one devised by Kapur and Pearson (1983). Several memory functions were listed including remem-bering to pass on a message and remembering the names of people Mark had known for a long time. For each of these functions Mark's parents had to decide whether their son was (a) as good as he was before his accident, (b) slightly worse or (c) very much worse. The ratings provided an indication of the severity of Mark's everyday memory problems. Mark also filled in the rating scale but it was noticeable that he tended to underestimate the extent of his diffi-culties. In common with many other head-injured people Mark experienced difficulty in remembering just how bad his memory had become. However, the information obtained from Mark did give an indication of his *own* insight into his memory problems.

Mark and his parents also completed a questionnaire about the methods he used to compensate for his memory impairment. This questionnaire was adapted from Harris (1980). It concentrated on questions about the use of aids such as notebooks and alarms. In fact Mark used very few methods to bypass or alleviate his memory difficulties, certainly fewer than most people *without* memory difficulties.

Mark's therapists were asked to complete checklists every day for two weeks. At the end of his twice-daily physiotherapy sessions his physiotherapist spent a few minutes going through the 19-item checklist, recording any memory failures noted during the session. The items included questions such as, 'Did he forget where he had put something?' and 'Did he forget what he was supposed to be doing?' Mark's occupational therapist also completed checklists at the end of her sessions. The information provided a detailed picture of the number, type, and extent of Mark's memory problems during his daily life.

Mark was also tested on a new memory test which combines the strengths of standarized tests with the strengths of behavioural measures. This test is called the 'Rivermead Behavioural Memory Test' (Wilson, Cockburn and Baddeley 1985). As well as an assessment tool the RBMT also indicated the severity of Mark's memory impairment. Finally, the information gathered from all the assessment procedures was used to design Mark's memory therapy programme.

TREATMENT

Introduction

People with physical handicap may come into contact with clinical psychologists for several reasons. Occasionally psychologists will be involved in the treatment of the physical or motor difficulties which all of these patients will experience. For example, psychologists may supervise biofeedback procedures used to improve foot drop in stroke patients. When physiotherapists and psychologists work together they can sometimes be effective in improving motor control by combining their skills. Thus, the physiotherapist's knowledge of muscles, joints, and physical therapy techniques can be combined with the psychologist's expertise in evaluating treatment programmes and knowledge of ways to improve learning.

Apart from physical handicap, which may or may not require treatment, there are other problems that require the attention of the clinical psychologist. For example, sensory difficulties such as impaired vision or touch may involve psychological intervention as well as the treatment supplied by physiotherapists, speech therapists, and occupational therapists. Behaviour problems, such as yelling and tantrums, are fairly common amongst patients who have suffered severe head injury, and other groups of physically handicapped people may exhibit similar behaviour in certain circumstances. Psychologists are often expected to devise programmes that will help patients overcome these disorders of conduct.

Emotional difficulties may also accompany physical handicap, leaving the patient fearful, anxious, or depressed. A patient with brain-stem damage, for example, is particularly likely to show emotional lability and will change from extreme tearfulness to loud laughter within minutes. Diseases of the basal ganglia, such as

Huntington's chorea or progressive supranuclear palsy, are also likely to promote emotional disturbances.

Cognitive deficits involving memory, language, and perception are commonly associated with certain kinds of neurological damage, including head injury, stroke, and encephalitis. Psychologists are becoming increasingly involved in the treatment of these disorders.

Finally, physical handicap may be associated with personality disturbances. These may develop as a result of neurological impairment such as bilateral frontal lobe damage, or because of environmental factors such as over-protection or rejection by the patient's family.

Treatment of a physical problem

Mrs A. was a 72-year-old widow who had her right leg amputated after several unsuccessful operations for vascular insufficiency. She was admitted for preliminary assessment to see if she was suitable for provision of a prosthesis and walking training. She was in moderately good physical health, but had some mild memory problems and was extremely anxious. However, she seemed highly motivated to walk, which was necessary if she was to return to her own home, which was unsuitable for a wheelchair. Emotionally, she seemed adjusted to the loss of her leg: she was able to examine her stump, touch it, bandage it, and was not worried about the appearance of it. She was cheerful and said she felt great relief in not having the continual pain she had suffered prior to amputation, which she regarded as a positive treatment rather than a devastating loss. She experienced minimal phantom sensation and, on provision of the artificial limb, experienced slight discomfort from rubbing of the stump in the socket—which was later modified by the prosthetist. After four days of walking and training she was referred to the clinical psychologist for fear of falling and for needing constant reassurance, and because she seemed unable to manage her own medication.

The fear of falling was tackled first and a hierarchy of fearful situations was drawn up by the psychologist and Mrs A. Following this, Mrs A. was taught relaxation techniques. She then practised the early items of the hierarchy, first by imagining them and then by carrying them through with the help of the physiotherapist. Mrs A. rapidly progressed up the hierarchy until she was able to walk up and down the parallel bars four times. At this stage the psychologist observed the physiotherapist and Mrs A. during three training sessions in order to assess Mrs A.'s constant requests for reassurance. Because Mrs A. was by now less afraid of falling, the number of requests had decreased to some extent, but when she did ask, the therapist spent a lot of time encouraging Mrs A., putting her arm around Mrs A's shoulders and patting her on the arm. However, when Mrs A. was walking successfully the therapist would speak to and touch Mrs A. less often. When this was pointed out to the therapist she changed her behaviour and gave Mrs A. attention and praise for *success* in walking, and removed attention when Mrs. A. complained or asked for help. In two weeks Mrs A. was successfully managing two lengths of the gymnasium using her frame, and by four weeks she had managed to transfer to two walking sticks, and could also managed to climb a short flight of stairs.

Treatment of a sensory problem

Gary was a 39-year-old divorced man who had been living alone, working as a self-employed businessman, when he received a spinal injury in a road traffic accident. He received six months treatment in a Spinal Unit and recovered sufficiently to be able to walk quite long distances with a frame. He managed all self-care activities except for his bowel routine. He was left with an incomplete sensory loss below the sixth cervical (C6) level, with diminished sensation over his trunk below the shoulder level, but with other areas of extreme sensitivity and intense pain. Because of increasing pain he did less and less and for the last month before admission he sat in a darkened room doing nothing at all. He had attended a pain clinic and, among other things, had been offered brain surgery. He was unwilling to accept this, saying 'My brain is the only bit of me that functions well, I would rather leave it alone.'

On admission he appeared depressed and complained bitterly of his pain. Assessment suggested that Gary had three kinds of pain. The first was a total body pain which affected him from the shoulders down, and this he described as aching, gnawing, and constant. The second was around the ribs, and he described this as stabbing, sickening and intermittment. The third pain, in his right leg, groin and buttock, he described as searing, burning, sharp, and unbearable. Gary was able to distinguish the three pains quite clearly and could relate the different pains to different stimuli. The stabbing pains which were intermittent around the rib area seemed to be related to muscle spasm in his left arm. The most intolerable pain, that in his left leg and groin, seemed to occur after a period when he felt hot or uncomfortable. The total body pain seemed to be most pronounced when he was inactive.

A programme was worked out for Gary by the physician, physiotherapist, and psychologist. The drug Lioresal was given for the muscle spasm, nerve stimulation techniques were adminstered by the physiotherapist to help relieve the leg and groin pain, and an increasing activity schedule in the gymnasium and assessment flat together with progressive relaxation exercises were used to help alleviate some of the general body pain.

Further investigation into the most unpleasant leg pain, which had responded slightly to the nerve stimulation, revealed that heat made Gary's pain intolerable. Even imagining a hot place worsened the pain. However, Gary learned to make the pain more manageable by imagining himself immersed in cold water.

Four months after discharge Gary was still using this technique and the nerve stimulation. He was living independently in a specially adapted flat, and planning to take a course in computer studies.

Treatment of an emotional problem

Jenny was a severely disabled 24-year-old woman with spinal muscular atrophy. She was confined to a wheelchair and dependent on others for all her needs except for the mobility provided by the powered chair. She was referred to an assessment unit to see if she could live independently in special accommodation, and to find out whether she was capable of directing live-in care attendants.

When assessed by the clinical psychologist Jenny was found to be intelligent. Her problem was that she was unhappy and felt that people did not like her. She also felt worthless. Her thoughts were concentrated upon two main themes (a) that she was worthless and unpopular because she was in a wheelchair that was regarded as a nuisance by other people and (b) that her appearance was unattractive and people did not like her because of this. In fact Jenny was a very attractive person who had beautiful hair, a lovely smile and good dress sense. She drove her electric chair with great skill and it was no nuisance in most small houses. Jenny's false assumptions were challenged, brought out in the open and discussed. The fallacies were pointed out to her. She was encouraged to monitor her thought about her wheelchair she was asked to bang her hand on the side and say, 'I am in a wheelchair, it is a very nice, neat chair, it looks good and I drive it very well, and it can get into even the smallest space and it is not trouble to anyone.' When she noticed she was thinking about being exceedingly thin and ugly she was to say to herself, 'I have kept myself beautifully slim, I look very good in these modern clothes, I have very nice hair, people look at me and think what an attractive girl.'

At first Jenny found this procedure difficult and she felt she would become conceited. However, it became easier and after two weeks she indicated that she was almost beginning to think the statements were true! She then watched the psychologist modelling a confident, assertive disabled, person, with one of the nurses playing the part of a care attendant. Jenny learned how to ask for her essential needs and to be satisfied without overly apologising or appearing too demanding or bossy. When discharged from the unit she stated that she felt much better about herself.

Treatment of a behaviour problem

Physically handicapped people, like any others, can have behaviour problems. In some cases these will be unrelated to the physical handicap and just happen to coexist with it. In other cases the behaviour problems and the physical handicap may both be direct consequences of neurological damage. For example, a patient with a large frontal lobe tumour may have difficulties in exercising motor skills *and* display behaviour problems, both directly resulting from frontal lobe damage. In another group of patients the behaviour problems may be indirectly related to the physical handicap. Thus a severely head-injured person who is unable to walk may develop problematic behaviour as a means of obtaining the attention of others.

M. B. was a young man who had received a severe head injury in a car accident. He was very ataxic and unsteady on his feet, had considerable intellectual handicaps and was very disruptive in his therapy sessions. His main behaviour problem was frequent calling out to his physiotherapist and occupational therapist. He appeared to want their attention all the time and interrupted the therapy of other patients as well as his own. The therapists and psychologist worked out a programme to try and reduce M. B's calling out. In the baseline period the number of times he called for the therapist was recorded. In the treatment stage staff explained to M.B. that they wanted him to call out less often, that they were going to count how many times he called out each session, and that they were going to count how many times he shouted out. They also informed him that when he managed to go two days without calling out, the physiotherapist, the occupational therapist, and the psychologist would take him to the pub for lunch. M.B. apparently found the idea of the pub lunch a powerful reward for he earned it very quickly. It was gradually made harder for him to earn the lunch, and staff also took turns accompanying him so that one or two staff members went on each occasion. With occasional lapses, M.B. continued to work reasonably quietly.

Not all patients will respond to treatment so quickly but behavioural approaches have been effective with a number of physically handicapped people. Several examples can be found in Ince (1976).

Treatment of a cognitive problem

These include difficulties with thinking, perceiving, remembering, and reasoning. These should not be confused with problems relating to emotional or physical behaviour, or to personality problems. Cognitive deficits are particularly likely to follow neurological damage affecting the brain, but they can also follow other handicapping conditions too. For example, some kidney patients show mild intellectual impairments, probably resulting from insufficient oxygen getting to the brain. Congenital handicaps can also lead to cognitive deficits, usually following on from interrupted or inappropriate education. Remedial education may be appropriate when cognitive difficulties occur in childhood. Similar procedures can be used with adults. There is currently a growing interest in cognitive rehabilitation for those patients who have been intellectually normal and whose problems result from brain damage acquired in adulthood (Wilson and Moffat 1984).

D.C. was a soldier who was shot through the head at the age of 23. He spent the next two years undergoing several operations and intensive rehabilitation. At the end of this two-year period he remained severely intellectually impaired and totally unable to read. He had been a normal reader before the injury. He never accepted the conclusions of the experts who told him that he would never read again. Three years after the injury an attempt was made to teach D.C. to read six useful, everyday words. He failed to learn any of them. Two years later, that is five years post injury, D.C. was taught the sounds and name of letters of the alphabet. These were taught one at a time and upper case letters were taught first. Following this, letters were presented in random order and D.C. was required to say the sounds. The next step was to teach him which letters were vowels. Then two and three regular words were introduced and finally irregular words were taught. The teaching method was simply practice, feedback, and teaching one thing at a time. D.C. failed to learn anything using the whole word method but quickly learned to read using the phonetic method. It took three weeks to teach the sounds and names of the letters and within six months D.C. had progressed from reading no words at all to reading at the level of a nine-year-old. He is still continuing to improve.

Treatment of a personality problem

It is not always easy to decide which problems are emotional and which are due to behaviour or personality disorders. We tend to judge people's personalities from the way they behave: describing a person who laughs a great deal as having a cheerful personality and someone who shouts and complains as bad-tempered. Similarly, if a person is fearful or depressed we might consider that this shows emotional disturbance or we might suggest that they have 'personality problems'. It is usual to regard emotion as connected with feelings; behaviour relating to conduct; and personality representing the characteristics or traits of an individual. Among the physically handicapped, 'personality problems' may be a direct consequence of neurological damage or they may represent a maladaptive response to a handicapping condition.

If a person is referred for help with 'personality problems' the psychologist will almost certainly identify some specific problem behaviours for treatment, and will not consider the personality as an entity that is capable of being damaged and therefore treated. Let us consider, for example, the case of A.F. who suffered a stroke, after which he became excessively demanding and asked staff dozens of times each day when his wife would be collecting him. She came each day at 4.30 p.m. and was never late. Treatment in this case consisted of (a) self-monitoring, whereby A.F. counted the number of times he asked the staff when his wife would be coming to collect him and (b) imaginal desensitization, whereby he imagined his wife arriving a few seconds later each day. His questions never ceased entirely but over a period of three weeks they dropped from over 40 per day to an average of five per day.

BEHAVIOURAL APPROACH TO PRESSURE-RELIEF EXERCISING FOR A PATIENT WITH SPINAL INJURY

P.W. was a 34-year-old man who fell from a tree and sustained spinal injuries which left him with a partial paraplegia. His sensation was impaired and he had no feeling at all in his buttocks. He spent long periods in a wheelchair and received advice from physiotherapists, doctors, and nurses on the necessity of lifting his buttocks regularly in order to prevent pressure sores developing. Despite considerable efforts to persuade him to cooperate with the recommended skin care, he failed to look after himself and developed a sacral pressure sore. More advice, encouragement, and persuasion followed but P.W. still failed to respond and soon afterwards staff noticed a new pressure sore developing. At this time P.W. was referred to the clinical psychology department with a request to seek ways of gaining his cooperation in the care of his pressure areas.

Pressure sores are a common complication after spinal injury and are difficult to treat. The patient has reduced circulation in the pressure areas but feels no discomfort, so has little motivation to help the circulation by moving or lifting the buttocks. When the patient does lift there is no immediate reinforcement such as relief from discomfort. Although, in the long term patients know that sores may develop and that these sores may prove to be life-threatening if gangrene sets in, the consequences are far removed from the actual behaviour required to avoid them. In these circumstances even the sores may fail to act as deterrents and the positive consequences of lifting may be obscured because the healing process is so slow.

Several methods have been used to encourage lifting in spinal patients. Most of these consist of some form of pressure-sensitive pad with an alarm to signal when lifts should be made. From the published reports it is often difficult to judge treatment effectiveness, but one important factor would appear to be the provision of immediate consequences for lifting. In P. W.'s case the immediate consequence was verbal feedback on the number of lifts made in a given period, and praise if he lifted often enough. On the basis of previous studies we decided that one lift should occur every 10 minutes. A lift was defined as a movement which involved P. W.'s buttocks leaving the seat of the wheelchair for at least 4 s. P. W. pushed himself up from the chair with his arms, which were not affected by the spinal injury. It was necessary to have equipment which would record the number of lifts made. This consisted of a pressure-sensitive pad attached to the seat of the patient's wheelchair. The pad was placed in a bag behind the wheelchair. Each time pressure was relieved from the pad for 4 s the counter registered a lift.

Before starting treatment baselines were necessary in order to know how few lifts were being made and how much improvement occurred as a result of treatment. P. W. was observed on two occasions in each of four different places: the woodwork shop, in the dining room during lunch break, in the canteen during coffee and tea breaks, and on the ward at the end of the day. The number of lifts made in all these places was recorded. During two of the baseline sessions two observers carried out the recording in order to test for reliability between different observers. The agreement was 100 per cent.

Following these baselines the equipment was introduced in the woodwork shop. The counter was set to zero, the pressure pad placed in the wheelchair and P. W. was told that this would count the number of lifts made, so he would know if he was lifting often enough. He was told that the equipment was only being used in one place, woodwork, in order to give him a chance to get used to it. At the end of the session P. W. was told how many lifts he had made and praised if the number was equal to (or more than) the minimum number required (six lifts per hour). During the next week the equipment and feedback procedure were introduced in the dining room during the lunch break. In the third stage the pressure pad and counter were used over tea and coffee breaks, and finally the equipment was introduced in the ward.

The reason for staggering the feedback procedure was to help decide whether increased lifting was directly related to treatment or was due to something else such as general improvement due to P. W. becoming more settled at the unit. If it was due to treatment then improvement should occur only after the introduction of the treatment. If, on the other hand, it was due to something else then lifting should improve throughout the period being monitored and show no relationship to the introduction of the feedback procedure.

As there was a strong association between the use of the intervention strategy and the number of lifts it appears that the feedback itself was effective rather than some general improvement. This method of staggering the introduction of treatment is known as a 'multiple baseline across settings' design.

Although the number of lifts made following the introduction of treatment was variable it was always above the minimum number required. Once equipment was being used in all situations we reduced the number of feedback sessions by combining two sessions together. At the same time P.W. began to take over responsibility for the recording. Increasing the number of lifts was, of course, a means to an end. P.W. was encouraged to lift to allow healing of his pressure sores to take place and to prevent further ones from developing. We were therefore interested to know about the condition of the skin around the pressure areas. Steady improvement took place soon after treatment began. Three weeks later the pressure sores were almost healed and four weeks after this P.W. was allowed to use the hydrotherapy pool, which had been impossible while his skin condition had remained poor.

P.W. was seen again 10 weeks after the end of the treatment programme. His skin was still in good condition, although he was not lifting regularly. However, by this time lifting was less important as he was spending periods on crutches and out of his wheelchair.[1]

COUNSELLING PEOPLE WITH PHYSICAL HANDICAP

The term counselling has different meanings in different contexts and for different people. It may refer to the giving of advice and information, which is the usual interpretation for the counselling offered to patients by doctors, health visitors, and therapists. Disabled people are often in need of information about drug and diet regimes, or apropriate appliances or new ways to carry out everyday activities. In each case the patient has to follow instructions from a professional, and it is the latter's responsibility to ensure that the

[1]This patient is also described in Carr and Wilson (1983)

information is clearly and unambiguously presented. Unfortunately, we know that much of the information given by doctors is forgotten or ignored. This may be due to anxiety, impaired memory, or some other disability on the part of the patient, or it may be due to an unfamiliar repertoire of language adopted by the doctor.

Psychologists can often help design the most appropriate format for the giving of information. For example, they may know whether a patient's verbal comprehension skills are sufficient to understand the language being used, or they can advise on the most readable form of written instructions for a particular patient. For people with language and/or reading problems it may be best to pass on information by drawings or diagrams, or even pantomime. For people with perceptual problems, however, these methods might be totally confusing and in these cases simple written lists may be the most suitable form of communication. An example of the latter situation occurred for a man who had a left hemiplegia following a right cerebral vascular accident. He was rendered incontinent because of difficulty in performing actions in correct sequence. In the lavatory he stood up, urinated, unzipped his trousers, zipped them up again, sat down and wondered why he was wet. When the instructions were written down for him he learned the steps by heart and repeated these aloud: 'Stand, up, unzip, pass water, zip up, sit down.' Eventually he was able to manage without saying the steps.

Counselling can also mean advocacy whereby the disabled person is given advice as to what to do or where to go to minimize a handicap. Understanding the complete range of health, social, educational, and employment services is beyond the scope of many people. Knowing what state benefits or allowances a person is entitled to is extremely difficult for newly disabled people and their relatives. Professionals may be expert in their own fields but very few of them know about all the resources available across all the services. Some clinical psychologists believe that they should make themselves knowledgeable and act as resource centres, thus being able in some degree to point each patient in the right direction in order to solve certain living problems. Before embarking on counselling they need to equip themselves with knowledge of the patient's condition, understand the genetics (if appropriate), the causes, and the likely prognosis. They also need to know the medical steps required in the management of the condition in order to achieve the most appropriate treatment. Those clinical psychologists who counsel patients in this manner will obtain useful guidance from the *Disability rights handbook* (Disability Alliance 1985) and the *Directory for the disabled* (Dornborough and Kinrade 1985), both of which will inform them of other services which may be helpful to their patients. These books will also help to create a dialogue which is structured to enable patients to make the best possible choices for themselves and their families. If patients have problems with bureaucracy when seeking access to certain services then the clinical psychologist should be prepared to give support and, if necessary, write back-up letters to gain the cooperation of other helpful people and organizations. Counselling of this type is of course often offered by members of several professions.

Counselling may refer to sexual advice in circumstances where a person with a physical handicap and his or her partner finds sexual activities increasingly difficult. Psychologists are frequently asked to help with such problems. It is first necessary to identify what is causing the problem. Sexual drive may be diminished because of general malaise, pain, muscle spasm, weak, paralysed, or contracted limbs. If any of these constitute the cause it will be necessary to consider changing or introducing the use of drugs, and prior consultation with the patient's medical practitioner will be important. However, many drugs such as anti-depressants, drugs for diabetes, pain-killers, can diminish sexual drive. Sometimes the drug can be changed or the timing can be modified. Other solutions could involved changing of positions, supporting limbs on pillows, or using other methods other than straightforward sexual intercourse. Encouragement of direct communication between the disabled person and partner play an important role in this type of counselling.

Another problem may be with the patient's sexual image. Some physically handicapped people may have a very poor opinion of their bodies and feel they are not desirable to their sexual partners, therefore they do not project themslves as sexual beings. Other people who have been disabled from childhood may never have been given adequate sex education, or they may have been treated as perpetual children. Psychologists can provide sex education and teach the skills involved in forming a sexual relationship. Difficulties in sexual relationships may result from reduced opportunities to express sexuality. Somebody with paralysed arms, for instance, will find difficulty in hugging a partner. Certain conditions may make sex painful and other methods of expression should be explored such as the use of sexual aids. Finally, there may be a psychosexual problem which is not related to the physical disability (as can, of course, be found in other couples without physical disabilities). In such cases a programme of re-education and psychosexual treatment such as that offered in sexual clinics may provide a solution.

Finally, counselling people with physical disability may mean supporting those who are dying. How people respond to terminal conditions will depend to a considerable extent on the explanations given to them. It is essential that anyone attempting this kind of counselling recognizes that people facing terminal illness pass through certain stages, although not necessarily in logical sequence. The spouse and children of the dying person also go through a form of anticipatory grief, and may show all the signs of bereavement. They may need as much help as the dying person at certain stages during the terminal illness (see Stedeford 1984).

CONCLUSIONS

Attitudes to the physically handicapped

Despite the professed goodwill towards physically handicapped people that is articulated in most European countries today, negative attitudes remain. This is shown, for example, by the lack of positive action on behalf of society to make it possible for physically handicapped people to take a full part in the community in which they live. Rehabilitation is often seen as the bottom of the hierarchy of medical specialisms, and one of the consequences of this is that services to the physically handicapped receive the worst cuts during periods when all public services are experiencing withdrawal of funds. Clinical psychologists should be prepared to use their skills to change the attitudes and behaviour of people in the Health Service, and in the general public, towards those who are physically handicapped. Similarly, disabled clients can be helped to change *their* negative attitudes and behaviour: they can be armed with information concerning their welfare rights can be informed of the services available to them. The learned helplessness seen in some disabled people can be reduced or avoided by encouragement to become more active in self-help groups. Physically handicapped people must be made aware of the control *they* can exercise over the environment in which they live.

Working with other staff

It is evident from this chapter that psychologists working with the physically handicapped do so in close collaboration with other staff, particularly physiotherapists and occupational therapists, and to a lesser extent with nurses, speech therapists, and social workers. At times the skills and interests of the psychologist may overlap with those of other disciplines. Some psychologists, for instance, are interested in motor problems, others may concentrate on language or perceptual deficits, others may prefer work connected with counselling. However, psychologists, having been trained in a different tradition, have few of the skills that are possessed by those other professionals with whom they work: for example, they do not have the speech therapists' knowledge of cleft palates and swallowing mechanisms; they do not have the occupational therapists' ability to make aids for the physically handicapped; nor do they possess the social workers' skills in sorting through financial benefits and future placements. Although this list of specific skills acquired and practised by other professionals is enormous, nevertheless, psychologists have a general training in learning theory and behavioural methods which can be put to good use in the field of physical handicap.

Most psychologists also have a commitment to evaluate the effectiveness of their intervention procedures through single-case experimental designs or larger research studies. A smaller number will also be interested in developing new assessment and treatment procedures for use with handicapped people. Rehabilitation of the physically handicapped will continue to improve as long as the different disciplines combine their specific skills and strengths for the good of their patients.

REFERENCES

Carr, S. and Wilson, B. A. (1983). Promotion of pressure relief exercising in a spinal injury patient: a multiple baseline across settings design. *Behav. Psychother.* **11**, 329–36.
Collins, F. L., Jr. and Gil, K. M. (1983). Behavioural approaches to visual disorders. In *Contributions to Medical Psychology* (ed. S. Rachman) Vol. III. Pergamon Press, Oxford.
Darnborough, A. and Kinrade, D. (1985). *Directory for the disabled.* Woodhead Faulkner with RADAR, Cambridge.

Disability Alliance (1985). *Disability rights handbook for 1986.* Disability Alliance, London.

Harris, J. E. (1980). Memory aids people use: two interview studies *Memory Cognition* **8**, 31–8.

Ince, L. P. (1976). *Behaviour modification in rehabilitation medicine.* C. C. Thomas, Illinois.

Kapur, N. and Pearson, D. (1983). Memory symptoms and memory performance of neurological patients. *Br. J. Psychol.* **74**, 409–15.

Stedeford, A. (1984). *Facing death. Patients, families and professionals* Heinemann Medical Books, London.

Sunderland, A., Harris, J. E. and Gleave, J. (1984). Memory failures in everyday life after severe head injury. *J. clin. Neuropsychol.* **6**, 127–142.

Wilson, B. A., Cockburn, J. and Baddeley, A. D. B. (1985). *The Rivermead behavioural memory test manual.* Thames Valley Test Company, 22 Bulmershe Road, Reading, Berkshire, England.

Wilson, B. A. and Moffat, N., ed. (1984). *The clinical management of memory problems.* Croom Helm, London.

FURTHER READING

Baddeley, A. D. B. (1984). *Your memory: A user's guide.* Penguin, Harmondsworth.

Brechin, A. and Liddiard, P. (1981). *Look at it this way: new perspectives in rehabilitation.* Hodder and Stoughton/Open University Press, Sevenoaks, Kent.

Crewe, N. M. and Zola, I. K. (1983). *Independent living for physically disabled people.* Josey-Bass, San Francisco.

Fordyce, W. E. (1976). *Behavioural methods for chronic pain and illness.* C. V. Mosby, St. Louis.

Ince, L. P. (1980). *Behavioural psychology in rehabilitation medicine.* Williams and Wilkins, Baltimore.

Nichols, K. (1984). *Psychological care in physical illness.* Croom Helm, London.

7

Working with the elderly
Jeff Garland

NEVER TOO LATE?

Directing a withering look at the book-lined walls of my office, a disappointed 86-year-old client told me: 'I never thought I'd end up . . . sitting here . . . listening to someone as knows everything and don't know nothing!'

At least specialists in work with people in late life can find a little comfort in the thought that even if inspiration is sometimes lacking, they never want for clients. Some 14 per cent of the population of the United Kingdom are over 65, official inhabitants of 'the country of the old' described by Ronald Blythe (1979). On a more positive note, Britain's Health Education Council has called for the involvement of health care professionals, including psychologists, in a continued campaign for better health in late life aimed at everyone over 50. Much work with the most severely impaired old people needs to be expended on supporting professional and paraprofessional carers, volunteers, neighbours, friends, and family drawn from most of the age span.

Geriatrics

This is a title properly used to define an area of medical specialization with patients usually over 65—geriatric medicine—but is sometimes misused to label the patients. In-patient provision usually includes acute beds in general hospitals for emergency admission; rehabilitation beds with fast or slow rates of turnover; and continuing care wards. Holiday or short-term care beds are widely used to give relatives relief. Day attenders are catered for by day hospitals in many localities. Outreach to the local community may include out-patient clinics, domiciliary visits to the homes of patients, and home-based support from geriatricians, geriatric liaison nurses, occupational and physiotherapists, and social workers.

It may often be difficult to tell if the problems of a given patient are primarily social, psychological, or physical, but as yet there are relatively few areas of the United Kingdom that offer a unified approach to care of the elderly, with social services, geriatricians, and psychogeriatricians working together. In some areas a start has been made by operating a joint assessment service or a review panel to make a shared decision on primary responsibility for an individual's treatment. Where there is no recognized joint approach, one or more members of a psychogeriatric team may be called in by geriatricians either in an *ad hoc* way or as part of a liaison service which tries to anticipate problems.

Psychogeriatrics

This refers to psychiatry specializing in patients aged 65 and over, although again it is sometimes used mistakenly to describe the patients themselves. A local service is likely to have some or all of the following types of in-patient provision. Continuing care wards look after long-stay patients, often with a mix of chronic psychiatric patients grown old as 'graduates' of the hospital system, and patients admitted in late life with psychiatric disorders related to ageing. Assessment units admit patients who, in theory if not always in practice, come solely for short-stay admission. Mixed wards may include continuing care, assessment, and medium-term care. 'Floating beds' on a rota system may be available so that, through planned periodic admission relief is offered to a number of patients and their supporters, and 'holiday beds' which offer short-stay admission responsive as far as possible to immediate needs.

Many such wards also serve a small number of day patients, usually attending for from one to five days each week, and more rarely, a few have a limited number of night 'hostel' beds catering for old people whose management elsewhere poses acute problems mainly at night.

Many psychogeriatric services also operate relatively small day hospitals, catering solely for day attenders, for one to five days each week, and may also support day centres run by local groups of national societies concerned with old people. Other psychogeriatric outreach services are likely to include local out-patient clinics, domiciliary visits and home-based support to patients and their family and friends, voluntary helpers, and professional carers. These services use a network of community psychiatric nurses, psychiatrists, psychologists, and social workers.

Social services

Local authorities may make provision for old people apart from the provision made by health authorities. Home care schemes enable the client to stay at home with varying degrees of support. Sheltered housing with a warden provides for those becoming frail but still able to cope largely unaided. Old people's homes are for those deemed to need full-time residential care. In some areas, selected homes for elderly mentally infirm residents are designated as such; in others *de facto* segregation may be imposed by reserving part of each home for 'confused' residents; in other parts of the country relative integration may prevail.

General practice

Those doctors responsible for health care in the community, the general practitioners, are in the U K paid extra for looking after older patients because this group makes a heavy demand on their time. While intensive screening of this age group may not be a cost-effective exercise, an increasing number of G Ps have special clinics for over-65s, and may wish to involve a clinical psychologist either in the health centre or in domiciliary visits.

Community hospitals

These are relatively small units serving a community and with beds controlled and serviced by local general practitioners. They usually have a large proportion of elderly patients, who are either receiving day care, in-patient rehabilitation, or long-term care. These units can usefully supplement the geriatric provision of large general hospitals and provide locally available care.

Voluntary societies

There are a number of national societies with local groups or initiatives related to local needs of old people. Age Concern, Help the Aged, and the Parkinson's Disease Society are examples. The psychologist and colleagues from other disciplines are likely to be found in such settings from time to time, offering consultancy or working with individual clients referred by the society or self-referred.

Private care

Provision of private residential care for old people in Britain is growing rapidly. State assistance is provided in some cases where, on completion of active treatment and in the absence of a health or social services unit able to accept transfer, the financial resources of a resident in a health service facility may be 'topped up' to enable that individual to transfer to private care, freeing a bed. Those residents are likely to be followed up, in some cases by visits of psychogeriatric team members. Private Homes may seek consultancy on general issues affecting staff training, management of difficult residents, and improving the quality of life in residential care.

TYPE OF PSYCHOLOGICAL PROBLEM

Physical, psychological, and social factors interact in old people to produce increased variability in behaviour and a wide range of reactions to ageing processes. Treatable physical causes should ideally be dealt with at an early stage, and social needs should also be met, leaving the psychologist free to home in on residual factors, but this rarely happens in practice. Continual awareness that psychological factors cannot be approached in isolation remains necessary. In listing the major types of psychological problem experienced by old people, we must recognize that these can occur in clients from other age groups. While old people do have some unique concerns, they are basically just people who have been around longer than the rest of us.

There is no widely accepted system of classification of the psychological problems of the elderly. The common behavioural distinction between 'deficit' and 'excess' categories, which can then be further subdivided, offers a basis for a helpful model, however, and is being actively developed in work with the elderly. Interview schedules, behaviour rating scales, and other psychological tests, have been widely used in large-scale surveys without as yet yielding a taxonomy that can be applied readily. This is hardly surprising when we consider the following selection of problems culled from the records of a recent series of 50 consecutive clients. Three main headings are used: *primarily psychological*, relating to an individual's thoughts and feelings; *primarily physical*, relating to physical activity and needs; and *primarily social*, concerning social functioning. Some of the problems quite clearly could belong to more than one category.

Primarily psychological

Forgetfulness and memory impairment become an increasing concern for many old people. Clients identify early forgetfulness with the first signs of 'going mad' or 'senility', and may develop unduly complex or drastic attempts to cover up or to cope which impose more burden than the actual memory deficit. Confusion, disorientation, and progressive inability to think straight may succeed failing memory but do not invariably do so. This type of problem may well be episodic and patchy, particularly in its early stages, so that relatively convincing attempts to cope alternate with lapses during which the client can be aware that something is 'wrong' without being able to correct what is happening.

Anxiety, whether diffuse or relatively specific, accompanies many of the problems listed here, and appears in many forms in older clients. Depression, one of the most frequent and serious psychological difficulties that can occur with ageing, similarly may appear in a variety of forms and degrees of severity. Often linked with depression, but worth considering as a separate entity, is demoralization. Low self-esteem and morale and a pervasive feeling of loss of control over one's own life, may to some extent reflect the low social value placed on ageing and the aged in our society. A preoccupation with bodily discomfort and the maintenance of physical functions, particularly excretion, is characteristic of some elderly clients, particularly those who are depressed. Often chronic pain is experienced, but the client's signals of pain complaining can become augmented, and may function not only as a response to bodily state, but also as a means of operating on others to gain reassurance. Reaction to actual or anticipated loss—of social status, economic or physical independence, of friends or family through relocation or bereavement, of one's own life—is of increasing concern in later life and is often linked with depression or demoralization.

Primarily physical

The following group of problems relate to physical needs and action, but have a strong psychological component since the behaviour, thoughts, and feelings of the client and others are intimately involved.

Maintenance of the activities of daily living, for example dressing or undressing, and performing domestic tasks can be disrupted in later life, so that the client requires retraining or other assistance. Maintenance of health, together with necessary compliance with medical or other treatment, may be interfered with through inability or unwillingness to act reliably in, for instance, maintaining body temperature by appropriate dress and heating. Sleep can be less satisfying in late life, with sleep dissatisfaction tending to increase after 50, sometimes involving an exacerbation of worry over lack of sleep, leading to reduced sleep, which leads to further worry. Apparent incontinence without a direct physical cause may occur in later life through inability to recognize a toilet, or failure to reach the toilet quickly enough because reduced mobility, or for many other reasons.

Mobility in the elderly may be impaired not only by physical damage, but also by reluctance to engage in rehabilitation, or by overdependence on a wheelchair or other aid either by client or by carers. Excessive movement, often labelled as 'wandering', may reflect a search for emotional security, looking for 'parents' or 'home'; or a continuation of occupational patterns—I've got my work to do'.

Physical or verbal 'aggression' is often complained of in the more severely impaired elderly client. Brain damage may reduce an individual's ability to inhibit violent impulses, understandable provocation may trigger violence, and the attention given to 'aggression' may make it more likely to recur. Inappropriate sexual behaviour, including masturbation, or unsolicited sexual approach, may involve loss of inhibitions. It may also illustrate the possibility that for some old people, while sexual needs are retained, the opportunities to gratify such needs in a socially sanctioned manner are drastically reduced.

Primarily social

The family system and network of friends to which an impaired old person belongs may be put under severe strain in coping with the major personality changes which Gilleard (1984) describes. Needs of the old person and supporters for information, access to services, general reassurance, and in some cases specific counselling and advice on management pose a series of inter-related problems.

Loneliness, almost certainly under-reported by the elderly, who understandably may be reluctant to admit social failure, can be linked with reduced mobility, loss of attractiveness, and lack of money. Excessive requests for attention, like repeated questioning, may function to force social responses from others, who pass by without comment when the attention-seeker is quiet, preferring to 'let sleeping dogs lie'. The stress of relocation and adaptation to institutional living represents a major upheaval for some older people, especially when the move is rapid, and the client is ambivalent and still in the throes of the life crises which forced admission.

CERTAINLY A CHALLENGE

This is the phrase usually breathed by the awed clinical psychologist new to working with the elderly, becoming aware that the above list of problems could be twice as long and still not cover all the psychological problems that can beset impaired old people.

However, the summary of practice which follows indicates that our resources are growing in response to the challenge. It remains the case that relatively few clinical psychologists devote most of their time to old people, their supporters, and carers. This imbalance is slowly being corrected as the positive contribution which can be made is recognized.

Describing the various tasks of a clinical psychologist concerned with old people, Gottesman (1977) points to the construction and administration of tests, particularly of competence in daily living, and carrying out therapy and counselling. Behaviour modification programmes and therapeutic environments have to be developed and a positive part taken within the multi-disciplinary team in administering and managing these. The psychologist has to work with community services in encouraging co-operation, new approaches, and in monitoring the cost-effectiveness of services; and act in relation to administrators as interpreter of research findings, advocate of the needs of individual clients, and as a change agent working for improved delivery of community care.

Assessment

It is of particular importance to use, and encourage others to use, a scientific approach to the assessment of old people. For this client group 'assessment' is too often invoked as a catch-all term, justifying emergency admission at the behest of hard-pressed community services or the client's despairing supporters. In these circumstances 'assessment' is rarely planned or related to design of treatment: it represents a breathing space while the multi-disciplinary team seeks inspiration or moves on to the next task in hand.

As Hussian (1984) points out, there is a shortage of psychological assessments that are relevant for old people, and that have ecological validity in sampling the experience of the elderly and the activities of daily living of particular importance for them. The tests available rarely have detailed norms for different age groups and backgrounds, so the significance of results is not easy to decide. The user of an assessment service, asking 'What will the results contribute to the management of this case?', needs guidance. Appropriately, the specialist psychologist is increasingly likely to offer a user's manual for his assessment service, since data on techniques or tests for use with the elderly can be complex and often conflicting.

An example of a useful short test is CAPE (Clifton Assessment Procedures for the Elderly), which consists of both a brief cognitive assessment and a behaviour rating scale. CAPE is unusual in translating scores into levels of dependency characteristic of estimated ability to cope with different environments, from independent living at home through to continuing care in a psychogeriatric ward.

Neuropsychological screening tests developed for the elderly are making a particularly useful contribution to diagnosis, prognosis, design of therapy to suit individual deficits, and certainly to the morale of some clients and their supporters. It can be a relief to hear that an observed specific impairment in cognitive functioning is not an indication of 'going mad' or 'becoming senile', that its cause can be understood and explained clearly, and that many other aspects of the individual's intellectual performance can be shown to be relatively normal. Tests such as the Kendrick Battery for Detection of Dementia in the Elderly (KBDDE) have shown the way forward for attempts to establish the sometimes difficult differential diagnosis between dementia and depression in old people.

Many clinicians use criterion-referenced testing, evaluating performance through individualized assessment, examining the client not in terms of comparison with group norms, but on his ability to meet a criterion specified in the test. For example, in the assessment of testamentary capacity, or ability to make a valid will, an old person's estimated ability to manage his own affairs, and make an informed decision on disposal of assets, is evaluated. This may be done most usefully not by administering a standard intelligence test and extrapolating from the results, but by constructing a personalized multiple-choice assessment of information and orientation directly demonstrating level of competence. There are also encouraging signs of progress in the objective assessment of family burden and strain felt by supporters of mentally frail elderly living in the community.

Direct observation of an old person's behaviour, and of overall levels of engagement or constructive activity in institutional settings, can quickly point to priorities for management. For example, an elderly man was admitted to hospital from an old people's Home, as 'physically aggressive' and 'incontinent'. The nurses did immediate event recording, carrying a small card when taking him to the toilet and recording occurrence of physical aggression and of incontinence. They noted that in 25 daytime visits he was wet once, and showed no aggression. Comparative observation of toileting approaches in the Home and in hospital revealed a more confident approach in hospital staff, pre-empting the frequent refusal and consequent incontinence which had been noted in the Home. Staff behaviour rather than resident's actions became the focus of intervention.

Frequency, duration, timing, or intensity of a problem behaviour can be established by observation, as a baseline against which future change can be evaluated. For example, an elderly woman who wandered around a ward was reported by staff as doing this 'all the time'. Structured observation for three days, using time sampling, taking in this case a 5-s observation hourly, revealed that this was not the case. She wandered on 47 per cent of observation, but settled behaviour coincided with activity such as feeding, washing, and conversation initiated by staff. Again, how others responded to her became a focus for action.

Observer ratings, self-rating scales, and the varied techniques of naturalistic informal observation may also be usefully involved at different times in work with old people. One major issue for the psychologist is to persuade clients, supporters, and care staff of the value of structured observation. Paradoxically, perhaps, it can sometimes be most difficult to involve care staff, many of whom have difficulty in fitting observation into their notion of 'the real work' of care, and feel uncomfortable with what looks like a passive role while their colleagues are being visibly active.

PRINCIPLES OF INTERVENTION

There are 10 guiding principles for psychological interventions, important for any client group but particularly valuable for this relatively disadvantaged and neglected population.

1. Emphasize early action, producing minimal disruption for the individual.
2. Maintain the client's independence as far as possible.
3. Consult fully with the client, principal carers, and supporters.
4. Establish the client's needs, and what incentives will help to meet those needs.
5. Reflect on the advisability or nature of an action before starting.
6. Work through carers and supporters in general.
7. Encourage objective assessment throughout intervention.
8. Set out action in small, specific steps, which are clearly understood.
9. Review progress with participants periodically.
10. Evaluate outcome and follow-up where necessary.

These guidelines are flexible. Despite point 6, for example, the psychologist needs to retain direct involvement with some clients to keep therapeutic skills sharp and to maintain credibility with other staff. For some of these 'difficult customers' that no one else wants, there will be no alternative. The following discussion of different types of psychological intervention illustrates some of the problems already described, selecting those which have received most attention in the literature.

Reality orientation

Reality orientation (RO), the best-known training approach for impaired old people, has two main forms. 'Classroom' RO is conducted with a small group or on a one-to-one basis, and cues, prompts, and selectively reinforces successive closer approximations to well-oriented behaviour. Information is shared with clients, recognition and repetititon of general or personal information is encouraged, sensory stimulation is given, the environment is clearly and attractively labelled, and trainers are active in drawing out responses and offering correction or praise.

Twenty-four-hour, or 24RO, extends this approach as a model for consistent practice around the clock. This is a philosophy of care rather than a specific treatment, and effectiveness has been difficult to evaluate. However, a specific aspect of RO, the use of directional signs to which resident's attention is drawn by ward staff, has been shown to reduce 'wandering' and clinical psychologists are currently concerned with refining RO and extending it beyond the confused elderly with whom it is generally used.

Counselling

Many clinical psychologists counsel demoralized clients, and the integrative model described by Sherman (1981) has won general respect. It is based on the capacities and strengths which normally develop in the course of growing old, to overcome the demoralization which can be produced by the losses and other problems of ageing. Sherman describes successive levels of counselling input: meeting the material needs of the immediate situation; offering support and promoting efforts to stabilize self-esteem and morale; assisting the client to feel more in control of his life situation; and building positive long-term changes in self-concept and self-esteem. For the client who is facing loss from bereavement, or who is in terminal care confronting loss of his own life, specialized counselling techniques may supplement this general approach.

Reminiscence and life review

These approaches, together with RO and integrative counselling constitute the main psychological interventions to be developed primarily for old people. Much remains to be done in clarifying the process, and refining evaluation of effectiveness.

In reminiscence, small groups are encouraged to share memories of national and local history, stimulated by old newspaper files, sound archives, and other sources such as photographs. Private as well as public recollections gradually emerge, and group members are prompted regularly to return to the present to compare 'things then' and 'things now', and appreciate the many challenges they have overcome. Life review is a more directly personal one-to-one therapeutic exercise, spoken or written, in collaboration with a therapist, enabling the client to see pattern and meaning in his unique experience of life, and to be able to relate past events to present state within a sense of personal integrity.

Improving intellectual functioning

Wisocki (1984) reminds us that we tend to exaggerate the effects of intellectual impairment in old age. Generally they are less severe, more specific, and more amenable to efforts to cope than we might suspect. For example, memory training programmes for old people have drawn with success on a variety of techniques. These include progressively lengthening by gradual increments the period of time over which memory is required; the use of external aids such as signposts, colour-coding of doors, use of diary or notebook, alarms or other cues to prompt recall; and the use of internal aids such as visual imagery to build face–name links or identify places needing association with items to be remembered. Clients with relatively early or mild impairment will probably benefit most from such approaches in out-patient 'memory clinics' but their lasting effectiveness for old people is still uncertain.

Coping with anxiety and depression

Anxiety is common with older people, and as in younger people may respond, however slowly, to a range of relaxation and self-hypnosis methods. Depresssion in late life is a major problem, yet anti-depressants have a risk of serious side-effects with old people, and the relapse rate after ECT is high. Prospects for cognitive therapy, in which the client is helped to identify and alter depressive patterns of thinking, are therefore of particular interest.

Cognitive therapy in a context of life review   Cecily, an 81-year-old widow living alone, referred herself by letter, after reading a news-paper account of a talk, 'Take Umbrage', I gave at an Age Concern meeting. I had recommended assertive behaviour by old people frustrated with health care services. Also I had outlined the psychology of doctor–patient communication, as indicating specific ways in which patients could make themselves understood.

Cecily had heart disease, cerebrovascular insufficiency, and arthritis as her main problems. Recurrently depressed (tearful, nega-tive, given to suicidal talk and gestures), she had been a psychogeria-tric day patient. Well-known at the health centre, she had been shuttled among the partners there.

After consulting her GP I visited her, to find her complaining that she was 'confused' about her medication. She produced a pile of 14 different drugs, with anti-depressants, tranquillisers, and sedatives prominent, given over the previous three years.

After most of these had been removed and her medication reviewed, we began life review interviews, indicated in view of her main complaint of feeling that her life had become 'useless to any-one, without meaning'.

Periodically, using life review material, we moved into cognitive therapy, confronting:

1. Her persisting belief that she was inadequate, 'just not good enough', so that she could not afford to get too close to people. We traced this back to when she was 10, had been in trouble at school for fighting the battles of smaller children, and her mother had begun to tell her repeatedly, 'You'll never come to any good!'
2. Her son in Australia had not written for a long time. He had abandoned her as unworthy! Eventually, we discovered that she had ended her last letter with, 'Don't come to my funeral.'

Did this sound like, 'I wouldn't be seen dead with you?'

Oh no, she had *meant*, 'Please come now, don't leave it until you come to my funeral!'

Understanding a misunderstanding, correspondence then restarted.

3. Her pattern of 2 am. 'depressive' thinking when she woke reproaching God for not having allowed her to die in her sleep. To replace her Job's lamentations, we arranged a comfort routine— flask of tea by the bed, radio with all-night programme ready tuned, her book of prayers, photo of her granddaughter, 'my reason for living.'

4. Recording and reflecting on her current achievements. These included giving support to her granddaughter in a chronic illness, befriending new attenders at her church, baby-sitting for neighbours. As anticipated, Cecily developed achievements, 'so I can have something *different* to write', she told me, as I admired a jaunty beret she had just bought.

After 12 sessions over 39 weeks, her self-rating on Brink's depression scale for the elderly had moved from an initial 23, indicative of clinical depression, to a relatively benign 7, within normal limits.

Old people have been shown to be able to respond to instructions so they develop positive patterns of thought, and the related ability to cope in stressful situations, such as their admission to residential care. Introducing unspoken self-statements such as 'This place is home now and I'm going to make the most of it' are one component of such cognitive therapy. In community health care studies clients aged 60 to 80 have been shown to respond well to classes on 'coping with depression', and, using cognitive methods, they have successfully faced many challenges.

Reducing preoccupation with discomfort

For old people it is vital to develop appropriate health-care habits and for them to recognize when they are not healthy so they can take appropriate action. While many impaired old people suffer increased bodily discomfort or pain, only a minority become excessively preoccupied, with consequent psychological distress. This minority can be extremely vocal, suffering and causing others to suffer, and becoming the target of intensive physical investigations and treatments which rarely yield long-term relief. Even when a treatable physical condition is found doctors may on occasion refrain from treatment, considering that for a chronic complainer the outcome of treatment would in itself become a focus for yet more complaining. A psychological intervention for this type of complaining thus involves systematically withdrawing attention for complaining, giving attention and other rewards for 'well' behaviour, and above all encouraging the client to engage in distracting activities. These activities may include relaxation and the use of mental imagery to view discomfort and pain as controllable.

Rehabilitation

Psychologists are often asked to design and implement programmes for chronic psychiatric patients who in late life face return to the community. These programmes include, for example, modules of training in activities of daily living, and social skills training.

It is increasingly common for psychologists to advise on incentive programmes for those older post-stroke patients commonly described as 'lacking motivation'.

The staffing of 'movers' groups is necessarily multi-disciplinary, but is often promoted by a psychologist. These groups integrate rehabilitation efforts by giving clients feedback on progress, using successful 'graduates' of the group as models, and by sharing information on requirements of the community settings to which moves will be made.

Behavioural deficits and excesses

As Hussian notes, many interventions by clinical psychologists working with old people in residential care have been directed at overcoming a lack of normal activity. Significant increases of activity have been achieved by behavioural management procedures in, for example, constructive occupation or 'engagement' and self-feeding. The basic procedures involved are those used for all client groups, such as helping the client to link specific behaviour with particular features of the environment (stimulus control) and selectively reinforcing desirable behaviours.

These behavioural procedures are also employed to reduce excess or high-rate behaviour, which has received less attention from clinical psychologists working in residential care settings, where deficit is more generally apparent. Excessive complaining has already been mentioned. Significant reductions have also been achieved in, for example, inappropriate undressing and inappropriate sexual approaches. Some of the main issues emerging in behavioural intervention with the elderly are addressed below, since the clinical psychologist's practice in this key area is essentially as consultant, teacher, and researcher. In some respects—for example, in carrying out family therapy with the client and immediate supporters—the psychologist will be found to be directly intervening to meet social and psychological needs. In general, though, his role in relation to these needs will be found in consultancy, teaching, and research.

CONSULTATION AND TEAMWORK

It is claimed that as clinical psychologists are generally in short supply for all client groups, the necessity of transferring psychological knowledge and skills to non-psychologists must be generally recognized. This must be particularly true for work with the elderly, where even in a relatively well-staffed area the number of psychologists working mainly with the elderly will be very few. Traditionally, the therapeutic process of developing knowledge and skills in the client (and, with family therapy, in immediate supporters), has been a direct intervention process. This has been seen as the 'real work' of clinical practice, fundamental to job satisfaction.

Less gratification has been perceived in consulting and teaching, viewed as a process of transfer of knowledge and skills to professionals, paraprofessionals, volunteers, and supporters. The traditional attitude has been fostered by a tendency to perceive a consultation and teaching role as being primarily enforced by lack of psychologists, and to consider the process one-sidedly as a 'transfer'. Rather it is a joint effort to achieve change which characterizes successful direct intervention.

Team or network?

With old people, as with other client groups, the 'multi-disciplinary team' is a generally recognized unit of clinical administration and management. In theory, such an entity should foster consultation and teaching, since shared problem-solving and collaborative effort is implied. In practice, the working of the 'team' may create difficulties for consultation: members may protect expertise rather than share it in a trans-disciplinary style; paraprofessionals from within the same agency may be seen as only marginal members; and, most importantly, the interests of client and supporters are not represented directly within the team.

In clinical practice the crucial venue for consultation and teaching is a specific health care network, consisting of the client and those other individuals who have clearly identified responsibilities in the assessment, management, and continued care of an old person. The most important criterion for effectiveness of consultation with regard to client then becomes the state of the network. If it is fine tuned and responsive to changes in the client's situation, consulting within that network should be efficient. Knowledge and skills 'given away' in conventional training, rather than earned by shared effort within a care network, may be less likely to be integrated effectively as an increased psychological-mindedness in the non-psychologist.

GERONTOLOGY

Clients need to be understood in the context of gerontology, the scientific study of normal and pathological changes occurring with ageing. The psychologist should be equipped as an information resource in the social and behavioural aspects of this science. A client may ask: 'Why is my memory failing?' A supporter: 'If we built a "granny flat" would it help?' A therapist 'Why do so many patients get "stuck" in our rehabilitation programme?' In some cases it may be desirable to offer access to information only, encouraging the enquirer to draw his own conclusions. Within gerontology, the following themes are of particular clinical interest.

Support for supporters

It has been wisely said that families of impaired old people in the community need to be supported by professionals but not supplanted. Such support is provided by many agencies in face-to-face contact with families, ranging from small *ad hoc* groups of supporters to national organizations such as the Alzheimer's Disease Society. While there are a number of excellent community care projects, there is also much muddle because many sources of support are involved, and beliefs about 'what supporters really need' differ.

Supporters appear to have three main types of need. Emotional support is needed, ranging from the reassurance of occasional contacts with 'someone who cares', to intensive and regular counselling where an individual care network is under intense pressure from guilt, anger, and/or physical exhaustion. Information about, and access to, resources such as social security benefits, aids, day care or holiday relief may be needed. Specific advice on techniques of managing disturbed feelings or behaviour in either client or supporters may be required. It has been suggested that the supporters who complain loudest get more than their fair share of assistance, that physical abuse of old people by their supporters is more frequent than is generally supposed, that precipitate support encourages families to lose commitment. The psychologist will then be involved both in direct consultancy to develop supporters' skills; and in indirect advice to them on how service and supporters' needs can be matched more closely, and in recommending how such problems as suspected physical abuse should be dealt with.

Assessment

The psychologist offers consultation to others who may wish to use, or adapt psychological assessment for their own needs. Consultation may be requested by community psychiatric nurses wishing to evaluate the level of burden on supporters, or by doctors dissatisfied with the brief 'mental state' measure handed down to them by tradition in their hospital. Some specialized types of assessment—for example, neuropsychological examination—may be retained by the psychologist, but the case for retaining psychological assessment as an exclusive function should be examined carefully, rather than be taken as axiomatic.

Behaviour management

Consultation on mangement of problem behaviour is a recurring issue, particularly with residential care staff who may be unwittingly maintaining an undesirable behaviour by inconsistent responding.

An illustration is offered by the case of 'Agnes', a geriatric patient who had been physically attacking fellow-patients and staff. Observation showed at least nine types of response from care staff: scolding; ignoring; separating antagonists; distracting her attention; secluding her; forcing her to apologise to the victim; slapping her lightly on the wrists with the injunction 'see how you like it!'; avoiding the situation by leaving the room; and even sitting 'Agnes' down for tea and sympathy and asking her reasons for attacking others (these in the classic delinquent response were usually given as 'I don't know' and 'I won't do it again'.) The only consistency in her management occured when she wasn't attacking someone. Then, she was consistently ignored. Consultation in this case focused on possible alternative responses by staff, and eventually led to an agreed minimal response to physical aggression, and using a variety of positive responses when she was otherwise engaged.

Consultation on behavioural problems of the impaired elderly can now draw from a 'menu' of procedures, from which selections may be made. An (abbreviated) illustration is given here, for the management of excess noise-making.

MENU: UNDERSTANDING AND MANAGING EXCESS NOISE-MAKING

1. If noise is because of delirium and/or terminal illness, it is unlikely to respond to behaviour management: physical treatment, possibly sedation, will be needed. However, if noise-making clearly is affected by events in the patient's surroundings, behaviour management can be applied. Share awareness of problem with patient. Attempt to get her views on what needs to be done. Begin taping and/or charting frequency and/or duration of noise, having notified the patient. Record for set periods at set intervals (from 1 to 5 min, at from 1 to 5-h intervals depending on resources). This is essential as baseline for measuring progress.
2. Ask whether the patient is being rewarded for noise: (self-stimulation; tension release, feeling of control over others; feeling of security when attention comes; satisfaction from stimulation attention brings; route to being sedated with relief from distress).
3. Find immediate causes, e.g. physical discomfort, worry about toileting. Correct if you can. Look for underlying causes, e.g. concern about disability, fear of death. Counsel or arrange counselling.
4. If noise-making persists, tell the patient changes in ward routine are to be made, 'because it's our job to see you get what you need without having to shout for it.' Repeat message at intervals, check

retention by cueing with first part, encouraging her to complete and to explain to you what is meant.

5. Tape noise and play back to the patient. This can help the patient who genuinely hasn't appreciated how her noise affects others. This may need to be done several times. Be prepared for her to disown the sound, denying responsibility.

6. Often the noise-maker is found to be isolated by sensory impairment. The problem can be compounded if the patient is permanently in side room to buffer others from effects of noise. Make the immediate environment as stimulating as possible to distract the patient. Reintroduce to ward gradually.

7. The patient must recognize that being quiet can have rewards. Approach if she has been quiet and awake her for a while; praise her for coping. Use repeated phrase such as: you're so peaceful, or it's best to be quiet. Identify treats for the patient (a sweet, a cigarette, a drink, newspaper, a back-rub), and link with the approach.

8. Do not respond to noise. If approaching during noise, use minimum standard response with neutral tone (unless real emergency).

9. Prompt the patient's listening to radio/tape recorder (headphones), to distract her. Use material of individual appeal.

10. If the patient is placed in seclusion when noisy this should be with a brief explanation and no further comment. Return her when quieter, within approximately 15 min. Be prepared to repeat the procedure.

11. Ward routine may be adjusted for her if necessary. Adjustment needs to be consistent.

12. Assess the effectiveness of management at intervals by further recording. Often the best that can be expected is reduction rather than elimination. Such patients need our patience, though they test it to the limits.

Adapting institutional care

While residents whose behaviour presents a major problem may need to be helped in adapting to their environment, the institutional environment itself needs to be shaped, like a prosthesis, to help residents be as independent as possible within the constraints of institutional life. Psychological approaches to reshaping care take four interrelated forms: stimulation and activity programmes;

planned changes to the physical environment of a care setting: 24-h reality orientation; and behavioural management that consistently attempts to shape and reward constructive independent behaviour, while limiting attention given to behaviour of a destructive or needlessly dependent nature. The significance of 'environmental docility' in the impaired elderly has been well documented by psychological research indicating that as competence decreases external environment factors become progressively more important in determining behaviour.

Occasionally a psychologist can be directly involved in planning the design of a new residential care setting for the elderly. In general, however, care settings and their staff are difficult to change. Change must be hard-won. For instance, the demands of 24-h reality orientation should not be underestimated. Working consistently to remind an impaired resident of reality and to maintain a positive attitude demands dedication from care staff.

Hazel, a care assistant, tried with me to build a personal relationship with a resident by teaching her name. Over several days the resident made 26 unsuccessful attempts, but No. 26 held promise: 'Something to do with nuts, dear? Brazil . . . No, Hazel!'. Hazel sat slumped. Somehow, for her, it no longer seemed to matter that much. With enthusiasm, born of relief, I congratulated the resident and Hazel, and managed to rekindle some of Hazel's interest. As this kind of experience illustrates, reshaping residential care takes time.

Psychologists have noted that certain care routines for the elderly such as bed making or drug rounds need little prompting. Others, such as activity programmes or reality orientation, appear remarkably subject to extinction through neglect. It has been suggested that the former are more stable because they are more visible so that neglect would be noticed, and they are in any case secure because they are seen as the 'real work' of care. Perhaps they also involve less close personal contact with residents who are likely to be severely impaired, and whose response to contact is at best hesitant and limited.

Staff support

To work with impaired old people demands adaptive skills of a high order. There is a heavy demand for services, while resources tend to be scarce or ill-coordinated. Health care networks are fragile and their problems complex, rarely admitting of straightforward solution. The 'burn-out' syndrome linked with high absenteeism and low morale is not unknown in teams serving the elderly, and it is not infrequent for a psychologist, or other members of a team, to consult with colleagues to give or receive help in this respect.

RESEARCH

In carrying out research the clinical psychologist is likely to be involved in fundamental research in clinical gerontology and in action research evaluating aspects of service provision, as well as participating in the work of other team members, offering advice, general support, and direct collaboration if necessary. There is now a substantial body of research with older people. Effects of impaired memory and problem-solving are beginning to be well understood and efforts to compensate for impairment are being explored. Action research effort is growing. However, there is a major need to sift and critically appraise the mass of research findings we have.

To illustrate this point, it has been shown repeatedly that increased occupational therapy resources in continuing care of the elderly brings a corresponding increase in the habitually very low level of constructive activity by most residents. When resources are withdrawn activity reverts to its original level. Important questions then arise. In cosmetic terms increased activity looks good, but can it be shown to benefit residents? If it does, how can we devise intermediate types of occupational therapy activity, which are attractive enough to engage both residents and the direct care staff who would be required to supervise in the therapists' absence?

Psychological research into intervention procedures with old people has been remarkably inconclusive in some respects. For example, reality orientation is a well-known procedure which has been widely researched. According to some studies it yields modest gains in intellectual functioning, and very considerable benefit for the morale of carers, who are able to interact with more confidence, and report greater satisfaction in their work. However, the rationale for RO is debatable, and it has been suggested that it is such a complex procedure that it has been impossible to date to conduct adequate research on it, as no study could implement RO comprehensively or consistently enough.

Another area of uncertainty relates to research on psychological management of apparent incontinence, that is incontinence where no primary physical cause can be demonstrated. Outcome studies have produced mixed results, and one factor in interpreting these variable results has been lack of care in screening subjects, so that in some cases clients were included who could not have been expected to respond to psychological retraining. However, there has been creditable progress in research into the effectiveness of behavioural treatments for old people, as Hussian (1984) and Wisocki (1984) illustrate.

In terms of priority for fundamental research in clinical gerontology, it might be generally agreed that investigation of early psychological correlates of chronic brain failure, 'this epidemic of our time', is of most urgency. A pressing target for action research would be to explore a model for appropriate provision and co-ordination of support for supporters. It is important for the clinical psychologist working with other people to retain a balanced perspective on ageing by maintaining some research interest involving the relatively healthy. In my own experience I have found of particular value the study of compliance by over-75s with their general practitioner's treatment, and investigation of sleep dissatisfaction in late life, which distresses but does not grossly impair psychological functioning.

ADMINISTRATION AND POLICY MAKING

Apart from internal administration of a specialist clinical psychology service, the psychologist is expected to contribute to planning of health and social service provision for old people. There are four major goals which would be recognized by many specialists.

1. To move towards a unified health care service for old people which recognises the identity of interest between the sectors already mentioned. Joint planning committees, joint-financed research programmes, and collaborative training exercises represent progress towards a unified service, but much remains to be done.

2. To establish a uniform data base for assessment of clients' physical, psychological, and social functioning, from objective appraisal. While retaining appreciation of the client as an individual, it would be helpful to establish a classification of the major types of problem

dealt with by services for old people.

3. To develop services' responsiveness to needs of clients and their supporters. The Niskanen Effect—systematic bias in providing what suits the service rather than what clients necessarily require—is too frequent in services for old people. There is a temptation to respond paternalistically to what is mistakenly seen as 'second childhood' in clients.

4. To introduce regular systematic audit of operationally defined care procedures. All too often, what is actually to be done in work with old people is left unresolved and unclear, and terms such as 'assessment' or 'support' conceal more than they reveal. Such audit would reduce rather than augment staff burn-out, since uncertainty about role requirements is likely to be more disabling than clarity.

CONCLUSIONS

Work with old people is a distinctive speciality for a number of reasons: the universality of ageing, so that we face in clients our own future; the aversiveness of ageing for many of us; relative frequency of premature termination of work through the client's death; nature of the required knowledge base in behavioural and social gerontology; need to grasp specialized assessment and treatment approaches; operating in age-segregated care settings; high frequency of physical symptoms interacting with social and psychological problems; and high frequency of iatrogenic complaints related to multiple treatments and idiosyncratic responding. Also, we must consider: tendency to work through carers rather than directly with client; family dynamics complicated by parent/child role reversal, and paternalistic care; clients with prolonged investment in current coping strategies, reluctant to change; old people less familiar with the concept of psychological intervention; barriers to communication—cognitive impairment, fatigue, sensory impairment—more evident.

Within this speciality, in which they have a relatively brief history of involvement, clinical psychologists have made a promising start, in drawing attention to individual psychological needs, developing assessment procedures, devising therapeutic interventions to produce demonstrable change, and in contributing to a literature in clinical gerontology which is growing rapidly in quantity, though rather more slowly in scientific quality.

Our need now is to ground our contribution more securely in tested theory within general psychology, most particularly that of adult development and ageing. Only on this basis can we make a considered and lasting contribution to a clearer understanding of the process of late life, and of the complex and often conflicting systems which enmesh old people, and their informal and formal carers.

Gerontophobia, a relatively common complaint among professionals in health care, is a suitable case for treatment. A treatment package may need to embrace not only *in vivo* exposure to a wide range of old people, but also the practical application of well-grounded theory as a form of cognitive therapy to probe and modify assumptions of clients and carers so that they fit fact rather than fancy.

Clinical gerontology, the scientific study of normal and abnormal changes in health care needs with ageing, can become the core knowledge unifying the many health-related disciplines concerned with old age. The future relevance of clinical psychology for late life will be measured in terms of practitioners' effectiveness in the development and application of this body of knowledge.

REFERENCES

Blythe, R. (1979). *The view in winter. Reflections on old age.* Allen Lane, London.

Gilleard, C. J. (1984). *Living with dementia. Community care of the elderly mentally infirm.* Croom Helm, London.

Gottesman, L. E. (1977). Clinical psychology and ageing: a role model. In *Geropsychology: a model for training and clinical service* (ed. W. D. Gentry) pp. 1–7. Ballinger, Cambridge, MA.

Hussian, R. A. (1984). Behavioral geriatrics. *In Progress in Behavior Modification* (ed. M. Hersen, R. M. Eisler, and P. M. Miller) Vol. 16, pp. 159–83. Academic Press, New York.

Sherman, E. (1981). *Counselling the ageing. An integrative approach.* Free Press, New York.

Wisocki, P. A. (1984) Behavioral approaches to gerontology. In *Progress in Behavior Modification* (ed. M. Hersen, R. M. Eisler and P. M. Miller) Vol. 16, pp. 121–57. Academic Press, New York.

FURTHER READING

Barrowclough C. and Fleming, I. (1986). *Goal planning with elderly people —making plans to meet individual needs. A manual of instruction.* Manchester University Press, Manchester.

Birren, J. E. and Schaie, K. W., ed. (1985). *Handbook of the psychology of ageing* (2nd ed). Van Nostrand Reinhold, New York.

Davies, A. D. M. and Crisp, A. G. (1985). The clinical psychology of the elderly. In *Principles and practice of geriatric medicine* (ed. M. Pathy) pp. 603–25. Wiley, London.

Hanley, I. and Hodge, J., ed. (1984). *Psychological approaches to the care of the elderly.* Croom Helm, London.

Mace, N. L. and Rabins, P. V. (1985). *The 36-hour day. Caring at home for confused elderly people.* Hodder & Stoughton and Age Concern, London.

Woods, R. and Britton, P. (1985). *Clinical psychology with the elderly.* Croom Helm, London.

8

Clinical psychology and primary health care

John Marzillier

Clinical psychologists have traditionally worked as specialists in health care. They have been attached to hospitals, special units, or other institutions and applied their psychological knowledge and principles to the problems of the particular client group. In the field of mental illness, for example, clinical psychologists have often been attached to psychiatric teams, carrying out specialized assessments and treatments (see Chapters 2 and 3). Mental handicap hospitals, neurology departments, adolescent units, Regional Secure Units, Special Hospitals, physical rehabilitation centres, paediatric departments, are all specialist services to which clinical psychologists have contributed a specialized service. Their work is illustrated in various chapters of this book.

However, the people seen by the various specialist services constitute only a small percentage of those who experience similar problems in the community at large. This relationship is aptly illustrated in the notion of different *levels* of care (see Fig. 8.1).

Goldberg and Huxley (1980), from whom the idea of levels of care is derived, suggest that of 250 people with psychiatric disorders found in the community (level 1) only 17 will in fact reach the specialist psychiatric services (level 4). Of these 17 only a certain indeterminate percentage will come to the attention of clinical psychologists. Goldberg and Huxley describe how between each level of care certain filters come into operation. For example, between the presentation of a psychiatric disorder in primary care (level 2) and its recognition (level 3) is a 'detection filter', indicating that a substantial number of psychiatric disorders remain undetected. Equally, of those detected (level 3) only a very small number are in fact referred on to psychiatrists (level 4), indicating the operation of a 'referral filter.' Clinical psychologists can receive direct referrals of patients from GPs and so be subject to a similar

	the community	primary medical care			specialist psychiatric services	
	level 1	level 2	level 3	level 4	level 5
	morbidity in random community samples	total psychiatric morbidity, primary care	conspicuous psychiatric morbidity	total psychiatric patients	psychiatric in-patients only
one-year period prevalence, median estimates	250	230	140	17	6 (per 1000 at risk per year)
		1st filter	2nd filter	3rd filter	4th filter
characteristics of the four filters		illness behaviour	detection of disorder	referral of psychiatrist	admission to psychiatric beds
key individual		the patient	primary care physician	primary care physician	psychiatrist
factors operating on key individual		severity and type of symptoms psycho-social stress learned patterns of illness behaviour	interview techniques personality factors training and attitudes	confidence in own ability to manage availability and quality of psychiatric services attitudes towards psychiatrists	availability of beds availability of adequate community psychiatric services
other factors		attitudes of relatives availability of medical services ability to pay for treatment	presenting symptom pattern socio-demographic characteristics of patient	symptom pattern of patient attitudes of patient and family	symptom pattern of patient, attitudes of patient and family delay in social worker arriving

Fig. 8.1 The pathway to psychiatric care. (Reprinted, with permission, from Goldberg and Huxley 1980.)

filtering system as psychiatrists or may receive many of their referrals from specialist physicians (e.g. neurologists, psychiatrists) and in the latter instance be subject to yet another filter. Operating as specialists in the health care system means that clinical psychologists will only see a fraction of the psychological problems presented by people at large. To a certain extent this protects the psychologist from being subjected to a larger volume of clients that she or he can cope with. But in other respects it results in a selective and at times idiosyncratic service to clients which is dependent more on the nature of the 'filters' than the applicability of the service to particular problems or clients. In one health district in the UK, for example, less than half of general practitioners referred people to the Clinical Psychology Department, mainly because they were simply unaware that such a service was available!

A recent development in clinical psychology has been one of establishing closer and more direct links with primary care staff. Some psychologists have carried out treatment sessions on general practice premises. Others have forged close links with health visitors and community nurses. There have also been occasional examples of a psychologist working full-time in primary care serving the needs of one or more teams (e.g. Johnston 1978). This 'move into the community' has also been seen in the work of other mental health professionals, psychiatrists and nurses in particular. It reflects a general climate of change in mental health in which the traditional reliance on specialized care, particularly in terms of large mental hospitals, is giving way to the idea of 'care in the community'.

PRIMARY HEALTH CARE

Primary health care describes the nearest contact that individuals have with their Health Service. It is one of a number of levels of care, as Table 8.1 indicates.

Primary health care is concerned with the delivery of services to a small local community of up to 50 000 people. In developed countries this is achieved through doctors, who act as 'gatekeepers' to the specialist hospital services, diagnosing and treating the vast majority of patients themselves and referring on those who need a specialist assessment or treatment.

The organization of primary health care differs from country to

Table 8.1 Population size, level of care, and professional service

Population	Level of care	Professional/premises providing care
Family unit (1–10)	Self-care	Friends; non-professional helpers; (only one in four of all symptoms are taken to professional medical worker)
50–50 000	Primary	Single-handed general practitioner; group practice; health centre practice; polyclinic
50 000–500 000	Specialist	General hospital and specialist clinic
500 000–5 000 000	Super-specialist	Regional or super-specialist hospital or clinic

country. For example, in some countries such as France the vast majority of doctors work single-handedly, whereas in the UK the majority of general practitioners collaborate in partnerships (i.e. groups of doctors co-operating together) or inter-disciplinary teams. The funding of primary health care differs too. In a few countries such as Denmark, New Zealand, and Britain, the service is centrally funded by government taxation. However, the majority of countries operate under a pluralist system of compulsory health insurance, private insurance schemes, and direct payment to doctors. In the UK the primary care doctor is a generalist (hence the term general practitioner) who provides personal and medical care to individuals and families within his practice irrespective or their age, sex, and illness. But in other countries patients may call directly on specialists such as paediatricians or gynaecologists who will have a specific responsibility for the category of patients within their area of expertise.

Primary health care team

There has been a trend in some countries for primary care physicians to work in collaboration with other professionals in the form of a primary health care team. This development has been seen in particular in the UK and an example of a primary health care team is given in Fig. 8.2.

The core of the team is a group of GPs, who directly employ the

Fig. 8.2 The primary health care team (UK).

practice manager, secretaries, receptionists, and practice nurses. In the UK 70 per cent of the salaries of these professionals can be claimed back by the general practitioners from central government. In addition, health visitors and, occasionally, 'attached' social workers and counsellors (e.g. marriage guidance counsellors) work directly on the practice premises, providing a service to their particular client groups. They do not come under the direct employment of the general practitioners but are responsible to their own managers. District nurses, community psychiatric nurses, and others operate in the local catchment area of the practice and will liaise with the various team members. Finally, consultants and specialists from local hospitals may occasionally visit the practice and hold clinics on the premises. It is here that clinical psychologists come in. They are one of a number of specialist professional groups who have deliberately set out to extend their services into primary health care.

PSYCHOLOGICAL PROBLEMS IN PRIMARY HEALTH CARE

What psychological problems present in primary care? This is a difficult question to answer because the term 'psychological problems' is vague and open to many different interpretations. The range of psychological problems that people have is considerable, from everyday problems of life such as marital discord, stresses at work, worries about bringing up a family etc., to major psychiatric disorders such as depression or schizophrenia. In addition, many purely physical illnesses can have psychological consequences, e.g. the need to adjust to a permanent disability, the impact of a chronic illness on family and friends, or the effect of surgical disfigurement on feelings of self-esteem and acceptance by others. Fortunately, people do not perceive most psychological concerns as problems for which they seek professional help. Most people cope with their psychological problems themselves, and, as far as we can tell, they cope reasonably well. This is an important point for health care professionals to remember, since many of the minor worries and concerns that people experience will 'resolve themselves' without the need for intervention. There is some risk that professional help can have a negative effect, crystallizing ordinary worries as 'illness' or 'disorders' with the implication that remedies need to be sought in order for these apparent 'illnesses' to be treated. For example, there is now a growing recognition that the prescription of minor tranquillizers, benzodiazepines, for anxiety has in many instances been unnecessary and potentially harmful, creating a state of psychological and physical dependency and reinforcing the view that emotional states are chronic disorders requiring treatment (Catalan and Gath, 1985).

Prevalence of psychological problems

Because of the vagueness of the term 'psychological problems', it is difficult to get a clear picture of their prevalence in primary care. In a questionnaire survey, over 1 000 general practitioners in the Oxford Region were asked the following question: 'Roughly what percentage of your consultations include psychological problems?' (Marzillier and Fowler unpublished findings 1986). On average, the GPs rated about 28 per cent of their consultations as including psychological problems, and of these, 30 per cent were rated as severe enough to warrant specific treatment, or about 8 per cent of all consultations. The range of estimates was large, however, varying from 0 to 100 per cent! In another study, a clinical psychologist sat in on 366 consultations and he and the doctors separately rated consultations for 'psychological relevance' (McPherson and Feldman 1977). The psychologist rated 12 per cent of all consultations as 'quite' or 'highly relevant' whereas the GPs rated 18 per cent. The correlation between the psychologist's and the doctor's ratings was very low, indicating substantial disagreement about which consultations were the psychologically relevant ones.

These subjective estimates may say more about the 'psychological mindedness' of the GP rather than be a reliable or accurate assessment of psychological disturbance in primary care. Not only will GPs differ in their readiness to perceive psychological problems, but patients will vary in their readiness to present such problems to particular GPs. In this way some doctors may genuinely never be presented openly with a psychological problem while others will be inundated with them. An alternative approach to the assessment of prevalence is to concentrate upon specific and discriminable categories of disorder, such as psychiatric illnesses.

Prevalence of psychiatric illness

A distinction can be made between 'formal psychiatric illnesses' such as neurosis, schizophrenia, manic-depressive psychosis, and those physical disorders or social problems with a psychological or psychiatric component. Even with regard to formal psychiatric diagnoses, estimates of their prevalence in primary care are quite variable. It has been estimated that between ¼ and ⅓ of all illnesses treated by GPs are psychiatric illnesses, and that in one year about 14 per cent of a GP's patients will consult for psychiatric disorders. By far the most common disorders are the minor affective illnesses, that is, anxiety, depression, and mixed anxiety–depressive states. Many psychiatric disorders that present in primary care will not be detected by the GP: this has been termed 'hidden psychiatric morbidity'. In a study by Goldberg and Blackwell (1970) a GP who was also a trained psychiatrist still failed to detect one third of psychiatric disturbances, primarily because psychiatric symptomatology was masked by somatic and physical complaints. Thus, although exact estimates of the prevalence of psychiatric illnesses are difficult to achieve, research has shown that these illnesses— particularly the minor affective disorders—are very common and, further, a substantial minority of them are not detected by the GP.

An example of 'hidden psychiatric morbidity'

Mrs Barnes is an example of 'hidden psychiatric morbidity.' She consulted her GP because of persistent insomnia and after a brief chat was prescribed sleeping tablets. However, Mrs Barnes's presenting complaint masked a more deep-rooted anxiety. She had been experiencing intrusive fantasies of harming her children and was terrified that she might be driven, against her will, to kill them. These fantasies kept her awake at night. Her anxiety was beginning to develop an obsessional quality; she hid away knives and sharp objects and would recite ritualistic phrases to forestall the possibility of harm occurring.

Mrs Barnes was eventually referred to a clinical psychologist and successfully helped to deal with her anxieties. Many patients present with a physical complaint (e.g. headaches, physical tension, skin problems, tiredness) which, on further analysis, reflects underlying psychological problems. These physical symptoms have been described as the patient's 'ticket of entry' to the consultation.

An alternative approach to attempts at assessing prevalence of psychological problems is to ask what sorts of problems would be most effectively dealt with by clinical psychologists. It is these problems that will then tend to be more usefully referred. Several clinical psychologists have sought to categorize psychological problems from this perspective. One of the most influential has been that of Kincey (1974) (Table 8.2).

Kincey's five categories describe the broad problem areas that clinical psychologists come across in their specialist work. The role of the psychologist is essentially that of therapist and in a sense they are simply transferring their normal professional skills to a different context (e.g. from psychiatric clinic to GP clinic). Surveys of GPs' attitudes to clinical psychologists suggest that these are by and large the problems that they would tend to refer. Thus, in a survey of GPs in Oxfordshire and Buckinghamshire the seven most common problems deemed particularly suitable by a sample of GPs for referral to a clinical psychologist were (in order): Phobias, Chronic Anxiety, Obsessional Disorders, Smoking Problems, Drinking Problems, Psychosexual Problems, and Interpersonal Problems (Marzillier and Fowler, unpublished findings 1986). The GPs also rated a therapeutic service as by far the most useful role for clinical psychologists. However, important as the therapeutic service is, it represents only one of a number of ways that clinical psychologists may work in primary care.

General practice has been the most fruitful ground for the work of clinical psychologists in primary care. Over the years GPs have

Table 8.2 Five categories of psychological problem amenable to clinical psychological intervention. (Adapted from Kincey 1974.)

Category	Description
(a) Problems of anxiety and stress	Generalized anxiety, panic attacks, phobias, obsessional ideas or rituals, psychosomatic or stress-induced illnesses e.g. migraine, asthma
(b) Habit disorders	Various habitual behaviours that lead to personal distress, ill-health or social problems e.g. smoking, obesity, bulimia, problem drinking, enuresis, encopresis, drug addiction
(c) Educational, occupational difficulties or decisions	Choice of transition points throughout life span e.g. leaving school, change of job, retirement. Problems that arise in the educational-occupational context e.g. study problems, lack of confidence and social skills
(d) Interpersonal–social–marital problems	Problems arising out of relationships with others e.g. shyness, unassertiveness, marital discord, psychosexual problems, antisocial and aggressive behaviour
(e) Psychological adjustment to physical illness and other significant life events	Adjustment to psychological trauma of illness and hospitalization. Adjustment to chronic disability. Childbirth. Accident. Terminal illness. Death

begun referring many more patients directly to specialist psychological services, rather than through the medium of psychiatric clinics, and this has resulted in a better knowledge of what the service can provide. Closer collaboration has been achieved when clinical psychologists have worked directly in general practices. One early example was the work of Johnston (1978). Johnston worked full-time as a clinical psychologist in a health centre attached to a Community Hospital, where she took referrals from the GPs. Johnston saw about five patients per day for appointments that lasted on average just over 40 min, using a behavioural approach to treatment. The majority of patients seen were female with a ratio of female to male of 3 : 1. About 15 per cent of the appointments were quite short, between 5 and 15 min, and quite a few patients were seen in their homes. Johnston reported favourably on the results of her work, commenting upon the greater flexibility that arose from being sited in the general practice, the easier access for patients, the greater opportunity to see relatives, the avoidance of the stigma of attendance at a psychiatric clinic, and the reduction in waiting times. These advantages of working directly in a general practice have been noted by other psychologists too.

There are four main ways in which clinical psychologists can work in general practice. These are:

(a) providing a specialist treatment service;
(b) acting as consultants and teachers to other professions;
(c) carrying out research;
(d) prevention and health promotion.

Specialist treatment service

Most clinical psychologists working in primary health care have worked in an essentially similar way to their traditional role in a clinic setting, that is, they have carried out specialist psychological assessment and treatment on the patients referred to them by GPs. Johnston's work falls into this category. Specialist assessment consists in the main of the assessment of cognitive abilities by means of psychometric tests, for example, the assessment of intelligence and memory. This is much less common than a therapeutic service, but it can be useful in physically handicapped or impaired patients where a formal assessment will reveal the pattern of their intellectual abilities and disabilities. Assessment of intelligence and attainments (reading, spelling, arithmetic) can also be of value in gaining a picture of the all round abilities of schoolchildren. (Educational psychologists, who are attached to schools, are usually the more appropriate professional group for this type of service).

Specialist treatment has been predominantly in the form of cognitive and behavioural methods for people with emotional problems such as anxiety, depression, obsessions and phobias, and for those habit disorders, relationship problems or problems in living (see Table 8.2. earlier). This approach consists of short-term treatments using psychological principles to achieve clearly defined and agreed goals. For example, for an agoraphobic patient with anxieties about going out on her own, the goal might be to go to the local shopping centre on her own with the minimum of anxiety. For a patient with an eating disorder such as anorexia or bulimia, the goal might be to establish a more normal eating pattern and to modify abnormal attitudes to eating, (For a fuller description of this approach see Chapter 2). Clinical psychologists working directly on general practice premises tend to spend rather less time in treatment sessions than when working in specialist clinics. In a careful study of clinical psychologists' work in general practices, it was found that, on average, a patient received 3.7 treatment sessions or about 2½ hs treatment time (Robson, France and Bland 1984). This was about half the time spent per patient in a local specialist clinic. An additional benefit of a treatment service on general practice premises is therefore that less time is spent with each patient. On the other hand, it is likely that the psychologist will see a wider range of patients, particularly those whose problems are less severe. The economics of a specialist therapy service in general practice are discussed below.

The effectiveness of psychological treatment

How successful has this move to general practice been? In the UK there have been several reports of both patient and doctor satisfaction with a clinical psychologist service in primary care. Studies such as that by Johnston have suggested that patients are significantly improved as a result of receiving psychological treatment. However, it is only recently that properly controlled evaluations of the work of clinical psychologists in general practice have been carried out. Two controlled trials have been carried out in the UK. In both studies patients were randomly assigned to either treatment by a clinical psychologist or 'normal' GP treatment.

In the first study (Earll and Kincey 1982), 50 consecutive referrals by the GPs to the clinical psychologist were randomly assigned to either treatment or control groups. Apart from patients needing to be 15 years of age of older, with no evidence of psychosis or organic brain disease and not being involved in any treatment elsewhere, no specific criteria for patient suitability were used. Kincey's guidelines were given to the GPs and the majority of patients had anxiety-based problems. Patients in the treatment group were seen by one clinical psychologist who followed a behavioural self-control approach. On average patients received 7.7 sessions of treatment over 16.3 weeks.

Patients in the control group were treated in whatever ways the GP felt appropriate.

The results of this study showed that during their treatment with the psychologist, the patients took significantly less psychotropic medication than the control patients, but that there were no other statistically significant differences between the two groups (e.g. in terms of prescription for other medications, consultation rates, number of out-patient attendances). At 7-month follow-up, 85 per cent of the treated patients reported that they had been helped to some extent or a great deal by the clinical psychologist. However, there were no statistically significant differences between the treated and control patients on psychological measures of emotional distress, life satisfaction, and personal control. Moreover, the difference between the groups in terms of prescription of psychotropic medication had disappeared, with the patients in the treated group tending to increase their medication during the follow-up period.

This study therefore failed to show that referral to a clinical psychologist was of clear benefit to patients. Although 85 per cent of the patients treated were satisfied with the service, and there was a reduction in the prescription of psychotropic medication during treatment, there were no significant differences between treated and control groups at follow-up. A major problem in interpreting the study is the fact that one psychologist carried out all the treatment, confounding the evaluation of a clinical psychology service with that of a particular clinical psychologist. The small numbers of patients in each group also made statistical significance between the groups difficult to achieve.

The second controlled study (Robson *et al.* 1984) avoided the methodological shortcomings of the Earll and Kincey study while following an essentially similar design. Four hundred and twenty-nine patients were randomly assigned to either a treatment group consisting of psychological treatment from one of four clinical psychologists working in the general practice or a control group, which consisted of management by the GP. Treatment was up to a maximum of 10 weeks, and, as reported earlier, averaged 3.7 sessions or 2½ h of psychologist time. Patients were assessed on psychological measures, prescription costs, consultations, and hospital appointments at various stages after the end of treatment up to one year follow-up. Kincey's categorization was used with the majority of patients having anxiety problems (47.9 per cent), interpersonal problems (17.4 per cent) and habit disorders (16.2 per cent). In addition, 13.7 per cent of patients were referred because of depression.

The results of this study were more favourable to psychological treatment. Patients treated by the clinical psychologists showed significantly greater improvement in their presenting problems than control patients immediately after treatment and up to 34 weeks follow-up. They made significantly fewer visits to the GPs during treatment and up to 24 weeks follow-up and received significantly less psychotropic medication during treatment and up to one year follow-up. Control patients improved steadily over time, but at a lesser rate than those treated by the psychologists; at one year follow-up the control did not differ significantly from the treated group on most measures except for the cost of psychotropic medication (higher for controls). Robson *et al.* (1984) concluded that the patients treated by clinical psychologists in this study showed an accelerated improvement compared to controls, with less frequent consultations and less expenditure on medication. Results, therefore, supported the value of a clinical psychologist service in a general practice setting.

Further research is needed to establish how beneficial a therapeutic service is. GPs and patients appear to value the service and many psychologists are prepared to offer it. The Robson *et al.* study gives some indication of the likely benefit to patients and to the practice. Economically is such a service viable? Robson *et al.* assessed the savings from reduced prescribing and translated this into a percentage of a psychologist's salary. They estimated that savings from reduced prescribing would pay for about 28 per cent of a senior clinical psychologist's salary (at 1981 rates). Other economies can arise, such as earlier return to work and reduced consultation time. A major obstacle to such a service, however, is the shortage of clinical psychologists in the UK and most other countries. There are too few psychologists for them to be attached to all general practices in this way, so that the current pattern in the UK is of a few practices being well served by clinical psychologists and many more not being served at all. Without a sudden and rapid increase in clinical psychologists, a specialized therapy service in general practice will remain a luxury for a few rather than a routine service for all.

Consultant–teacher role   A clinical psychologist may work collaboratively with GPs and other members of the primary health care team either by working together on individual cases or carrying out specific projects. There are some obvious advantages to a collaborative approach not least of which is the fact that it makes more efficient use of clinical psychologists' time and skills. One example of a collaborative project is that of a GP and a psychologist who worked together running a weight control group for overweight women in a Scottish town (Coupar and Kennedy 1980). Patients were recruited by advertisements and, although there was a large drop out after the first session, those who persisted in the treatment successfully lost of least 10 per cent of their initial weight. Most interestingly this weight loss was maintained for all but one of the attenders at follow-up 18 months later. GP and psychologist working together meant a useful sharing of expertise for a problem that has both psychological and physical aspects.

Consultation between clinical psychologists and primary care workers can be at various levels. At its simplest there may be informal meetings over coffee and lunch in which cases are discussed, possible referrals mooted, and information about treatment (medical and psychological) shared. A step up from this is joint work on individual cases (e.g. marital disorders, sex therapy) or in running a group as in the weight control group discussed above. The extent of joint work will largely depend upon the interests of the primary case worker since (s)he will need to put aside time specifically to take on treatment cases or run groups. At another level clinical psychologists can run training courses or workshops for GPs and other primary care workers with the aim of teaching specific skills. One example is the teaching of anxiety management skills (relaxation; target setting; planned practice) to primary care workers with the aim of their using these skills as an alternative to medication or simple advice. Care must be taken to evaluate how effective primary care workers are in the use of such skills.

Behavioural group treatment for sleep-disordered children: a collaborative project between health visitors and clinical psychologists

The health visitors attached to a practice in a small market town reported that a large proportion of their time was taken up with sleep problems in the pre-school child and that although they could offer support to parents, they did not know what constructive advice to give on management. Could clinical psychologists help? This request led to a collaborative project evaluating the effectiveness of a group-based behavioural management programme run by health visitors and psychologists.

Sleep problems in pre-school children are quite common and consist of difficulties in settling, frequent waking, and disturbances to sleep routines, e.g. being taken into the parents' bed. While many parents will cope without help, others find the disturbance to their own sleep and the child's sleep distressing and emotionally draining. Health visitors, because they routinely visit parents with young children, are often the recipients of the parents' worries and are frequently asked if they can help in any way.

Behavioural management of sleeping problems involves careful record keeping, analysis of the individual's problem in terms of contingencies maintaining the behaviour, establishing agreed goals and working gradually towards their attainment, an approach which has proved helpful when carried out by psychologists (Douglas and Richman 1984). There is evidence that this approach is effective when carried out on an individual basis. In this project a group approach was developed and assessed.

The behavioural management groups

Since three health visitors were attached to the Health Centre, it was decided to run three groups in each of which the clinical psychologist worked in collaboration with a health visitor. Parents and children were assigned to the group run by their own health visitor. The groups were held on a weekday morning in the Health Education Room at the Health Centre. Between five and six mothers and their children attended each group. At the first meeting the parents were informed about the project and information systematically collected on each child's sleeping problem. Various assessment measures were filled in which the parent recorded in detail her child's sleeping pattern in the form of a diary. The group met weekly over the next six weeks, during which time the principles of behavioural management were introduced and parents advised how to apply them to their children's problems. Five weeks after the final session the group met again for a follow-up session.

An example of the behavioural management was a 4½-year-old girl, Linda, who refused to go to bed in the evenings and fell asleep on the settee in front of the television each evening after which she would be taken up to bed. She then woke between 12.00 and 1.00 a.m. and wandered as if sleepwalking into her parents' room. Linda would then get into her parent's bed and sleep the rest of the night without waking. If her parents attempted to put her to bed in the evening or at night she screamed and if left alone would come and find them. The main goal established was that Linda should go to sleep in her own bed. The advice on management involved:

1. Bathtime to precede bedtime immediately;
2. Linda to have a story read to her in bed for about 20 minutes;
3. The parent reading the story was then to stay in the room until Linda was asleep, but was to have minimal interaction with her e.g. they could read a book, knit, etc.

Later advice involved the parent gradually withdrawing from the room before Linda was asleep, e.g. sitting outside the room, then on the landing and finally downstairs. These procedures successfully led to the resolution of the settling problem.

Outcome of the project

Parents in all three groups attended consistently and all bar one rated the groups as useful. The main criterion of success was an increase in the number of 'clear nights', i.e. nights without any form of disturbance from their child. Parents in all groups reported an increase in clear nights over the course of the treatment, from an average of between 0 and 1 night per week prior to the groups, to an average of 2.5 to 4.1 nights per week at the end of the group. Follow up at one month showed that progress had been maintained and improved upon.

The positive effects achieved in this project encouraged the health visitors to apply behavioural management principles themselves in the course of their normal work (Mercier, unpublished findings 1984).

Research in primary health care

An important part of the training of clinical psychologists is in research skills and methodology. In their undergraduate degree psychologists are taught experimental methods of inquiry, and are required to carry out and report a research project using appropriate statistical analysis. In their postgraduate training they are taught to apply these research skills to clinical problems and are required to carry out a major research study (see Chapter 1). Carrying out clinical research may be part of a clinical psychologist's job description (though not in all cases) and up to one day per week be made available for research. For various reasons—the pressure of clinical commitments, competing interests, awareness of the snags and pitfalls of research work—the majority of trained clinical psychologists is not actively involved in research. Yet their contribution as researchers may well be of particular value in primary care. Some ways in which clinical psychologists could carry out collaborative clinical research are considered.

Detection and identification of psychological problems

Knowledge about what psychological problems present in primary care is still only rudimentary. The problems of definition and categorization of psychological problems were noted earlier. By focusing on discrete and widely identifiable categories of disorder such as anxiety, depression, obsessions, where standardized assessments have been developed, there is scope for psychologists to uncover the extent to which such problems present in the community and to primary care workers such as health visitors, district nurses, and GPs. It is also of interest to find out more about the 'natural history' of psychological problems since, as mentioned earlier, many problems will be resolved without any professional intervention. Clinical psychologists, with their knowledge of psychological problems and ways of assessing them, could fruitfully collaborate with other specialists, particularly those with experience in epidemiology such as community physicians. The knowledge gained from this type of inquiry will be of practical use in, for example, helping to determine what problems need intervention.

Psychological aspects of the work of primary care professionals

It has been increasingly recognized that a large part of the work of doctors, nurses, receptionists, health visitors, and others who work in primary care is 'psychological'. At its crudest this refers to the importance of interpersonal skills and behaviour in professional work which, of course, would also apply to medicine in general. But a singularly important feature of primary care is the frequency of contact with people, over 95 per cent of whom will visit their GP at least once in five years. A large part of primary care work entails dealing effectively with people whether it is in making appointments, in changing dressings, in one-to-one consultations or in clinics. Psychologists and other social scientists have become interested in the process of communication in primary care and in particular what factors aid and what impede effective communication (Pendleton and Hasler 1983).

The failure of many patients to adhere to the treatment regimens suggested by doctors and others is in part due to deficiences in communication. While most patients report being satisfied with the communication they receive from their doctors, a substantial minority (between 35 and 40 per cent) report dissatisfaction. Psychological studies of doctor–patient communication have highlighted some of the factors that affect satisfaction. For example, many communications from doctors are too complex for patients to understand, too long to be adequately recalled, and delivered in a way that fails to take into account the patient's existing knowledge and beliefs. Psychological studies of the processes of remembering and forgetting can be useful in designing more effective communications. People tend to remember information presented at the beginning of a message (the primacy effect) and at the end of a message (the recency effect) whereas the bit in the middle—which often contains important information about treatment and its effects—is less well remembered. Equally, information that is concrete, emphasized as important and repeated will be more easily remembered. It is obvious that well-established psychological knowledge such as this can be practically applied as indeed it has begun to be. For example, a collaborative project between a social psychologist and a group of GPs has led to a training programme focusing on teaching key inter-personal skills in the consultation (Pendleton, Schofield, Tate, and Havelock 1984).

Prevention and health promotion

There has been an increasing awareness that primary health care is one of the most fruitful fields for the prevention of illness and the promotion of health. The GP in particular has been seen as potentially a major agent of change, although other primary care workers such as practice nurses and health visitors are also important (Gray and Fowler 1983). About two-thirds of patients consult their doctors in one year and the availability and accessibility of the GP creates many opportunities for health education and promotion. The doctor too is generally a respected and trusted figure whose advice is taken seriously. For example, studies of GPs giving advice to smokers to quit smoking have clearly demonstrated that a small but significant number of smokers successfully give up directly as a result of that advice (Jamrozik, Vessey, Fowler, Wald, Parker, and Wnakis, 1984) In recent years, doctors and other primary care workers have become more and more involved in promoting health, from straightforward activies such as immunization and screening to education and advice on aspects of lifestyle.

Clinical psychologists have also begun to direct their attention to prevention and health promotion. This makes sense since it is primarily psychological change that is necessary to achieve a healthier lifestyle. For example, there is an accumulating body of evidence linking diet, particularly one high in saturated fat and low in fibre, with coronary heart disease and certain cancers. If people can shift their eating habits, then they will reduce the risk of these very common diseases. What is required is a change in attitude (e.g. being prepared to recognize that a change in diet is important for health) and in behaviour (e.g. adopting a healthier pattern of eating). The GP, practice nurse, or health visitor may well be the best means of seeking to instigate change, but how should his/her advice be given? Clinical psychologists, whose daily business is seeking to change attitudes and behaviour, could work closely with the primary care worker to maximize the effectiveness of their intervention. One such project is currently being carried out in Oxfordshire, in which practice nurses are giving advice to smokers during a 'health check'. The psychologist's role is to promote more effective advice by training the nurses in basic counselling and interpersonal skills.

COMMUNITY SERVICES

The work of clinical psychologists in primary care has predominantly been with the general practice team. This is not surprising since clinical psychologists are health care professionals with already established links to GPs, nurses, and other health care staff. In the transition to primary care clinical psychologists have extended their customary ways of working and general practice has been a most fertile ground. However, as was illustrated earlier in Fig. 8.1., many more psychological problems exist in the community than actually present or are recognized in general practice. Awareness of this has led some clinical psychologists to work directly 'in the community.'

Community teams

The slow transition from the institutionalized care of the mentally ill and mentally handicapped to 'care in the community' has been accompanied in some instances by the setting up of community teams. Community mental handicap teams (CMHTs) are a good example of this development. A CMHT consists of personnel from both the NHS and from local authorities, whose main role is to provide specialized advice and help with problems related to mental handicap. The team consists of a core of two or three full-time professional staff, usually a community nurse and social worker, with back-up support from clinical psychologists, consultants in mental handicap, and other specialist professional staff (e.g. occupational therapists, physiotherapists). The CMHT functions are: (i) to act as the first point of contact for parents and families of the mentally handicapped providing direct help and advice; (ii) to co-ordinate access to services; and (iii) to establish close working relationships with relevant local voluntary organizations. CMHTs deal directly with problems in the community as they arise and in addition act as intermediaries between the primary care teams (who can refer patients) and the specialist services (to whom the team can refer people for longer term and more specialized work).

The major role taken by clinical psychologists on CMHTs has been to provide psychological advice and training to the core members of the team in their work with mentally handicapped people and their families. This is acting in a consultant–teacher role as outlined above. Occasionally, psychologists may also act as 'key workers' in CMHTs and work directly with clients on skills training or behavioural programmes. CMHTs have the virtue of being community based rather than institution or hospital based and, in theory at least, can be more responsive to the needs of the community. For clinical psychologists, it has meant the opportunity to work outside the umbrella of a medical bureaucratic system and deal directly with psychological problems in the community. Other examples of community teams are community alcohol teams and community drug abuse teams which, although differently organized to CMHTs, have similar aims of a greater involvement in the community and a move away from an excessively medical perspective on psychological and social problems.

Community mental health centres (CMHCs)

CMHCs were first established in the USA in the 1960s in response to widespread dissatisfaction with the then existing methods of care and treatment of mentally ill people, particularly the large state mental hospitals, and out of an awareness that many of the most needy people (the poor, the disadvantaged, ethnic minorities) were simply not gaining access to any form of professional treatment. CMHCs served a small community catchment area (between 75 000 and 200 000 people) in which professional staff worked alongside non-professionals providing a psychological service that was designed to be accessible, flexible, primarily educational, short-term, and open to all members of the community. Although there have been criticisms of the extent to which CMHCs achieved these aims, over 800 CMHCs had been established in the USA in the early 1980s.

In the UK the development of CMHCs has been a sporadic one and largely dependent on local initiatives. In some health authorities CMHCs have been seen as a direct alternative to institutional psychiatric care; in others, as a development taking place alongside the traditional services. The latter development is by far the commonest and one example, the Newbury Mental Health Unit, is described to illustrate how such a centre works in practice.

The Unit was set up in 1983 as a result of a successful application for Joint Funding (Health Authority and Local Authority finance). It is staffed by two occupational therapists, one community psychiatric nurse, one clinical psychologist, two social workers, and clerical staff. Two consultant psychiatrists hold regular clinical meetings at the unit. The major work of the unit is applying a broadly educational model of treatment on an individual or a group basis to people referred by Health and Social Services professional staff. The main problems seen are anxiety and phobic states, depression, family relationship difficulties, sexual and marital problems, bereavement reactions, eating disorders, and difficulties in social adjustment. The staff at the Unit work closely together combining to run various groups, e.g. anxiety management group, agoraphobic group, bereavement group, tranquilliser withdrawal group, social skills group. The clinical psychologist plays a central part in planning and implementing the various treatments and in the training and supervision of other staff. In addition, she takes responsibility for monitoring and evaluating the work of the unit.

The advantages of CMHCs such as the Newbury Mental Health Unit are their greater accessibility to people, the reduction of stigma associated with psychiatric services, the benefits of a multidisciplinary approach, and their ability to offer psychological interventions that are pragmatic, brief, and effective. It remains to be seen, however, to what extent CMHCs provide a radical alternative to traditional medically based systems of care, for example, by taking in people 'off the streets' rather than through referral, by being able to respond to the needs of all the people in the community not just a select few, by focusing on mental health education and promotion rather than conventional treatment. These activities demand a different role for clinical psychologists and other professional staff, one which looks more to social and environmental change rather than to the treatment of the individual.

Community psychologists

Community psychology is a term that first appeared in the USA to describe a radical shift in applied psychology away from individual psychotherapy in a professional health care context to an approach that views psychological problems from an ecological viewpoint. Community psychology emphasizes the critical importance of social and environmental forces in the determination of human behaviour problems and favours what is loosely described as a 'systems-oriented' approach to intervention. There is also the recognition that many mental health problems are the product of social and political conditions such as poverty, unemployment, racism, urban deprivation, and that changes in these social conditions are required in order to make much impact on these psychological problems. Community psychology, therefore, seeks to embrace a broader perspective on mental health and illness than is currently adopted by most clinical psychologists.

There are in fact few community psychologists *per se* outside of the USA, probably because there does not exist a career structure in the health and social services. Some clinical psychologists have sought to take more of a community psychology perspective in their work. This entails a deliberate move away from individual treatments to attempts to produce or provoke changes in social systems, for example, by working closely with voluntary groups seeking social and political change, by taking an advocacy role in the pursuit of the rights of the mentally ill and handicapped, by working in or with Social Services Departments, and by helping to establish and support self-help groups. To date this community role has been relatively little developed, but as political and financial constraints directly affect the health care system, this is a role that may become increasingly important.

SUMMARY

Clinical psychologists have only recently begun working in primary health care. There are four main ways in which they have worked. Firstly, a treatment service is offered similar to that provided in out-patient clinics. This has been the commonest and most preferred service. Recent research has provided some support for the effectiveness and efficacy of such a service. Secondly, a consultant–teacher service can be provided. An example of this is described in which a clinical psychologist worked closely with health visitors to teach behavioural methods for managing sleep disorders in pre-school children. Thirdly, research can be carried out into various aspects of primary care work; doctor–patient communication is one example. Finally, clinical psychologists can participate in health promotion and prevention programmes, many of which are carried out in primary care settings. Advice on diet and smoking are two examples. While clinical psychologists have on the whole worked in primary care through the medium of general practice, this is not the only way of working. Some clinical psychologists have begun to work directly in the community either as community psychologists or as part of community teams.

REFERENCES

Catalan, J. and Gath, D. (1985). Benzodiazepines in general practice: time for a decision. *Br. med. J.* **290**, 1374–6.

Coupar, A. M. and Kennedy, T. (1980). Running a weight control group. Experiences of psychologist and a general practitioner. *J. R. Coll. gen. Pract.* **30**, 41–8.

Douglas, J. and Richman, N. (1984). *My child won't sleep*. Penguin, London.

Earll, L. and Kincey, J. (1982). Clinical psychology in general practice: a controlled trial evaluation. *J. R. Coll. gen. Pract.* **32**, 32–7.

Goldberg, D. P. and Blackwell, B. (1970). Psychiatric illness in general practice. A detailed study using a new method of case identification. *Br. med. J.* **2**, 439–43.

Goldberg, D. P. & Huxley, P. (1980). See 'Further reading'.

Jamrozik, K., Vessey, M., Fowler, G., Wald, N., Parker, G. and Wnakis, H. V. (1984). Controlled trial of three different antismoking interventions in general practice. *Br. med. J.* **288**, 1499–1503.

Johnston, M. (1978). The work of a clinical psychologist in primary care. *J. R. Coll. gen. Pract.* **28**, 661–7.

Kincey, J. A. (1974). General practice and clinical psychology—some arguments for a closer liaison. *J. R. Coll. gen. Pract.* **24**, 882–8.

McPherson, I. and Feldman, M. P. (1977). A preliminary investigation of the role of the clinical psychologist in the primary care settling. *Bull. Br. psychol. Soc.* **30**, 342–6.

Pendleton, D. and Hasler, J., ed. (1983). See 'Further reading'.

Pendleton, D., Schofield, T., Tate, P. and Havelock, P. (1984). *The consultation. An approach to learning*. Oxford General Practice Series No. 6. Oxford University Press, Oxford.

Robson, M. H., France, R. and Bland, M. (1984). Clinical psychologists in primary care; controlled clinical and economic evaluation. *Br. med. J.* **288**, 1805–8.

FURTHER READING

Bloom, B. L. (1984). *Community mental health. A general introduction* (2nd edn). Brooks/Cole, Monterey, CA.

France, R. and Robson, M. H. (1986). *Behaviour Therapy in Primary Care*. Croom Helm, London.

Goldberg, D. P. and Huxley, P. (1980). *Mental illness in the community. The pathway to psychiatric care*. Tavistock, London.

Pendleton, D. and Hasler, J., eds. (1983). *Doctor–Patient communication*. Academic Press, London.

9

Clinical psychology and physical health

Louise M. Wallace

INTRODUCTION

Physical illness

Modern concepts of diseases such as cancer and heart disease are described in somatic terms, which imply that the cause can be traced to a lesion or breakdown of the structure and functioning of an organ system. The distinction between physical and mental disorder, between somatic and psychological diseases, is readily accepted by health care practitioners and lay people alike. However, it is also recognized that entirely somatic models of disease to the exclusion of psychological processes provide an inadequate picture of how illnesses develop, and how people who are ill experience their illness and adapt to it. The recognition that both physical and psychological factors play an important part in the causation of physical disorder, the patients' response to treatment, and to their ultimate adjustment to illness, provide a rationale for the contribution of clinical psychologists to the health care of people with physical health problems.

Clinical psychological services and physical health

People of all ages suffer physical health problems, and it is not surprising that psychologists working in mental health and handicap services should also be concerned with those patients who have both mental and physical problems. For example, within child and adolescent services, clinical psychologists have developed expertise in managing patients' behavioural problems. These skills are applicable not only to children who present behaviour problems at home as a result of family problems, but also to the patient who becomes disturbed when faced with the prospect of repeated hospitalization

213

as part of the treatment of a physical disorder. In Britain, the establishment of District Psychological Services, which provide psychological services to a given geographical population rather than to a specific hospital or ward, has enabled psychologists to respond to the demand for psychological advice from patients and from staff caring for the physically ill patient.

Similar assessment and therapy skills may be called upon to help the patient who is depressed as a result of a recent bereavement or the diagnosis of a potentially fatal illness. Not only are psychologists concerned with improving patients' psychological adjustment to physical disorder, they are increasingly concerned to modify the psychological factors which may contribute to the development of physical disorders and to the exacerbation of the symptoms of a chronic physical illness. It is perhaps expected, for example, that the occurrence of a heart attack in a young fit person can cause considerable anxiety which may require psychological intervention. Further, whether the patient carries out the instructions of his doctor to change his diet, alcohol intake, exercise, and smoking behaviour may well influence that patient's subsequent morbidity and mortality. Psychological factors are clearly at work in the development of health attitudes and behaviour which can become a focus of intervention with an individual patient.

The recognition that all health care staff use psychological skills, and that their interactions with patients can greatly influence the patients' well-being and physical recovery and response to treatment, has created demand for psychologists' teaching and research skills. For example, through direct clinical work with individual cases, as well as research into the quality of care of all patients on the unit or ward, the psychologist can show that specific types of information are required by the patients about their illness and treatment. The psychologist may then teach the nursing, medical, or other staff how to use communication and counselling skills to overcome regularly occurring problems and to improve the overall quality of care.

For example, in a coronary care unit, patients are particularly concerned about their immediate survival, and yet the nursing and medical procedures which are designed to save life may endanger the patient's life by causing additional fear. In a patient with a compromised cardiovascular system, the occurrence of an acute anxiety state may influence the electrical activity of the heart. The importance of clear and reassuring communication with the patient is, therefore, paramount. Wallace and Joshi (in press) reported that the staff of the coronary care unit in Dudley in the West Midlands were interested in learning from the psychologist how to detect which patients were most anxious and in learning how to reassure them effectively. In this case, the clinical psychologist carried out some systematic observation of nurse–patient interaction to determine the degree to which staff were able to detect and manage patients' fears. One particularly effective method of changing these interactions was to provide a counselling course for newly qualified staff, which incorporated role-played demonstrations of accurate and reassuring communication by the most competent nurses.

The research skills of a clinical psychologist are employed in many ways within this speciality. For example, new medical treatments are typically tested in clinical trials by assessing whether the patients given the treatment show improved health or remission of disease compared with patients given a placebo or standard treatment regime. Psychological treatments can also be tested in this way. For example, the author and her cardiologist colleague, Robert Nagle, are testing their clinical impression that patients who suffer greater degrees of stress and have difficulty in controlling anger and frustration tend to show more frequent and severe symptoms of angina than patients who are less prone to get stressed. The usual way to evaluate a new drug for the treatment of angina is to ask the patient to keep a diary of their angina symptoms, and to ask them to perform a standard medically supervised exercise test to the point where chest pain prevents any further exertion. The investigators are now examining whether the patients who are taught how to manage their reactions to stressful and anger-provoking situations have fewer angina episodes. They are also expected to take more regular activity and show improvement in their general well-being, in comparison to the patients who receive standard medical care.

Clinical psychologists are not only concerned with the identification and amelioration of physical disorders. Where psychological factors such as stress and unhealthy lifestyles are significant causes of physical diseases such as coronary heart disease, clinical psychologists have been involved in health promotion programmes. For example, Walsall Psychological Service runs anti-smoking advice classes in schools as well as groups for people who want to give up smoking. Stress has been shown to have a causal role in the development and exacerbation of many disorders including asthma, angina, high blood pressure, eczema, and irritable bowel syndrome. Similarly, clinical psychologists have set up classes to teach people how to identify and control stress, which may be offered in Health Centres or as part of an adult education programme.

TYPES OF PROBLEMS

Psychological problems presenting as physical disease

Somatic symptoms are usually perceived by people as a sign of physical rather than mental ill health, and yet psychological problems can be confused with physical disorders where they produce similar symptoms, as illustrated in the following case study.

Mrs Hartfield is a deputy headteacher in a large comprehensive school. She had been experiencing some slight but sharp pains in her chest at irregular intervals. One day she collapsed at school after experiencing a pain in the middle of her chest while giving a lesson. She was taken by ambulance to the coronary care unit of the District General Hospital. However, after two days, when all investigations were complete, the doctor told her she had not had a heart attack, 'it was just nerves'. She felt foolish that she had caused so much fuss. However, she was not convinced that there was nothing wrong, particularly as her father had been taken ill suddenly and it had been too late before anyone could get medical help to him. The clinical psychologist working in the District General Hospital was asked to see her. Discussion revealed that the patient had been experiencing many symptoms of anxiety including feelings of physical tension, agitation, breathlessness, and poor sleep, and she reported being troubled by quite small problems which she found difficult to put into perspective. In addition to the periodic chest pain, she was also troubled by tension headaches. In a joint session with the clinical psychologist and cardiologist the nature of the physical symptoms, including the muscle tension problem causing sensations of tightness and ischaemic pain in the muscle of the chest were discussed with her. It was further explained that these symptoms were not indicative of an underlying heart condition, and that she had now had a complete medical check-up. She was prepared to accept psychological treatment for her problem of anxiety.

This case serves to show how patients can present with a problem which may not ultimately be explained by the presence of a disease process. In this case, chronic work stress produced a state of chronic arousal which manifested in a number of minor unpleasant physical sensations. There are other situations where the clinical psychologist may be called upon to help determine whether a problem is a result of an organic disease process or non-organic causes. For example, elderly people who are depressed are very often more restrained in expressing their feelings than younger people. Sometimes a person who is depressed is not aware of this, and may believe their forgetfulness, concentration, poor appetite, lethargy, and sleeplessness are a result of physical disease. Here, the training of a clinical psychologist can be useful in helping staff to detect those elderly patients whose physical problems are a result of an emotional rather than a physical problem. Similarly, bed-wetting in a child who has been able to sleep through the night without wetting the bed for a period of time could be due to a physical problems such as a urinary infection. However, these common behavioural problems may result from emotional difficulties such as anxiety. Additionally, the child may learn to maintain the habit if there are positive consequences for bed-wetting, such as being taken into the parents' bed for the rest of the night. The inadvertent provision of rewarding consequences for the habit may account for the maintenance and continuation of behavioural problems even after the physical cause of the symptoms has been identified and treated.

The skills of the clinical psychologist in detecting the presence of mental health problems in people presenting the symptoms commonly associated with physical disease processes are similar to those employed by the clinical psychologist in community and mental health services (See Chapters 2 and 3).

Psychological problems secondary to physical disease

Physical diseases usually involve discomfort and disruption of current activities and plans at best, and protracted pain, perhaps disfigurement, loss, and death at worst. Research into the causes of mental illnesses, life-threatening illness, and long-term disability give examples of the kinds of stressful life events that are associated with the development of mental illness problems such as anxiety and depression. It is therefore to be expected that people with physical illnesses will have more psychological problems than physically well relations. Studies of patients consulting their general practitioner, or undergoing hospital treatment for heart attack, ulcer, and a variety of disorders such as asthma, diabetes, and stroke, showed that approximately one third of the patients had detectable mental illness problems severe enough to warrant psychological treatment. However, very few of those patients are referred for psychological or psychiatric help, as Maguire has shown in his study of depression in women receiving surgical treatment for breast cancer in an Oxford hospital (Maguire, Julier, Hawton, and Bancroft 1974). He believes that this neglect of the psychological consequences of severe physical illness may reflect the limited skill of the staff, who are trained to treat physical disorder. It may also reflect the lack of psychological services available in general hospitals, and also the reluctance of staff and patients to assign a 'psychological' label to people who are already in the unenviable position of having severe physical disorders.

As noted above, the author provided a psychological service to the staff and patients on a local coronary care unit. The case of Mr James is typical of the patients about whom the staff would consult the clinical psychologist.

Mr James was 57 years old when he experienced his first heart attack. There had been no indication beforehand that he suffered from heart disease, but he smoked 30 cigarettes per day. He was a Heavy Goods Vehicle driver and was shocked to find that he automatically lost his licence when he received the diagnosis of myocardial infarction (heart attack). He recovered well in hospital, and gave up smoking with little difficulty. However, he found it difficult to distinguish between those symptoms of chest pain that were attributable to anxiety, and those that were early warning signs of strain on his heart. He was advised by the cardiologist to attend an exercise class to build up his physical fitness to compensate for the damage to his heart but he declined, saying he was too busy finding another job. Later he admitted that he was terrified that the physical exercise might cause a second heart attack. He experienced occasional breathlessness, tiredness, and occasional aches and pains in his chest, and he began to lose weight. He became reluctant to go out on his own, fearing that if he collapsed there would be no-one to summon medical help. Within six weeks of his heart attack he was unable to leave the house alone. In his case it was not possible to distinguish neatly between the bouts of chest pain due to anxiety and those due to decreased blood supply to the heart muscle. However, helping the patient to overcome his anxieties and also to undertake the physical exercise programme could be expected to improve his overall physical and psychological well-being.

Some physical disorders not only affect how people feel emotionally and how well they carry out their normal activities, they may have direct effects on patients' cognitive functioning. Chronic renal failure is associated with high rates of depression, which may be attributable to the very realistic fear of imminent death and long term disability, but also to neuropsychological processes. The symptoms of fatigue, apathy, drowsiness, irritability, anorexia, and dysphoric mood can in some circumstances be attributable to uraemia. Occasionally, salt depletion or hypertension can lead to symptoms typical of dementia. Other symptoms of hallucinations and delusions can occur as a result of the cerebral effects of uraemia. In practice, although in some patients the symptoms will remit when the uraemic condition is controlled, in many circumstances the patient continues to feel depressed and psychological intervention is warranted.

Major illness may not only influence the patient's mood and ability to cope, but also influence activities that are important to them, such as achieving satisfactory sexual relations. It is accepted now that people develop difficulties in achieving satisfactory sexual relations for many reasons, including lack of sex education, unpleasant early sexual experiences, and concurrent family and marital problems. However, even couples with many years of satisfactory sexual relations can find that difficulties arise when one partner becomes physically ill. As physical appearance can be particularly important in maintaining sexual attractiveness, it is predictable that people who receive treatment which results in disfigurement to the face, hands, and genital areas may experience self-revulsion and also rejection by their partners. Illnesses that result in disfigurement as well as disrupting normal functioning can be expected to produce sexual problems.

Mrs Hatton was referred to the clinical psychologist working in the gynaecology department when it was discovered that she had a severe form of cancer to her internal and external genitals which required urgent surgery. In this case, as the gynaecologist knew that most if not all women experience difficulties in sexual relationships after this mutilating surgery and that there is also a high rate of suicide, the couple were referred for preventive sexual counselling.

Psychological problems exacerbating existing disease processes

There are many disorders where the patient's lifestyle and methods of coping with stress lead to an exacerbation of the disorder or a delay in remission of symptoms. The occurrence of one or more stressful events can be associated with the occurrence of symptoms of disorders such as psoriasis, eczema, allergies including asthma, cardiovascular diseases such as essential hypertension and angina pectoris, vascular disorders such as migraine headache, and even endocrine disorders such as diabetes, which can be exacerbated by stress.

Generally, the occurrence of recent stressful events is said to have a triggering effect on people with undetected early signs of disease. For example, although myocardial infarction (heart attacks) can occur out of the blue, if the patient dies there is usually evidence of atherosclerosis or 'furring up' of the coronary arteries. There is evidence that chronic life stress is associated with increased occurrence of cardiovascular diseases. Stress-related disorders have many causes, but some people may be more susceptible than others. For example, mild hypertension may be caused by increased cardiac reactivity and there is some suggestion that repeated stressful situations may lead to repeated hyper-arousal associated with sympathetic nervous system stimulation. Whatever the cause of high blood pressure, clinical psychologists have shown that teaching patients with essential hypertension how to avoid stressful situations and how to relax to reduce overall muscle tension and sympathetic nervous system response can lead to reductions in arousal and in blood pressure. These reductions occur not only during practice but during the patient's everyday life. This can lead to remission of the symptoms of high blood pressure. Stress management training for early essential hypertension can prevent the long-term problems associated with high blood pressure such as increased risk of cardiovascular disease, and also reduce the side effects of long-term antihypertensive medication.

Not only can patients' habitual ways of coping with stress influence their symptoms, but patients' moods, health beliefs, and health behaviours can dramatically influence how people seek and respond to medical treatment. Faulty health beliefs and the expected value of health-promoting actions when balanced against expected risks of not following advice or of maintaining unhealthy habits, contribute to the decisions which people make as to whether they will follow their doctor's advice. Several models of patients' health beliefs and attitudes have been researched, the best known of which is the Health Belief Model as proposed by Becker and Maiman (1975). The patients' beliefs about the course of their illness and the likely effectiveness of treatment, their assessment of the cost/benefits of health action and inaction are very useful in understanding when patients often fail to seek health care, and when they do not follow advice which is, according to accepted medical wisdom, apparently in their best interests.

Gary Adams was badly burned on his legs, face, chest, arms, and hands as the result of an accident. He and two other teenage friends had been drinking and smoking marijuana in a disused house in which one of the teenagers was living. The gas fire exploded and they were unable to react quickly enough to save themselves. All three teenagers were burned and one died subsequently in hospital. Gary was admitted to the Regional burns unit. He received intensive treatment including several surgical procedures to clean and cover his burns and to graft new skin into place. While in shock he was provided with the necessary fluids and nutrients, and after this phase he was required to eat up to twice his normal daily calorie intake as burn injury raises the body's metabolism and results in the loss of protein and calories through the burns. He was required to remain in bed with restricted movement of some body parts to avoid damage to his grafts and to follow the physiotherapist's exerises to stretch other areas to prevent the skin from contracting. He experienced pain from these exercises and soreness from bed rest, and pain from the burned areas and from where his own skin had been removed to cover the burned areas. However, when he was beyond the critical state, 14 days after the burn his wounds became badly infected. His new grafts failed to 'take'. This meant that he would need to have more operations as the surgeon would need to 'harvest' some new skin to cover the old wounds. After one month he was losing weight, he was refusing to eat and pulled out his nasogastric feeding tube. He refused to exercise and his grafts were not 'taking'. He also wanted to know about the fate of his friend but the staff were avoiding telling him that he had died several weeks ago as they felt he would become further depressed and would also no longer trust them.

When the clinical psychologist interviewed Gary she discovered that he had been depressed from the moment he began to suspect that his friend had died. He suspected that staff were not telling him the truth about his own future. He was terrified of looking at his disfigured face and believed the future was hopeless for him. He believed that as his grafts were not taking and he was losing his appetite that he was slowly dying. As he had been the ringleader of the gang he felt that the staff were sadistic and blamed him for the accident and the fate of his friend. He did not see why he should eat or follow the physiotherapist's advice when all of these things made him feel more discomfort. Discussion of the patient's feelings about his responsibility for the accident and his responsibility for his own future, discussion of his health beliefs concerning his prognosis and the likely costs and benefits of following medical advice were the starting point of the clinical psychologist's psychological treatment of this case.

Psychological factors as causal of physical disease

Epidemiological studies in the USA and The Netherlands have shown that a stress-prone behaviour pattern known as 'Type A' behaviour is a risk factor for coronary heart disease in the same way as a family history of coronary heart disease, high blood pressure, smoking, and high blood fats. 'Type A' behaviours include impatience, time urgency, hostility, and competitiveness, which contribute to a state of chronic stress. There is evidence that similar unhealthy habits such as over-eating, eating a high fat and a high salt diet, smoking, lack of exercise, excessive alcohol intake, and perhaps the 'Type A' behaviour pattern do contribute to the very high rate of coronary heart disease in the UK.

These findings have given impetus to the work of clinical psychologists in designing health promotion programmes aimed at promoting the health behaviours of the population and of helping people with many risk factors to change entrenched and unhealthy habits such as smoking, and to modify their response to stressful events as discussed earlier.

There are also psychological factors not immediately under the intentional control of the person which may lead to the worsening of symptoms. This in turn may lead the person to reject potentially life-saving treatments because of their unpleasant side effects. Chemotherapeutic treatments for several types of cancer are toxic. That is, in order to kill off diseased cells, the drug also kills normal tissues. This can produce very unpleasant side effects such as hair loss, tiredness, pain and discomfort, poor appetite, nausea, and vomiting.

While most patients feel sick during treatment on drugs such as Adriamycin, several studies in the USA have shown that approximately 25 per cent of people felt sick at the *thought* of treatment. That is, the smell of the hospital ward, the hospital food, the sight of the hospital, the thought of the treatment can make some patients not only feel anxious but feel nauseous and vomit. In some cases this can lead to anorexia, debility, and fatigue. Psychologists believe that a conditioned aversion may account for this process, that is the patient's feelings of nausea have become conditioned to the hospital environment by the process of classical conditioning (see Fig. 9.1).

If untreated, many patients are unable to complete the chemotherapy, and can be expected to suffer further physical consequences of their untreated disease. Psychological treatment involves using anxiety management techniques such as relaxation and systematic desensitization developed in the treatment of phobias (Morrow and Morrell 1982).

Physical health problems are not only caused directly by disease processes, but also by trauma. The staff of a hospital casualty department, a head injury unit or burn unit, are usually aware that accidents are seldom random events. That is, there are accident-prone environments and accident-prone people, and the combination of the two put some people more at risk of accidents than others. While it is possible to be burned in a truly accidental way such as in an earthquake, it is much more likely that a burned person will live or

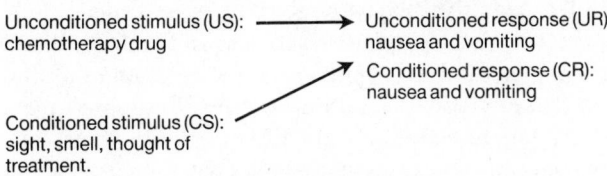

Fig. 9.1 A model of conditioned anticipatory nausea to cancer chemotherapy

work in a hazardous environment. It is also more likely that they will be careless or ignorant of safety precautions. The case of Gary Adams above illustrates the combination of a hazardous environment and accident-prone behaviours. It is also well established that the commonest cause of death in children is through accidents of which burns injuries are second only to road traffic accidents. Many of these occur in the home, and in pre-adolescent children the cause of the injury is often traced to a poor and hazardous physical environment with evidence of social disruption and family tension at the time of the accident. Some accidents may be the result of neglect; others may be more directly attributed to intentional child abuse. While the causes of accidents are multi-faceted and involve an interaction between the individual and the environment, approximately 75 per cent of burn accidents are preventable through legislation and engineering to change physical environments, and through social policy and health education to improve the psychological environment and the promotion of accident prevention behaviour.

THE WORK OF CLINICAL PSYCHOLOGISTS IN PHYSICAL HEALTH

Assessment

Just as in other areas of clinical psychology, assessments are carried out to answer questions. Usually the questions involve determining if the particular patient needs psychological help, and what form of help is indicated. Assessments may also be made of groups of patients or environments such as a ward in order to determine if changes in services are required or if new changes are effective.

Cognitive behavioural analysis

The aim of a cognitive behavioural analysis is to determine the problem, enumerate the patient's responses, and evaluate the effect of the patient's methods of coping. The frequency and duration of symptoms, the antecedent conditions, and the responses and consequences are determined. There are many methods of carrying out such an analysis. In some cases information is gathered using a questionnaire in which patients identify situations that are associated with the occurrence of symptoms. This may be combined with a self-monitoring diary kept each day for several weeks in which the patients record their activities, their symptoms, and responses. From such a diary, it is often possible to determine whether there are predictable relationships between antecedent conditions and behaviour, and between behaviour and consequent conditions.

In order to assess Mrs Hartfield's problem of anxiety-related chest pain and headaches, she was asked to keep a self-monitoring diary over a period of weeks. From such a diary, it is possible to determine whether pairs of antecedent stimuli and behaviours or symptoms are apparent. For example, the record showed that Mrs Hartfield most often experienced headaches while driving to school, but seldom while driving at weekends. She also experienced more symptoms whenever she anticipated conflicts with staff or pupils. Such a record can also reveal associations between behaviours and consequences. That is, certain behaviours may be associated with pleasant or unpleasant consequences, which if repeated over a period of time, may lead to a well established habit. For example, Mrs Hartfield reported that she regularly lay down for an hour or more when she experienced chest or head pains at home, and this usually resulted in solicitous behaviour from her husband and avoidance of household duties. Thirdly, such a record can be useful in assessing the apparent efficacy of the patient's preferred method of coping with symptoms. When changes in the patient's lifestyle are suggested, or new coping strategies such as relaxation or self-hypnosis are introduced to alleviate symptoms, a self-monitoring record helps to provide some evidence of the degree to which the patient is carrying out the suggested change, and also the consequences of such change.

Where patients' cognitive processes are believed to be particularly problematic, it may be important to encourage patients to record their thoughts as well as their behaviours. For example, where patients show a consistent pattern of undervaluing themselves and of their ability to control their symptoms, it may be important to ask them to record their thoughts, so that the therapist can teach them how to dispute these thoughts and substitute more appropriate coping self-statements. It can be helpful to provide patients with a list of typical thoughts that people have in response to stressful situations, as many people are reticent to record their thoughts verbatim. Other methods include encouraging patients to re-enact typical problems in imagination, and to verbalize their thoughts as they occur.

Behavioural observation

Observational methods are most often used where the clinician is concerned with the circumstances in which a behaviour occurs, rather than the patient's interpretation of the event. In the case of a young child in a burn unit where verbal communication is severely restricted by the patient's age and physical condition, behaviours such as excessive crying, self-destructive actions, or violence towards staff can be problematic. Systematic behavioural observation may be important in determining the frequency, antecedents, and consequences of these behaviours, and the alternative behaviours that the patient could be taught to substitute. In a burn unit where dressing changes and physiotherapy are painful, but non-compliant behaviour of patients only serves to prolong the treatment and exacerbates the painfulness of the procedure, the staff are often concerned to minimize excessive pain behaviour. Behavioural observations could include direct observation of the patient and recording the number of physiotherapy exercises completed in a given time period. More indirect observation could be made after the exercises are completed by recording the mileage gauge on an exercise cycle used by a burn patient instructed to increase movement of the lower limbs. (Varni 1983)

Behavioural observations can be important in determining the baseline of activities from which improvement in activity can be negotiated as part of the treatment. For chronic pain patients the aim of treatment is often to maximize activity, since many patients show relatively stable patterns of pain irrespective of activity, and yet their activity levels have often diminished since the onset of their pain problem as they believe that activity is necessarily limited by the occurrance of pain. In an in-patient chronic pain treatment facility, such as exists in the Walton Hospital in Liverpool, self-recording of activity and staff observation of activity may be combined to get a clear picture of the patient's activity level prior to setting appropriate treatment goals. An operational definition of activities is usually made, with categories such as sitting, reading, talking, and so forth. Where a patient's problem consists of lying down too often, a distinction may be made between 'up-time' (activities carried out when the patient is taking weight on their feet) and 'down-time' (when the patient's weight is taken off their legs as in sitting or lying). Clear definitions of behaviour are necessary in order to enable reliable observations to be made which are used to monitor the effectiveness of the treatment.

Psychophysiological methods

Measurement of psychophysiological processes, such as parameters of arousal level, can be particularly important where abnormal functioning is believed to underlie the illness. For example, some investigators believe that excessive muscle tension, which can be measured by monitoring electrical activity of the muscles, may underlie certain types of tension headache. Measurement from various sites taken when the patient is at rest and under circumstances of psychological stress may help to locate the particular muscle groups where abnormal tension is believed to occur. With biofeedback techniques, where the level of muscle tension in specific muscles is 'fed back' to the patient, it may be possible for the patient to identify the physical sensations associated with build-up of muscle tension, and to learn to apply preventive relaxation techniques prior to the onset of a muscle tension headache. Recordings of other physiological processes such as blood pressure, respiratory rate, and heart rate, which along with muscle tension are all believed to be influenced by sympathetic nervous system arousal, can be used to determine if patients who are being taught relaxation training for stress-related diseases are achieving an adequate level of therapeutic response. In conjunction with these direct psychophysiological methods, an indirect method of assessing compliance with relaxation may be employed. For example, patients may be instructed to use a relaxation tape with a cassette recorder in which a device is fitted which records the amount of times the cassette has been played. Such indirect methods may be useful where direct methods may have a reactive effect. That is, where a patient believes that they are being recorded, social factors such as a will to please the therapist may produce a bias in the response under investigation.

Psychological tests

The standardized questionnaire method of assessment may be used for research purposes in order to describe a sample in a way that can be replicated by other researchers. When investigating a clinical problem, standardized questionnaires may be useful in order to cut down on the amount of therapist time, or in order to obtain information which may be biased by the presence of the therapist. For example, some therapists use standardized questionnaires in order to take a sexual history.

Standardized questionnaires can be particularly useful in providing methods of screening patients for psychological help, and to evaluate the effects of psychological treatment. Since much of the work of a clinical psychologist is concerned with detecting patients who are psychologically distressed, and the aims of many interventions are to improve their overall well-being and reduce symptoms of distress, a relatively well-researched area is the measurement of psychological disturbance. Unfortunately, most of the available measures have been developed for psychiatric populations and it is difficult to interpret the meaning of these scores for other populations. This is particularly so when the patient's physical illnesses can cause them to have somatic symptoms such as fatigue or loss of appetite, which on some psychiatric inventories are automatically taken as indicators of psychiatric syndromes such as depression. One solution is to use questionnaires developed for use with physically ill populations, which exclude somatic items. The Hospital Anxiety Depression Scale was developed to screen patients for overall levels of disturbance, and problems of anxiety and depression in particular in the patients attending a mixed medical out-patient service (Zigmond and Snaith 1983). It is increasingly being used with patients suffering from psychologically traumatic illnesses such as cancer, and shows some promise.

Other methods of psychological assessment are used to determine degrees of disability, based on an assessment of the frequency with which patients carry out activities of daily living as determined by investigation of samples of disabled people living in the community. From such a measure it is possible to provide an overall score for a given patient which can be compared with their pre-morbid level of functioning and with scores typical of normal and disabled people in the community. This type of measure is useful in evaluating the effects of treatment. For example, many cancer patients are subject to noxious treatments for cancer such as surgery, chemotherapy, and radiotherapy. Comparison of the relative effects of treatment on the patient's mood and his ability to return to normal activities in between courses of chemotherapy can be very important in helping clinicians to determine which form of therapy has the least deleterious effect on the patient's quality of life.

Treatment

Cognitive–behavioural treatments of physical disorders have a number of common elements (Turk, Meichenbaum, and Genest 1983). It is most important to conceptualize the problem and its treatment in a way that patients understand and that will motivate them to participate actively. Any physical problem is 'bad news' to some degree, and help-seeking usually involves much anguish and self-questioning. The first step, then, is to elicit the patient's perspective on the problem, its aetiology and its likely treatment.

The second step is to carry out a full assessment, and using this shared knowledge, to formulate an understanding of the problem. This 'translation' of the patient's knowledge into the working model of the therapist can reduce helplessness in the patient by explaining the unexplained. It also recasts the problems in a form that has feasible solutions. This step leads naturally to the third which is the formulation of therapeutic goals and treatment strategies in a *collaborative* relationship.

This collaborative endeavour can be encouraged by having patients collect data on themselves (for example, using diaries or reporting anecdotes). Patients are encouraged to monitor their behaviour, emotions and cognitions, and using feedback from the therapist, to develop a more objective view of their problem and of their coping strategies. Patients are often taught to employ old strategies more effectively, and are taught new ones. Most therapies involve patients in changing their overt behaviour (for example, learning to be more assertive with the boss who overworks them) and their cognitions (such as learning to put their thoughts into perspective when under pressure).

A number of strategies are employed to help maintain therapeutic gains. A collaborative relationship helps ensure the patient feels responsible for their improvement, particularly if the therapist is able to clarify how changes made are attributable to the patient's actions. Finally, unlike many medical treatments, which are assumed to be superfluous once the 'lesion' is 'healed', most psychological problems require continued effort. This effort is facilitated if the patient is taught to monitor their problem and anticipate and plan for relapse.

Examples of the cognitive–behavioural treatment of a gynaecological pain problem and of an acute burns injury illustrate some of the applications of this treatment perspective:

COGNITIVE-BEHAVIOURAL TREATMENT FOR CHRONIC PELVIC PAIN

Pearce and Beard (1984) report the surprising finding that approximately two-thirds of women presenting with pelvic pain to a gynaecology clinic proved to have no obvious organic pathology. Explanations for the cause of the illness include as yet undetected physical pathology such as infection in the fallopian tubes and abnormal psychophysiological processes such as stress induced vascular congestion in the pelvic area. As with other chronic pain syndromes, such as low back pain, the longer the pain has been experienced the weaker the relationship between noxious stimulation and pain intensity. For a given patient the original cause of pelvic pain may have been resolved, but pain may still be experienced even where there is little evidence of a pathological process. In a proportion of patients, however, physiological processes such as vascular congestion are implicated. Patients who have been trained in relaxation methods, which are known to influence vascular flow to the pelvic region, show improved pain control.

Social influences may also be important in the control of the subjective and behavioural components of chronic pain. Laboratory experiments have shown that instructing people to expect pain is associated with subjects reporting a given level of stimulation as painful, whereas in other circumstances where no such expectation is given the same level of stimulation is not reported as painful. For chronic pain patients it may be expected that patients with prior experience of pain may be more attuned to physiological changes and may expect particular activities to be painful, and therefore they may more readily label sensations as painful. In a patient with a history of abdominal disease such processes may partially account for pain reporting in the absence of profound or continued pathology.

Experimental studies have shown that where subjects believe they are in control of the occurrence of painful events greater tolerance of pain is achieved. For the chronic pelvic pain patient repeated procedures and investigations may induce a sense of helplessness. A therapeutic goal therefore is to improve the patient's perceived control over pain. This may be achieved through preparing the patient so that they are able to understand the likely effects of invasive investigations and physical treatments, and by helping the patient to gain control over pain levels by reducing the anxiety component of pain through relaxation training. Control over the anxiety component may be particularly important as anxiety is known to reduce the threshold for the detection of pain, and it may also act by triggering abnormal blood flow to the pelvic region, and hence influence the physiological component of the condition.

Pain is a subjective experience, and the observer only knows a person is in pain by their behaviour. Even for acute pain induced in a laboratory or by medical/dental procedures, social influences affect pain expression and other pain behaviours such as guarding movements, limping, and taking analgesics. Fordyce, a clinical psychologist in Seattle, USA, has shown that pain patients exhibit more pain behaviours when they believe their spouse is watching them through a one-way mirror than when they were told they were in the company of less sympathetic persons. The degree to which patients' normal activities are impeded by pain behaviours is also subject to psychological control. This is put to therapeutic effect where staff attention is switched from pain behaviours such as lying down and disengaging from physiotherapy exercises and switched to the achievement of therapeutic activity goals. Where systematic application of social reinforcement is carried out by the staff and the patient's spouse, patients can learn to improve their overall functional capacity. These techniques have been used to great effect with mixed chronic pain patients in in-patient facilities, and discussion of the relationship between patients' pain behaviours and social reinforcement are an integral part of the behavioural treatment of pain problems such as chronic pelvic pain (Fordyce 1976).

Pearce, Knight and Beard (1982) compared relaxation training with behavioural counselling, non-directive psychotherapy and a no-treatment control condition for 32 patients suffering from chronic pelvic pain with no obvious pathology of six or more months duration. The patients kept a record of pain for one month before surgical investigation, throughout psychological treatment, and for three months afterwards. All patients were seen for four to six sessions over two to three months. Patients in the three treatment groups all showed some improvement in pain-free days, but relaxation training and non-directive psychotherapy showed greatest improvement by one year follow-up.

Additional techniques that have been effective with patients suffering other chronic pain syndromes such as headache include stress management training, similar to that described earlier in the treatment of stress disorders. Direct modification of the patient's experience of pain by hypnosis similar to that described below for acute burns pain can also be useful, particularly if patients are taught to induce a hypnotic state for themselves. This is particularly useful where the patient's pain diary shows that pain occurs at predictable times or in response to specific stimuli such as stressful meetings at work. In this way, patients can not only apply hypnosis once the pain has started, but it can be applied preventatively.

Psychological treatment of acute burns injury

Gary Adams' problems were discussed earlier, and were identified as:

1. Failure to comply with the medical regime of increased protein and calorie intake leading to delayed healing, and failure to comply with physiotherapy exercises leading to reduced movement and the development of contractures.
2. Depression.
3. Fear of repeated painful procedures.
4. Distress and fear for his own life and guilt associated with the accident and the prospect of long-term disability.

Initial discussions focused on explaining the interrelatedness of his problems, and how his own emotional behaviour could influence his recovery.

A behavioural contract was drawn up which specified the behavioural goals (i.e. the behaviours required of the patient) plus the rewards for achievement of the goals. The patient agreed that the main reward would be seeing his grafts 'take'. A short-term reward such as being accompanied by a nurse he had befriended on trips in a wheelchair outside the hospital would be useful. Staff were also instructed to comment on his progress.

The anaesthetist was reluctant to increase his medication, which could further reduce his appetite and could lead to the possibility of morphine addiction and of respiratory failure. Gary was instructed that he would have to tolerate the painful burn dressing changes with only the help of mild analgesics such as paracetamol. In order to relieve the patient's fear, he was taught to identify fearful thoughts and substitute less fearful thoughts. For example, he was taught to substitute 'I know it will hurt' with more positive self statements such as 'it will not be worse than before'. He was taught to practise using more positive thoughts and also to reward himself when he coped well. He felt it was difficult to concentrate during the dressing changes so a guided imagery technique was used. He was taught to distract himself and dissociate his thoughts away from his body. He found he could concentrate on imagining himself walking along the bank of a river, which he used to do when he wanted to relax and unwind.

To reduce the muscle tension caused by involuntary tremors and involuntary muscle tension or guarding movements, he was taught behavioural relaxation techniques. As he was unable to tense up certain muscle groups he was taught a simple self-suggestion method focusing on increasing feelings of warmth and heaviness in each muscle group and by deep breathing exercises. Finally, a self-hypnosis procedure was taught in order to enable the patient to remain in a light trance. He was a responsive subject and also learned not only how to dissociate himself from his body, but also develop feelings of numbness in the most painful parts of the body. The psychologist attended several burn dressing changes in order to coach Gary and encourage him to use the techniques.

Finally, the patient was most fearful for his own safety. He began to discuss the fate of his friend with the clinical psychologist. Although he was shocked to learn that his friend had died, he had suspected this. Now the matter had been brought up he was able to grieve for his friend openly and was encouraged to discuss his feelings. When it became apparent that his thoughts included a number of cognitive distortions typical of depression, a cognitive restructuring approach was initiated to help the patient learn to substitute more rational thoughts for irrational thoughts associated with his dysphoric mood. As much of his depression was associated with helplessness, the principle of behavioural contracting in order to encourage Gary to develop a feeling of control over his environment was extended to other activities. For example, where there was some particularly important social goal, such as having a visit from a friend who was only able to visit at certain irregular intervals, he was able to earn access outside the normal visiting arrangements provided that he had achieved the behaviour specified in the contract, such as wearing an uncomfortable pressure garment, eating, or attending to his personal hygiene as required.

Although many psychological hurdles remained for this patient at the time he was discharged from hospital, such as the problems of being disfigured, he reported that he no longer felt depressed, and he attributed most of his improvement to the feeling of self-control which was engendered by learning to control the fear of pain associated with the many painful procedures which he had repeatedly undergone for several months. He also resolved his feelings of guilt concerning the accident by 'trading off' his painful hospitalization against his past misdeeds.

The psychological assessment and treatment of Gary Adams illustrates some of the complexity of the relationship between psychological and physical problems and of the multi-faceted nature of clinical intervention.

Consultation

Where there is limited time available from the clinical psychologist, and where other staff are in more direct contact with patients on a regular basis, the clinical psychologist may choose not to accept individual referrals of patients, but to advise staff on the management of particular patients, or on strategies for preventing or managing frequently occuring psychological problems. The example noted earlier of the clinical psychologist looking at staff communication in the coronary care unit is one such example.

In some renal dialysis units, a clinical psychologist has provided support and advice to nursing and medical staff as an indirect means of providing a service to the patient. Nichols' works in a renal unit in Exeter provides such a service. A major concern of the staff who have regular contact with the patients while on dialysis is to find ways of helping the patients to cope with chronic illness and with the strain that this puts on the families of the young and old patients alike. Making a determined effort to retain and regain ability to carry out normal activities rather than to sink into the role of a chronic invalid requires considerable motivation. Psychologists may counsel individual patients, but they also have a role to play in training staff to detect patients who are under severe stress and to develop and support their ability to counsel patients appropriately (Nichols 1981).

Staff may also request help in dealing with service problems. The author was invited to investigate whether the trend towards shorter hospital stay for minor gynaecological surgery was harmful, and whether it was beneficial for some women (Wallace, in press). It was found that day-case patients were more anxious before surgery, and more often unable to be discharged on the evening surgery than expected. These unplanned overnight stays were costly to the hospital, and caused social disruption for the patients. Interviews with patients before and after the operation showed that anxious patients had slower or more complicated recovery. The next stage was to find a way of reducing fear and increasing patients' ability to cope with post-operative pain and other minor complications. It became clear from interviews with the patients that much of the fear was the result of fear of the unknown. Most of the patients had little idea how much pain to expect, or of the effectiveness of post operative medication or of other methods of relieving post-operative pain like lying in particular positions or by using relaxation tapes. The staff believed they were already giving adequate verbal informa-tion to the patients, and yet much of this information was not under-stood or remembered. The staff were willing to assess whether a booklet containing information about surgery, how to cope with fear and pain, and the particular ward routines associated with being a day case or an overnight stay case would be effective in improving patients' adjustment to surgery and recovery. A subsequent study showed that patients who received the informative booklet, in comparison to patients receiving a minimally informative 'placebo' booklet or who received a routine verbal explanation only, were less anxious before the operation, experienced less pain after the opera-tion and recovered faster both while in hospital and during the first week after discharge home. Consultation with the staff in this way suggested several options for improving the service, such as provid-ing information for day case patients prior to their admission to hospital, in order to avoid unplanned overnight stays.

Research

The research skills of clinical psychologists may be used to investigate the causes of health problems such as the role of stress in coronary heart disease, or the development of psychological treatment such as stress management training, or the more effective medical management of ill patients by using psychological models of patients' understanding of their illness in order to tailor information to patients about their illness and the benefits of treatment. Research skills may be used to investigate service problems such as the causes and some solutions to staff stress in particular medical environments, such as Intensive Care and Coronary Care units.

An example of theory-based research is provided by Grossmarth-Maticke and colleagues in Heidelberg who have been developing a model of the relationship between psychological adjustment and development of cancer. Much of their work is based on research supporting the view that cancer-prone patients are characterized by a particular cognitive style involving suppression of emotions, particularly aggression, low self-esteem, and lack of assertion. They have carried out recent studies examining whether the psychotherapy aimed at changing these characteristics will alter the course of the disease. Patients suffering advanced breast cancer were offered chemotherapy. Those patients who accepted and those patients who refused were further divided into two groups and given 30 h psychotherapy or no psychotherapy. The results showed that chemotherapy improved the survival by an average of 2.8 months, while psychotherapy improved survival by 3.6 months. The combination of chemotherapy and psychotherapy had a synergistic effect. That is, the improvement in survival time was on average 22.4 months, which exceeded the expected improvement in survival of 4.7 months which would occur if the effects of chemotherapy and psychotherapy were simply additive. In a second study the authors showed that a specific type of cognitive behavioural treatment aimed at improving patients' expression of emotion, their interpersonal behaviour, and self-esteem was associated with greatest survival (Grossmarth-Maticek, Schmidt, Vetter, and Arndt 1984).

This work is new and requires replication. However it shows not only considerable promise as a practical form of clinical intervention, but also demonstrates how research can lead to specific psychological treatments linked to a careful analysis of psychological factors involved in the development of the disease. If these methods are as effective as the study suggests, clinical psychologists may contribute not only to the reduction of the stress associated with cancer treatments and diagnosis of cancer, but also to improving patients' survival.

Planning and evaluation of health care systems

The clinical psychologist's research and clinical skills can make a useful contribution to the design of health care systems. For example, the clinical psychologist can draw upon research into patient's health beliefs and their response to fear-provoking health messages in designing health promotion programmes. In the case of smoking cessation programmes, research suggests that in the UK most people understand the link between smoking and cancer, and that most people have made several partially successful attempts to give up smoking. Health promotion messages designed at helping people who want to quit and to plan to prevent their relapse are effective as well as health promotion messages aimed at motivating patients to making further attempts to give up smoking.

A number of health authorities now have health promotion teams which include a psychologist. The clinical psychologist's role in this instance is to help bring about change in health authority policy, thereby facilitating changes in the behaviour of health care professionals as well as changes in the behaviour of individual people.

SPECIAL ISSUES

A recurrent theme in this chapter is the extent to which patients should be involved in their health care. This includes whether they should be informed in order to take decisions affecting their treatment, their rights to refuse treatment, their responsibility to accept and comply with treatment, and the extent to which information about patients' prognosis or treatment will adversely or positively affect their health. Such issues involve complex physical, legal, and psychosocial factors and are not solved by putting the responsibility entirely on the staff or on the patients. However, some of the issues are capable of clarification by systematic clinical observation and by clinical research. For example, an extension of the concern of doctors about the effect of cancer treatments on patients' quality of life is to investigate the patients' judgments of the overall worthwhileness of treatments. Some clinical trials have shown that most patients did not judge as worthwhile a treatment which promised only a moderate improvement in survival of a few weeks when they underwent chemotherapy that caused considerable side effects. An intriguing study of patients in Liverpool by Jennifer Ashcroft (Ashcroft, Leinster, and Slade 1985) sought to establish whether patients who were given the choice between two apparently equally effective treatments for breast cancer had better psychological adjustment than patients who were not given such a choice. Interestingly, she found that initially the patients experienced considerable difficulty in taking this decision. A form of structured decision-making analysis, including analysis of the individual's perceived costs and benefits of the two treatments which formed the basis of a counselling interview, enabled all patients to make an informed decision. The results showed that patients were more satisfied and showed fewer signs of depression than would have been expected from previous studies of patients where no such choice has been given. Later work may show whether these benefits are maintained if and when disease re-occurs, or whether the greater perceived responsibility for treatment choice results in greater anger on reoccurrence, and therefore to greater adverse psychological effects. Other ethical issues such as the types of information patients need to achieve informed consent are also susceptible to empirical analysis.

CONCLUSION

The clinical psychologist as a member of the health care team for physical diseases is a new development. The development of psychological services will depend on continued research into the processes of psychological factors in illness and health behaviour and the quality of life of physically ill patients, particularly those suffering from chronic disease, which are so seldom completely remedied by medical treatment.

REFERENCES

Ashcroft, J. J., Leinster, S., and Slade, P. D. (1985). Breast cancer—patient choice of treatment. Preliminary communication. *J. R. Soc. Med.* **78**, 43–6.

Becker, M. H. and Maiman, L. H. (1975). Sociobehavioural determinants of compliance with health and medical care recommendations. *Med. Care* **13** (1), 10–14.

Fordyce, W. E. (1976). *Behavioural method in chronic pain and illness*. Mosby, St Louis.

Grossmarth-Maticek, R., Schmidt, P., Vetter, H., and Arndt, S. (1984). Psychotherapy research in oncology. In *Health care and human behaviour* (ed. A. Steptoe and A. Mathews). *Health* Academic Press, London.

Maguire, G. P., Julier, D. L., Hawton, K. E., and Bancroft, J. H. J. (1974). Psychiatric morbidity and referral on two general medical wards. *Br. med. J.* **I**, 268–70.

Morrow, G. R. and Morrell, C. (1982). Behavioural treatment for the anticipatory nausea and vomiting induced by cancer chemotherapy. *New Engl. J. Med.* **307**, 1476–80.

Nichols, K. A. (1981). Psychological Care in general hospitals. *Bull. Br. Psychol. Soc.* **34**, 90–4.

Pearce, S. and Beard, R. W. (1984). Chronic pelvic pain. In *Psychology and gynaecological problems* (ed. A. K. Broome and L. M. Wallace). Tavistock, London.

Peace, S., Knight, C., and Beard, R. W. (1982). Pelvic pain—a common gynaecological problem. *J. Psychosom. Obstet. Gynaecol.* **I**, 12.

Turk, D. C., Meichenbaum, D., and Genest, M. (1983). *Pain and behavioural medicine: a cognitive behavioural perspective*. Guilford Press, New York.

Varni, J. N. (1983). *Clinical behavioural paediatrics: an interdisiplinary biobehavioural approach*. Pergamon Press, Oxford.

Wallace, L. M. (in press). Day-case laparoscopy: patient preferences, adjustment and recovery. *Eur. J. Psychosom. Obstet. Gynaecol.*

Wallace, L. M., and Joshi, M. (in press). Video-tape modelling of communication skills in a coronary care unit. *Intensive Care Nursing*.

Zigmond, A. S. and Snaith, P. P. (1983). The Hospital Anxiety Depression Scale. *Acta psychiat. scand.* **67**, 361–70.

FURTHER READING

Bernstein, N. R. (1976). *Emotional care of the facially burned and disfigured*. Little, Brown and Company, Boston.

Broome, A. K. and Wallace, L. M., ed. (1984). *Psychology and gynaecological problems*. Tavistock, London.

Everly, G. A. and Rosenfeld, R. (1981). *The nature and treatment of the stress response: a practical guide for clinicians*. Plenum Press, New York.

Meichenbaum, D. (1983). *Coping with stress*. Century Books, London.

Nichols, K. A. (1984). *Psychological care in physical illness*. Croom Helm, London.

Steptoe, A. and Mathews, A., ed. (1984). *Health care and human behaviour*. Academic Press, London.

Wallace, L. M. (1982). The heart of the matter: a clinical psychologist in coronary care. *Bull. Br. psychol. Soc.* **35**, 379–382.

Wilson-Barnett, J. (1980). *Stress in hospital: patients' psychological reactions to illness and health care*. Churchill Livingstone, Edinburgh.

10

Working with other professions
John Hall

It is just about possible to imagine a clinical psychologist practising in isolation, seeing patients who refer themselves directly with minimal contact with other health care staff. However, in most settings a psychologist will be involved with members of other professional groups from the very moment that a referral is made. Apart from a psychologist's concern with identified patients and their families, many psychologists will be concerned with other aspects of the local health care system, such as helping to run a day centre, or planning a new service for people dependent on drugs. If a doctor makes a referral, or a manager makes a request, this suggests they have some knowledge of the contribution that psychologists can make to the care of that patient. How was that knowledge acquired?

WHO ARE THE OTHER PROFESSIONALS?

Professions and professional boundaries relate mainly to particular diagnostic or therapeutic skills; they may also relate to pay and status, or to patterns of authority. They have arisen because the amount of technical information on health care is so great, and the range of clinical skills so varied, that no one person could possibly be expected to be conversant with them all.

These boundaries are not fixed, nor are they impermeable. New health care professions arise, such as Health Educators, and old health care professions, such as nurses specially trained to care for people with infectious disease, decline. Relationships with and between similar professional groups can change. Some people may be trained in more than one health-care profession. Indeed, a proportion of clinical psychologists have previously been nurses or therapists of some sort (such as occupational therapists) before retraining.

But these boundaries do exist, and an important part of a clinical psychologist's job is to recognize the boundaries, and to work with people on the other side, maybe changing the boundary in the process. This suggests identifying the main other professional groups with which a clinical psychologist will work, and the main ways in which collaboration can and does occur.

The concept of 'profession'

The latter part of the nineteenth century saw the emergence of groups such as engineers and architects, complete with their own institutions. As striving for 'professional' status has been a constant theme in this century, sociologists have tried to identify the characteristics of a profession, suggesting that a profession is defined by possession of a body of specialized knowledge; a monopoly of practice in a field of work; an acceptance that fellow members of a profession are adjudged competent to assess the work of a member; and an ideology of service to clients.

The two major professional groups in health care, doctors and nurses, developed gradually from the middle of the last century, in England dating from the establishment of the General Medical Council for doctors in 1858. However, the development of a profession's standards has to take account of external pressures, the realities of finance, and availability of people able to do the job. An examination of the variation in length and type of training of clinical psychologists in different European countries shows how these pressures and realities continue to operate today. Even now, the length and standard of training of some professions is changing, as some therapist groups have moved to a graduate-level degree training course.

The introduction of the term 'semi-professions' by Etzioni indicates that some professions may be more professional than others! Certainly within health care professions, medicine has achieved an ascendancy over most other clinical care groups, to the extent that they may control, or 'prescribe' the therapeutic actions taken by members of other groups. Where the medical profession does not have prescriptive or legal control over another group, and where it cannot be seen to possess knowledge which encompasses that of the other group, then negotiation has to take place on how members of each profession relate to doctors, and negotiation has to take place between members of each of those professions generally.

Since professions have a strong internal organization, trainees of each profession pick up the assumptions and views of their trainers, and can develop a distinctive ethos of their own quite early in their training. This professional ethos may have an influence greater than bare details of training would suggest. For example, rehabilitation is a major area of involvement of occupational therapists and physiotherapists, the two major remedial therapy professions in Britain. Alaszewski (1979) gives a fascinating account of how these two professions view their contribution to the rehabilitation process differently. He suggests that there are three modes of performing the medical task: by preventing disease, by curing it, or by alleviating it. Also staff may approach a medical task either by concentrating on the whole person—taking a holistic approach—or by concentrating on techniques—taking a technique-oriented approach. Alaszewski points out that, in general, physiotherapists favour a curative, technique-oriented ideology, while occupational therapists favour an alleviative holistic ideology. He points out the difficulties this would lead to in merging the two present groups into one new integrated profession, although some degree of joint professional training could reduce these differences. Similar issues could arise between those clinical psychologists who may have studied sociology or social psychology as undergraduates, and their undergraduate classmates who have become social workers.

Professional views and standards thus have a range of functions. They clarify the nature of the task each group can perform; they provide a set of guidelines of inter-professional conduct; they can protect both professional and client. Conversely, professional differences can be over-rigid, and can fail to cope with changing patterns of health need and professional skill; they can hamper collaboration in helping individual patients; and they can lead to confused communication. Understanding the ethos of other professions is a prerequisite for working with them.

Working with doctors

Doctors are, in virtually every country, the most influential professional group in health care. Because of the central position of doctors in any health care system, it is essential that as a group they are aware of the clinical implications of developments in psychological theory and practice, and aware how psychologists both can provide a service and can assist them to modify their own practice accordingly. Chapter 9 gives examples of the relevance of psychological procedures for some clinical problems in general medicine.

In most countries there is a clear separation between the 'general practice', 'family medicine', or 'primary care' type of practice, and the specialist practice of a particular branch of medicine, such as neurology. While in Britain these two areas of practice are highly, but not totally, separated, in many European countries a family doctor will also have an associated specialist practice. The relationship between these two branches of practice has changed in recent years, but the family doctor usually occupies a key position in the care of the individual patient. Chapter 8 describes Goldberg and Huxley's 'Filter model' of referral by family doctors, indicating the pivotal role of family doctors in steering patients to specialized treatments.

Patterns of training for doctors are also changing: although different countries have a differing emphasis on pre-clinical experience, traditionally the neophyte doctor spends a period of two to three years studying ' pre-clinical' subjects, such as anatomy and biochemistry, before being exposed to 'clinical' subjects by direct contact with patients who are attending clinics and wards associated with the medical school. This separation means that the trainee doctor cannot be expected to easily integrate his medical 'clinical' knowledge with his pre-clinical knowledge. There have thus been attempts to introduce some clinical contact much earlier in the basic 'scientific' training, and correspondingly to introduce scientific topics at a time when they can be related to clinical phenomena. All of these developments have prompted a growth of interest in the process of professional acculturation by medical students and in the process of acquisition of the relevant skills, and thus promoted a development of behavioural science teaching from the very beginning of the medical course. From a psychological viewpoint, the more that relevant teaching of topics such as doctor–patient communication can be integrated with early clinical experience, the more trainee doctors are likely to absorb a psychological perspective to their work.

Following basic training, doctors usually follow some course of specialized training. Some medical specialities have a high proportion of psychological content in their future training, the best examples being paediatricians and psychiatrists. In these specialities some knowledge of developmental psychology, (for example, parent–child bonding and normal language development) and normal psychology (for example, psychology of small groups) respectively is essential, so that clinical psychologists come to have a specialized teaching role for these specialities. This implies that psychologists with the relevant professional knowledge are themselves available, not only to become familiar with the clinical practice of the speciality but to make the trainee doctors aware of some of the conceptual difficulties in their fields.

Working with nurses

Nurses constitute the largest staff group in a health care system. They are the people who will have the closest day-to-day contact with patients in hospital, and who both in hospital and in the community have to carry out the most personal tasks for people who cannot look after themselves. A group of nurses on a ward often have to provide a 24-h service every day, so that at any time of the night they may have to deal with medical—or psychological—emergencies or sudden outbursts of disturbed behaviour. While a particular doctor will have medical responsibility for a patient, many of the minor —and indeed major—worries of the patient will be shared with and solved by the first available nurse, who may be relatively junior and inexperienced.

Because nursing is the key caring health profession, continued recruitment of nurses is essential to a health care system. A lot of psychological attention has accordingly focused on the way in which interest develops in potential nurses, and why nurses withdraw from training. It has been suggested that a third of all 18-year-old girls in Britain, for example, have been interested in nursing at some time in their lives. Yet the young nursing student is confronted with illness, suffering, and dying in a way that young people starting other jobs are not, exposing student nurses to considerable personal stress. Perhaps as a result, voluntary withdrawal from training is much more common for nurses than for other health care groups. Another study suggested that many nurses who smoke may start to smoke during their nursing training: together these findings suggest that day-to-day contact with patients is personally demanding, and those nurses should be helped to develop support mechanisms for coping with this stress.

BURN-OUT IN HEALTH CARE STAFF

One of the appeals of working as a doctor or a nurse is the idea of 'working with people'. Many texts on psychology and nursing, for example, focus on the interpersonal elements of nursing, often described as nurse–patient interaction. From the patient's point of view, the quality of the human relationship with those looking after him is extremely important, as evidenced by such phrases as 'a good bedside manner'. Qualities such as warmth, sensitivity, and respect for the patient are encouraged in all sorts of care situations, quite apart from their value in more intense one-to-one therapeutic relationships.

However, while the patient may want such qualities in the staff about him, it is not easy for those staff always to display them. Particular types of setting are associated with higher levels of stress, so that nurses on medical wards show higher levels of stress than nurses on surgical wards. Wards with high rates of death on them, such as intensive care units and terminal care units, are also associated with high stress levels. The end result of this type of stress has been called 'burn-out'. Burn-out describes a range of responses to increased emotional demands, such as emotional detachment, cynicism, and an unwillingness to admit to having emotional needs. Burn-out can be seen, of course, in a number of other professional groups where there are high personal and emotional demands, such as clergymen and policemen, and where there may be a lack of support from others.

What can be done about this? From a psychological point of view, it may be possible to offer a psychological analysis of burn-out, and then do something to relieve the problem. Llewellyn (1984) describes an approach to helping cope with burn-out based on Personal Construct Theory, a theory put forward by Kelly which proposes that people are essentially trying to make sense of the world around them, and relate events according to their own constellation of 'constructs', which are based on each individual's own life history and beliefs. A valuable part of this theory is the way in which it has yielded a technique known as a Repertory Grid, which is a graphical way of representing the construct system of an individual. The relevance of this to coping with the burn-out is that it helps to explain what is happening to both patient and nurse in what may be a very confusing situation. For the patient, all sorts of strange things will be happening, with threatening medical procedures and an endless stream of strange new people, each anxious to ask about this or take a drop of blood for that. A general approach to the patient which accepts that they will interpret these events differently, and positively need help to make sense of their experiences, will offer more support to the patient. For the nurse, it emphasizes the value of exposing hidden anxieties: a hidden anxiety cannot be tested or rejected. The nurse in the frontline then needs to be supported by others alive to these anxieties and stresses, and with some skills in resolving them.

Another psychological analysis of this issue has been made by Winefield (1984). She points out that social support consists of information and practical components, as well as emotional ones, and that social support does not just happen, but has to be obtained or elicited from those about us. People who feel unsupported in a stressful professional situation may therefore have help potentially available to them, but be unsure how to elicit that help. Drawing on the literature concerning patterns of social interaction in lonely and depressed people, Winefield goes on to suggest how to help people elicit help. If some people in a situation feel support, and others do not, what can we observe about the supported people that differentiates them from the others? 'Remedial help' for unsupported people would, for example, focus on social norms of intimacy and its reciprocation, knowing when and how to complain. This type of analysis, applicable to patient and staff alike, could give an added dimension to more straightforward advice usually given to staff feeling under pressure.

The demands made on nurses vary widely from one setting to another so that some nursing, such as in operating theatres, is highly technical while other fields of nursing, such as work with mentally handicapped people, is primarily interpersonal and social. Some nurses work entirely within a specialist unit , such as a coronary care unit, and others, such as community psychiatric nurses, work entirely in the community. Some countries train nurses as polyvalent; some specialize from the start of basic training; some specialize after a common basic training. Basic standards of training vary greatly, ranging in Europe from completion of primary studies to university admission level, although those countries who are members of the EEC have signed an agreement which will lead to more consistency in standards of training. For all these reasons, the assumptions that can be made about the level of psychological knowledge and skill in nurses vary greatly. Yet there are an increasing number of reputable nursing journals and texts that demonstrate an increasing psychological sophistication among at least a proportion of nurses. As more nurses become psychologically informed—partly a product of a number of people being doubly qualified as nurses and psychologists—this sophistication, and demand for more psychologically orientated training and support, is likely to grow.

Nurses are the people who potentially have the greatest knowledge of a patient's day-to-day behaviour. They also often have the closest, if not the only, knowledge of patient's relatives. Equally important is the fact that careful observation of ward interaction between nurses and patients shows that it is the more junior or less well-trained staff who usually interact more with patients. From a psychological viewpoint perhaps the less well-trained staff actually have more potential to change patients' attitudes and behaviour than the better trained senior staff who are necessarily involved in other tasks. If that view is correct, it carries major implications for the design of staff training programmes, both for who should be trained, and the level of knowledge and literacy that can be assumed of trainees.

Working with remedial therapists

After doctors and nurses, the members of the various therapeutic professions are the most numerous, dignified by such catch-all phrases as 'paramedics' or 'ancillary professions'! The diversity already noted in nurse training and differentiation is even greater with this group. While in Britain the two major professions in this group are called physiotherapy and occupational therapy, kinesitherapy and ergotherapy are parallel titles used in other countries. Since the professions use complementary techniques, despite the differences in attitude already noted, they are often grouped together as the 'physical therapies'.

The importance of these professions is that, for many patients, they provide the main rehabilitative daytime activity for patients in hospital. Many of the activities are highly intensive, and may involve a lot of physical contact between therapist and patient. Apart from the technical nature of therapy offered, a physical therapist also potentially offers a strongly supportive relationship to their patient, this being particularly apparent when patients are recovering from traumatic accidents. People—often active young men—who have, for example, had a severe spinal injury will spend several months having regular physiotherapy with usually young women therapists. In this setting, as in others, physical therapists need to know how to use the relationships they become involved in, and how to cope with the problems that arise.

There are many specific issues in different branches of physical therapy that can be analysed in psychological terms. Measurement of progress in rehabilitation requires careful assessment of such subjective or complex phenomenon as pain and gait. Just as many people do not comply with a prescribed medical regime, so some people do not use a prosthesis or physical aid as prescribed, and need instruction and guidance to use it properly. Should activity regimes provide a relatively modest level of stimulation for, say, 2 or 3h, or provide a more demanding level of stimulation for ½h?

Speech therapists are a particular group of therapists concerned to alleviate defective speech patterns, and to correct acquired speech defects after, for example, a stroke. They have a special training in speech development and linguistics, and thus necessarily need to be familiar with a number of psychological concepts. For all these therapists, and others such as audiologists, their significance to psychologists lies in the length of time they are in contact with the patient, and the significance of a particular skill they offer to the patient.

Working with social workers

The boundary between health care and social care has always been loose and moveable yet people's needs often require that the two systems of care work closely together. Different countries organize the two sets of services differently, so that even within the UK there are major differences between England, where the health and social services agencies are separated, and Northern Ireland, where one agency organizes both services. Depending on differences between the organization of the health services and social services, issues such as differing degrees of responsiveness to local political opinion, differing methods and time-scales of financial budgeting, and differing styles of professional accountability, may loom large as matters requiring resolution.

This suggests that a certain degree of political sophistication is required from a clinical psychologist working with both health and social care agencies.

To the extent that the organization of services dictates the training and roles, there is thus a huge diversity in the range of work undertaken by 'social workers'. There may be generic field workers providing a comprehensive service to a population including everything from arranging adoptions to supporting the families of people currently in prison; there may be specialist field workers funded by religious or voluntary bodies providing services to a particular client group such as alcoholics; there may be specialist workers attached to day or residential units, such as a day centre for elderly people.

In some of these functions, a social services department may lack staff with skills to provide the best sort of help. Indeed, it is noticeable in Britain that one of the greatest uses made by social services departments of clinical psychologists is in providing advice on day care, or in special residential settings for children. It is likely that a social services department will be presented with other highly specific demands, such as improving the selection of foster parents, or of developing a community programme for substance abusers— glue sniffers— which a clinical psychologist may be best equipped to manage. These two examples give an indication of the type of advice that a wide range of voluntary agencies may also seek from clinical psychologists, so that the psychologist's role with respect to these agencies becomes that of a true 'consultant'.

Other professions associated with clinical psychology

The main professional groups with which clinical psychologists work are doctors, nurses, remedial therapists, and social workers. In addition, they work with a number of other professions, or people working in health care who do not readily fit into existing professional 'slots'. This is due to the appearance of totally new techniques, the realization that a specific established technique does not require more than a specific range of skills to apply it, or the wish to utilize existing skills outside the conventional health care system.

Chapter 4 indicates some of the work done by educational psychologists with children; depending on the way in which countries organize their health and education services, there may be an integrated profession of child psychology, seeing children with problems irrespective of how the problems present, or two separate professions. In a similar way, clinical psychologists may often have very close links with teachers, particularly if the psychologists are working in a special day or residential unit (e.g. for disturbed adolescents, for children who have committed serious offences and are in special units, or for multiply-handicapped children).

Another allied profession is that of 'health educator'. Until the last 15 years or so, positive public education in health promotion was very limited, and in Britain often carried out by health visitors, a group of community nurses often known as public health nurses in other countries. A positive decision was then made to encourage health promotion, and many people now working as health educators have a background in nursing, teaching, and increasingly in psychology. Their concerns with 'health care routines' and 'health beliefs' can be seen as highly psychological, and there is plenty of scope for collaboration between psychologists and such workers. Indeed, members of many professions may have a mutual concern for health-education, prevention, or promotion—perhaps relating to a common problem such as smoking—which overrides their profession of origin.

TEAMWORK

Good teamwork has been mentioned in several other chapters in this book, such as the chapter dealing with work with physically handicapped people. Teamwork obviously assumes the existence of a team—a group of people who work co-operatively with each other. Teams in health care vary in their composition, and fall into three categories. They may be made up of groups of people of the same profession, who usually are of varying levels of expertise and experience within that profession. Thus nursing teams will consist of one or more ward charge nurses or head nurses who clearly organize the work of registered or qualified nurses, and a number of assistant or learner nurses. Secondly teams may be made up of members of different professions, where a member of one specified profession —usually medical—specifies the work of the whole team: an excellent example is the group of staff in an operating theatre, where the operating surgeon is very clearly in charge of the operation.

A third option exists: where members of different professions are in the team, but where no one profession inevitably carries prime responsibility for all the work done by a team. Such multi-disciplinary teams may have either a management function or a clinical function—sometimes both. Where clinical psychologists work as team members it is very often in teams of this third and last type. A team of workers at Brunel University in Britain have been working to clarify some of the organisational and structural concepts implicit in team working, and a series of publications by them illuminate a number of difficulties inherent in team working (Øvretveit 1984). Multi-disciplinary team work is seen by some as impeding clear executive action, and by others as the only acceptable way for members of different professions to work together. In either case the issues it raises are central to the way in which psychologists relate to members of other professions, and work with them.

As far as management teams are concerned, any health authority will lay down clear lines of authority, and should establish clearly where, in the last resort, responsibility for action lies. Management needs to be constantly reviewing services priorities, and interpreting data on the efficacy of different types of treatment, for example. Clinical psychologists obviously have a role in contributing to management in this way, and if they possess the confidence of their employers or colleagues can appropriately be the chairperson of such teams in, for example, planning a new type of service for mentally handicapped people, or can become the manager of the range of services for mentally ill people.

More typically, however, a clinical psychologist will be contributing to a multi-disciplinary clinical team, where staff are appointed to or seconded to the team for all or part of their work. The activities of this type of team includes the acceptance, diagnosis, and assessment of new cases; the discussion of cases as a group; the determination of appropriate treatment; and the organization of follow-up after treatment. The key questions which immediately arise in such groups are: Who does what? Who is the leader? and Who is responsible for what? The allocation of tasks among members of a team is determined by a number of factors. Usually members of a team will contribute specific skills and knowledge derived from their particular professional training, and will have other more personal knowledge, such as knowledge of a particular locality or of a particular local voluntary group, which may be highly relevant to who does what with a particular patient. A psychologist working in a community mental handicap team, for example, might be expected to contribute particularly to decisions on individual care programmes, and to the design of treatment programmes for specific behavioural problems.

The concept of a 'key worker' is becoming increasingly widely accepted, so that one person is designated as the main link or liaison with an identified patient, so that specific professional skills are seen as secondary to the development of a positive one-to-one relationship between key worker and patient. The 'practice assumptions' of a profession also dictate how work is allocated. Some professions, of which medicine and clinical psychology are examples, organize their work on the assumption that a patient expects to see one individual member of that profession exercising their professional skills during their episode of illness. Nurses, on the other hand, are organized on an 'agency' assumption, so that nurses will change shifts and even wards during the course of a patient's illness.

Leadership of teams may be vested in a member of any professional group who possesses the relevant experience and knowledge. Sometimes leadership in such groups rotates among members according to a set pattern. Sometimes the appropriate leadership of a team may apparently be settled by appeal to the purpose of the team. The example of child guidance teams—teams of child psychiatrists, psychologists, psychotherapists and social workers—in Britain illustrates how different professional orientations may then impose their own pressure on leadership questions. A health-centred orientation, stressing the child's health, suggests medical leadership; an educational orientation, suggesting classroom adjustment and attainment, might favour psychological leadership; a social orientation, emphasizing the effects of family and social conditions, might indicate social work leadership . Yet the nature of child guidance work is such that for any group of children seen, some will have presenting problems mainly in one sphere, other children problems in other spheres. There is no uniform solution to leadership in such teams; what is certain is that as professions other than medicine—not only psychology—offer an increasing proportion of experienced and competent staff, so their claims for leadership of teams are bound to increase.

The title of teamwork is often applied to what is in reality a different style of joint working, which is described by the Brunel workers as a network. In a number of settings, a professional will be a regular contact with members of other professions, but contact will be primarily by telephone or by letter. It is vitally important that communication is good between members of a network, as in a team; but in networks, the total team need not, and often do not, meet face to face. With the move to community services, as opposed to hospital services, health care staff inevitably move away from patterns of joint working, produced by working on a common site, to patterns of working more resembling a network than a team. If this shift is not recognized, staff may be left working with little personal support, with the associated risk of work dissatisfaction and loss of morale.

Since teams are groups of people, a number of findings of social psychology, particularly of the psychology of small groups, help to explain why teams do what they do. Leadership styles, as already implied, are important in inducing members of the group to adopt a unified approach to problems. In any group there needs to be a balance between activities aimed at achieving the group's common objectives, and activities aimed at meeting the social and interpersonal needs of group members. Different group tasks require different levels of thinking and working, so that some group members will then be satisfied with one type of activity, while other group members will be satisfied by others. Team loyalties can become so strong that they supersede other loyalties or responsibilities that individual members should at least bear in mind, so that group tasks become subtlely modified, and a team heads off in a direction different to that which was intended (Øvretveit 1984).

TEACHING AND TRAINING HEALTH CARE PROFESSIONS

A major issue in meeting rising expectations of health care is the limited supply of teachers, not only for training the major health care professions but also for training auxiliary workers. Traditionally teachers at the highest levels of the education system in most countries have not been trained as teachers: whatever skills as teachers they may possess have been obtained by apprenticeship, or by trial and error. However, limited skills obtained in this way are often not adequate to design an educational programme that may be trying to produce a range of specific skills from a student body highly heterogeneous in ability and prior experience.

A World Health Organization report, published in 1973, paid particular attention to the training of teachers in the health care field. The report pointed out the need for teachers, for example, to be able to plan objectives relevant to local needs and to plan instructional strategies to provide varied routes for achieving these objectives. They must also be able to evaluate their own teaching and consider such issues as teacher effectiveness. All of these activities presuppose some knowledge of the extensive educational and psychological literature on these topics. Thus clinical psychologists are often closely concerned with curriculum design and course evaluation, together with members of other professions, to increase the effectiveness of teaching. To take but one example, knowledge of educational evaluation techniques is important to any health care professional who has to do any teaching. Evaluation of a teaching course is usually limited to some assessment of how much knowledge the student has acquired, largely because this type of assessment, involving some sort of set essay or factual questions, is easy to set and use. In many situations, of course, some sort of skill is the desired outcome, whether it be a specific clinical skill, such as learning how to take blood pressure with a mercury sphygmomanometer, or a more interpersonal skill such as knowing how to comfort mothers who have just been delivered of a stillborn child.

Both these types of assessment focus on the gains of skill the student has made: they do not focus on the educational methods used to produce those gains, and thus would not be helpful in designing an improved teaching method. In the example of comforting a mother, a clinical psychologist would explore the range of teaching procedures that could be used: observing an experienced clinician carry out this difficult task; formal teaching on typical reactions of mothers in those circumstances; talking with mothers, or seeing videotapes of mothers, who have been through this painful experience and who can now look back on it and reflect on their feelings; asking students to role play with a 'stooge' mother and videotaping the attempt; or any combination of these. Finding out which combination of methods works best, and working out how to design a practicable training module from the results, requires some evaluation of the methods used, not just of the student.

Psychological knowledge is thus relevant to a wide range of teaching and training situations in a health care system. More specifically we can consider teaching and training members of other professions in psychological knowledge and skills, not forgetting the training of psychologists by members of other professions in *their* skills.

Teaching psychology to other professions

The demand for teaching of psychological topics from other professions is growing: the statutory training syllabuses for many health care professions now require what may be dozens of hours of psychological teaching. Some such syllabuses still imply that the best way to introduce psychology is by teaching a watered-down academic course on general psychology. This approach is nearly always inappropriate: the trainee comes to psychology expecting it to provide the answer to questions his discipline prompts, so a more appropriate introduction is to immediately explore, from a psychological viewpoint, practical problems the trainee encounters. This might include the problem of compliance with medication; how to prepare someone for surgery; why people respond to placebos; how to control pain. Most of these topics can be presented in a way that integrates theory with practice, and presents psychology as relevant to the trainee.

The boundary between psychology and related disciplines such as ethology or anthropology is sometimes unclear, and increasingly psychology is taught as one component in a 'behavioural sciences' course embracing these related disciplines, especially medical sociology. It is usually important that a clinically experienced psychologist is involved in both planning and teaching such a course. There may be an excellent teacher locally available, not technically a clinical psychologist, who can cover some of the teaching, but an increasing number of colleges and training schools for health care professions now employ clinical psychologists for this purpose.

Psychology does pose some problems, when deciding how to teach it. Many students come to the subject ignorant of the experimental nature of the subject; some come with what almost amount to fantasies about the subject, and imagine the subject has a mystery and power that is quite unrealistic. As with any discipline, the subject has its own vocabulary, but the need to define terms carefully can be overlooked by students used to everyday concepts of 'emotion', or 'learning', or 'reward'. The importance of animal experimentation in some fields of psychology can be off-putting to some students, who see reference to animal studies as a reductionist account of human behaviour. For all of these reasons, careful thought has to be given in planning the teaching of psychology to other professions, especially at the beginning of the course.

Training in psychological treatment skills

One important consequence of the development of treatment procedures by clinical psychologists is the realization that members of other professions can, and in some circumstances should, themselves learn to use those procedures. A good example of this development is the training of psychiatric nurses to carry out behavioural training programmes with psychiatric inpatients. Twenty-five years ago a key study by two American clinical psychologists, Ayllon and Michael (1959), showed how nurses were instructed to respond to a range of odd behaviour, such as hoarding rubbish and talking in a 'psychotic' way: the authors themselves acknowledge how casual these instructions were, and how crude a behavioural model of reinforcement was presented to the nurses.

Psychologists are also involved in training in other types of skills to other groups of staff or would-be therapists. The range of skills is considerable, including basic counselling skills; treatment of sexual dysfunction; psychological care of children in hospital; and educational techniques for severely handicapped children at home. The range of people so trained is also wide: family doctors, community nurses, clergy and church workers, parents, marriage guidance counsellors, and voluntary workers in day centres.

When a psychologist becomes involved in direct skill training a number of practical issues become important. Very often the learners have never read a psychological book in their lives, and need to acquire some sort of general psychological perspective along with the particular skills they are acquiring. Scheduling teaching or training sessions into the lives of often very busy learners means that considerable flexibility in fitting in the sessions may be needed—including sessions at 10 or 11 p.m. for night staff. Some learners become over-enthusiastic, so they do not appreciate the limitations of some techniques, and have to be restrained from over-zealous application of the techniques. Despite these demands and problems, many psychologists find this form of training to be one of the most stimulating areas of their work.

A good illustration of how this essentially simple idea has been developed is given by a series of studies by Milne (1986) in a book also concerned with the training of parents and teachers. He carried out a series of carefully planned experiments aimed at producing an effective training package for ward-level staff. He considered the level of sophistication and skill which the nurse needed to acquire: some nurses might only need to become 'applicators' of behavioural techniques, so they could dispense tokens in a highly structured token economy programme. At the other end of the scale, some nurses could become 'nurse therapists', able to assess and treat a wide range of complaints without supervision. This latter level of training has been particularly developed by Professor Isaac Marks and his colleagues at the Institue of Psychiatry at London, who has shown how nurses can function successfully at this level.

Milne examined in detail several components of training nurses in behavioural skills. A five-day training package was developed, which covered 16 main topics in the general areas of assessment of behaviour, learning theory, and techniques of therapy. The training package was designed to use a range of educational techniques, and to be acceptable to nurses who had little or no prior experience of these techniques.

In evaluating the effectiveness of such a training course, it is necessary to use a range of measures of the skills the nurses acquired during the course—obviously a pen-and-paper test could assess knowledge, but a different approach is required to assess skills. Milne used a range of measures, three of which were: a simulated proficiency test, consisting of 10 videotaped nurse–patient interactions, to which the nurse students had to respond; a functional analysis test required the nurses to select a behaviour of their choice from a short videotape, and then to note the frequency of that behaviour and what happened immediately before or after the selected behaviour; and a formulation and treatment plan were to be prepared, again following observation of a videotaped vignette.

Milne found that a first version of his training course did not produce the desired change in behaviour of the nurses when they returned to their wards: the benefits of training had not spread, or generalized, from the teaching setting to the ordinary ward setting. He therefore increased the attention paid to a special project, carried out on the ward by the student, to make sure that these projects were carried out, and then found that the benefits of training were found in the ward.

This series of studies demonstrates very well the detailed attention to content, teaching method, and evaluation which is necessary to make sure that a staff training programme achieves what is intended. The lessons learned from this type of experimentation are of course relevant to the training of direct care staff in *any* treatment modality, and to the training of staff working with the elderly and mentally handicapped, as well as with psychiatric patients.

There is a continuing debate within clinical psychology on the advisability of training other professions in psychological techniques. However, most psychologists in Britain take the view that psychological skills can be usefully acquired by others. In view of the relatively small number of psychologists compared to doctors, nurses, and other therapists (let alone parents and spouses!) perhaps most clinical psychologists should be actively engaged in 'giving away' or sharing their skills.

EVALUATING THE SERVICES PROVIDED

Other chapters have described some of the ways in which psychologists have evaluated their services they themselves provide. For most psychologists, such an evaluation of their own effectiveness, or the effectiveness of the particular unit or team with which they work, will be relatively limited in scope, often concerned with outcome for the patient. There is now an increasing pressure for health care services to demonstrate their effectiveness on a much broader scale, often under circumstances where close experimental control or manipulation of the service is impossible.

This pressure derives from a number of sources. There is public concern about the extent to which widespread discharge of institutionalized patients has not been accompanied by proper community provision. Government may be concerned that public money is used in the most cost-effective manner. Professions may themselves be aware that new patterns of service cannot be convincingly demonstrated to be superior to the old. A spreading interest in some so-called 'fringe' therapies and in the use of non-statutory charities or service-providing agencies is generating new techniques and services that also need appraisal.

Clinical psychologists have a number of contributions to make to evaluating the work of other professions in concert with them. One accepted definition of evaluation is 'the formal determination of the effectiveness, efficiency, and acceptability of a planned intervention in achieving stated objectives' (Holland 1983). Those objectives should be a set of desired outcomes which are attainable, measurable, and sufficient to justify a programme. These definitions indicate the areas where a psychological perspective is most relevant.

First of all, can clear objectives or desired outcomes be stated, and stated in advance in such a way that relevant baseline or pre-intervention measures can be obtained? A psychologist can work with other colleagues to identify and clarify specific goals, which are shared by all—or most—of those concerned with a project.

The evaluation approach also turns attention away from what one profession alone might see as a desirable outcome, to those outcomes which might be desired by patients and by others, such as direct-care staff. This requires that all those groups contribute to the evaluation procedure, and that the results of the evaluation are comprehensible to all those who contribute. Evaluation reports then have to be readable by direct care staff, not just published in scientific journals; they have to be readable by the planners and managers who may have to make difficult decisions of resource allocation on the basis of those results.

One matter of continuing debate that is central to many evaluation projects is what constitutes 'quality of life'. Quality of life is a concept used to supplement the usually simple but essentially rather arid measures of survival or cure rate relevant to some conditions or operations, such as stroke or coronary bypass surgery, where the patient may still encounter significant limitations of everyday activity. In some fields of physical rehabilitation indices of Activities of Daily Living (ADL) have been used as global outcome measures. These are less relevant for people with a primarily non-medical disability, where more comprehensive indices including information on social activity are required, such as the Index of Well-Being (IWB) suggested by one team of workers. All of these more comprehensive measures raise issues of reliability, validity, sensitivity to bias, and utility under service conditions with which psychologists are likely to be familiar.

COMMUNICATING WITH PATIENTS AND WITH STAFF

Some forms of health care can be given without any spoken or written communication, such as emergency resuscitation or giving an injection. However, most care of treatment involves some spoken communication, even if it is only to require some simple response such as opening your mouth or rolling over. For most patients, there will at some stage be a complex series of communications, intended to establish a diagnosis or to advise on treatment, which may include detailed questioning about symptoms, issuing of detailed guidance on, for example, diet, or giving instructions to direct care staff on what they have to do.

Psychologists have been interested in several aspects of this information exchange system, not least because many health care staff do not appreciate how difficult many patients find it to both provide and retain the relevant information. Some patients may have defective senses, so that some artificial communication aid—such as an electronic aid to give a visual display of what is required—or artificial language may be needed. A substantial proportion of patients, certainly 10 to 15 per cent, will not be highly literate, and will simply not understand high-level vocabulary words. This suggests the use of various indices of 'readability' to make sure that instructions are generally comprehensible, although the simplistic application of such formulae is open to criticism.

Another approach is to look at the amount and type of information conveyed to the patient, examining, for example, whether fear-arousing messages to patients work—in other words, do they lead to more compliance with prescribed treatment by patients? Some studies suggest that fear-arousal cannot be strongly advocated on present evidence. However, an approach which examines just the way in which the doctor or patient evaluates that information, is criticized by Tuckett and Williams (1984). Their social–psychological or sociological analysis also draws attention to the social setting within which information is exchanged, particularly

examining the degree of control exerted by doctors in their communication with patients.

There is now a wealth of useful psychological guidance on many
aspects of patient communication, relevant not only to highly
qualified staff but to portering or domestic staff who may have to
deal with a violent patient or visitor. The guidance may relate communication with compliance—how to improve the often 50 per cent
rates with which out-patients take oral medication as prescribed.
The guidance may make sure that the huge range of forms used in
any hospital are comprehensible to the wide range of both staff and
patients who must use them (Wright 1983).

CHAPTER SUMMARY

Clinical psychologists work closely with a wide range of other
professions and people. The significance of these other people to
the life of the individual patient varies considerably—they may
be making a highly sophisticated diagnostic decision, or they may
be engaged in practical 'hands-on' care. There is a psychological
component to all of these tasks. How does the diagnostician obtain
the fullest possible information from the patient? How can direct-
care staff be helped to maintain an individualized and relevant ward
regime month in, month out?

Current practice suggests that clinical psychologists have a
number of key functions with respect to other staff. They can facilitate team-working. They can disseminate psychological knowledge
and skills. They can help to ensure that the most effective treatments
are chosen. Lastly, they can help to promote clear and uncluttered
communication between everyone concerned with the individual
patient.

REFERENCES

Alaszewski, A. (1979). Rehabilitation, the remedial therapy professions and
　social policy. *Social Sci. Med.* **13A**, 431–443.
Ayllon, T. and Michael, J. (1959). The psychiatric nurse as a behavioural
　engineer. *J. Exp. Anal. Behav.* **5**, 343–52.
Holland, W. W. (1983). *Evaluation of health care.* Oxford University Press,
　Oxford.

Llewellyn, S. P. (1984). The cost of giving: emotional growth and emotional stress. In: Skevington, S. *Understanding nurses: the social psychology of nursing*. Wiley, Chichester.

Milne, D. (1986). *Training behaviour therapists: methods, evaluation, and implementation with parents, nurses and teachers*. Croom Helm, London.

Øvretveit, J. (1984). *Organising psychology in the NHS*. Brunel Institute of Organisation and Social Studies, Uxbridge.

Tuckett, D. and Williams, A. (1984). Approaches to the measurement of explanation and information-giving in medical consultations: a review of empirical studies. *Social Sci. Med.* **18**, 571–80.

Winefield, H. R. (1984). The nature and elicitation of social support: some implications for the helping professions. *Behav. Psychother.* **12**, 318–30.

World Health Organization (1973). Training and preparation of teachers for schools of medicine and of allied health services. Geneva. *WHO Technical Report Series No. 521*.

Wright, P. (1983). Informed design for forms. In *Information design the design and evaluation of signs and printed material* (ed. R. Easterby and H. Zwaga). Wiley, Chichester.

FURTHER READING

Bligh, D., Ebrahim, G. J., Jaques, D., and Warren Piper D. (1977). *Teaching students*. EUTS, Exeter.

Davis, H. and Butcher, P. (1985). Sharing psychological skills: training non-psychologists in the use of psychological techniques. *Br. J. med. Psychol.* **58** (3) (Special Issue).

Jaques, E. (1978). *Health services: their nature and organisation, and the role of patients, doctors, nurses, and the complementary professions*. Heinemann, London.

11

Overview and implications

John Marzillier and John Hall

In Britain 40 years ago there were only a handful of clinical psychologists, working as technician scientists in psychiatric hospitals. Like physicists and biochemists they were 'backroom boys' whose contribution to health care consisted of highly specialized scientific investigations, mainly in the form of psychometric tests and investigations. In many other countries in Western Europe clinical psychologists did not exist. Only in the USA had clinical psychology any appreciable history and the development of a professional identity. In the 1980s, the picture is very different. Clinical psychology has become an established profession in many European countries and in the English-speaking areas of Australia, New Zealand, and South Africa. Some countries such as Britain have seen a rapid increase in the number of clinical psychologist particularly over the last decade. Most importantly, as illustrated in the chapters of this book, clinical psychologists have shed their backroom image and have become front line workers in many spheres of health care. Clinical psychologists have had a practical impact on such diverse fields as child health and the elderly, in drug addiction and physical handicap, in psychotherapy, and in staff training. There has been a recognition amongst health care workers, sometimes slowly and painfully gained, that psychology is important and sometimes vital to health care, and that psychologists can and do have a direct and useful influence on health in diverse fields.

The preceding chapters of this book have provided illustrative accounts of the practical working of clinical psychologists in various settings. In this chapter we describe some of the common themes that emerge from those working practices and tentatively discuss their implications for both clinical psychology and for health care in general.

THEORY AND PRACTICE

Clinical psychologists see themselves as 'scientist–practitioners' whether their work is in teaching basic skills to mentally handicapped people, in carrying out intensive psychotherapy with disturbed adolescents, or in evaluating the success of a new environmental programme for institutionalized elderly residents. What does the term 'scientist–practitioner' mean? In Chapter 1 we described how the profession of clinical psychology is based upon a growing knowledge base (the science of psychology) and how the training of clinical psychologists entails using that knowledge for beneficial ends. The application of scientific knowledge is therefore a fundamental feature of clinical psychology, which distinguishes it from the practical 'common-sense psychology' that all of us use in everyday life. For example, in Fielding's chapter we can see how knowledge of normal child development is essential to understanding when a particular behaviour such as encopresis becomes a significant problem. Understanding of the stages and processes of developmental change in young children enables the psychologist to assess a problem in its appropriate context and to tailor interventions to suit the developing child. The same point may be made for adults too, though the process of development takes place over a longer period of time and reflects social and cultural influences, as in the transition from young adult to parent or from worker to retired person. Models of 'science' too are changing, so that psychology has itself grown by, for example, the adoption of ethological concepts and the development of more qualitative, as opposed to quantitative, methods of assessment.

Scientific knowledge consists of facts embedded within theory and psychology is driven by various often competing theories about human behaviour. Theories are vital. They are the lifeblood of our attempts to make sense of our behaviour. Clinical psychology has been influenced by several theories, notably theories about learning processes, and many have directly guided clinical practice. Tennant and Cullen, for example, describe how as psychologists they use learning principles to teach a mentally handicapped person to tie a bow successfully. The behavioural treatment of anxiety illustrated in Chapter 2 arose directly from experimental studies of conditioning in the laboratory. Theories about the way memory operates in terms of different stores and processes directly influence the memory retraining programmes that Wilson and Staples use for their head-injured patients. The interplay between theory and practice is not simply a one-way relationship, but a reciprocal one. Studies of the way memory is disturbed in head-injured patients help psychologists understand more about the way memory normally works.

The plethora of different theories can sometimes be confusing. This is evident in the field of psychotherapy, where Freudian theories sit side by side with behavioural theories, humanistic theories, cognitive theories, and many other variants. This is partly a reflection of our ignorance about the complexities of human experience and the real difficulties in testing theory in the complicated world of clinical practice. Yet despite the confusion, theories are essential in order that scientific progress can be made. In recent years there has been a growing recognition of the central importance of cognitive processes, notably disturbances of thinking, in various emotional disorders such as anxiety and depression. This has led to new theories about therapeutic change and, as was illustrated in a recent book (Mahoney and Freeman 1985), a re-thinking of established psychoanalytic and behavioural theories. We can anticipate perhaps a synthesis of different psychological theories in the area of psychotherapy, which may help dispel some of the current confusions.

The development of new theories, and the modification of existing theories, inevitably means that some older theories are of little relevance to present clinical practice. For example, the classic work of Sheldon on the relationship between bodybuild and personality, known as somatotyping, did not lead to the discovery of links of value in the individual case, and has not been widely pursued. Indeed, the decline in the use of personality measures for clinical use has been accompanied by a reduction of interest in general personality theory by clinicians.

The scientist–practitioner model also entails the application of *scientific principles* in clinical practice. The development of behavioural assessment batteries such as REHAB in the assessment of psychiatric disability (See Chapter 3) involves the scientific procedures of item analysis, scaling, correlation, and factor analysis in order to produce an assessment tool that is scientifically reliable and valid. Many other psychometric instruments or tests have been developed using similar scientific principles, such as the British Ability Scales used in assessing the intellectual abilities of children.

Attention to these scientific principles enables the psychologist to develop an assessment measure that is free from gross errors such as bias, poor reliability, or invalid inferences, so that greater confidence can be placed in the results of the assessment.

The use of scientific principles is also evident in the systematic evaluation of treatment methods. This can take the form of clinical research trials such as the evaluation of a clinical psychology service in primary care reported in Chapter 8, or in the careful assessment of individual cases. Data on the problem in question are collected by means of a self-monitoring record (by observation, or by other means), before, during, and after treatment, thereby providing evidence on the extent to which change occurred. Wilson and Staples provide several examples of systematic evaluation applied to single cases. In recent years research strategies suitable for the single case have been developed which give the clinician–researcher greater confidence in the validity of the treatment outcome (e.g. Barlow and Hersen 1984).

The 'practitioner' component of the scientist–practitioner model should not be overlooked. Working with clinical cases demands many practical skills. These range from the subtle, interpersonal skills involved in psychotherapy to diplomatic skills required for working with other staff. These skills are acquired not so much from scientific principles and procedures, but as a result of practical experience. Clinical psychologists, like other professionals, can only be scientists to a degree. They must also learn to be creative and sensitive practitioners, and while some skills training occurs in professional courses, many are learnt from personal experience.

Psychology is about people

Underpinning the work of clinical psychologists in various settings is a fundamental concern with the rights and values of patients as people. As Garland states in his account of work with the elderly: 'While old people do have some unique concerns, they are basically just people who have been around longer than us'. Tennant and Cullen describe the 'normalization' philosophy which has come to influence work with the mentally handicapped. It is strongly asserted that mentally handicapped people should not be segregated from the community, but treated as equal members with equal rights and privileges. This is all too rarely achieved. A similar argument can be made with respect to the care of psychiatric patients (see Chapter 3).

Concern about the rights and values of people can be found in different aspects of the work of clinical psychologists. It can be seen in the respect for the dignity and worth of the client in psychotherapy, where an open and non-judgemental attitude is adopted by the therapist and the client is able to discuss painful, personal concerns in an atmosphere of acceptance and trust. It is very much a part of the advocacy role suggested by Wilson and Staples with regard to the rights of the disabled and physically handicapped. It underlies the concern expressed by Wallace that hospitalization and medical treatments should take into account the personal concerns of the patient as well as their medical needs (see, for example, the case of Gary). It can be found in the need to protect children and young people from abuse and exploitation by parents and other adults.

This essentially ethical statement is also reflected in the view that most psychological problems are not different *in kind* from the problems all of us experience. For example, problems of anxiety, depression, sexual difficulties, addictive behaviours, are part of a continuum and are experienced by most of us. Professional help may be sought when the problems become too intense or severe to be managed on their own, or cause too great a disruption to normal life. Even in cases where there is clear evidence of a biological deficiency (e.g. some mental handicapping conditions), the psychological approach is to emphasize the communalities with normal experience. Mentally handicapped people have to learn skills like non-handicapped people, following the same principles of learning. People with physical illnesses experience the normal psychological reactions to pain, trauma, and isolation that all of us experience from time to time. This is not to say that there are not unique or peculiar features to being mentally handicapped or severely depressed or in undergoing major surgery. But it is with the experiences and behaviour of *people* that psychology is ultimately concerned, and there is much to be gained from recognizing the continuity of such experiences across all conditions and problems.

ASSESSMENT, INTERVENTION, AND EVALUATION

The common clinical strategies of assessment, intervention, and evaluation are exemplified again and again in the various chapters of this book. Whatever the setting or whatever the population worked with, clinical psychologists are concerned to provide a thorough assessment of the problem, a psychologically based method of intervention and a systematic evaluation of the outcome.

(a) Assessment

Three important characteristics of assessment stand out. Firstly, assessment is always in response to a significant clinical question. In the past clinical psychologists were sometimes asked to assess the patient's 'IQ' or 'personality', often without any real consideration of the value of such information. These essentially descriptive assessments have been replaced by more practical and specific questions, the results of which will have a direct bearing upon the patient's clinical state. In the case of mental handicap, for example, Tennant and Cullen contrast an IQ assessment, which is of little practical use, with an assessment that seeks to understand why a mentally handicapped child might giggle and run away whenever she is asked a question. This type of information is of practical use since the information can be used to help the child improve her communication skills. In the field of physical health Wallace illustrates how a simple diary record sheet can be used to assess what factors provoke a woman's anxiety about chest pains and headache. Understanding the factors that lead to such anxiety (antecedents) can not only help to understand it better but to plan methods of change.

This leads to the second major characteristic of assessment, which is that it contributes to an analysis of the factors that cause and maintain problems. This is known generally as a *functional analysis*, since it is concerned not merely with the description of the problem, but with the function it has for the patient in question and for the patient's family. This type of analysis can be applied to very precise patterns of behaviour, such as the triggering of an aggressive outburst in a psychiatric resident or to more complex psychological relationships. The successful treatment of the problems such as depression, anxiety, and eating disorders depends upon a sensitive and careful assessment of how these problems relate to other important aspects of people's lives. If a person's self worth is strongly determined by believing themselves to be slim and attractive, as was the case of Susan illustrated in Chapter 2, then understanding that relationship is necessary for successful therapy.

It is precisely because a functional analysis provides information about the causes and consequences of a problem that it leads on to the third major characteristic of assessment, which is that it provides the basis for intervention. The information provided is useful precisely because it suggests ways of achieving change. Fielding illustrates this well in Chapter 4 with respect to parental reactions to John's encopresis (see pp. 98–101).

Assessment is not simply confined to an individual and his problems. There are various levels of assessment, e.g. intrapsychic, interpersonal, social, institutional, familial etc. In Chapter 3 Hall illustrates how assessment can be concerned with the characteristics of the institution (in this case a psychiatric hospital), taking into account the behaviour of ward staff, administrators, doctors as well as the residents. Such an approach has sometimes been called a *systems* approach since the assessment is concerned with the inter-action between various systems. Thus a child's antisocial behaviour can be seen in terms of the relationships between him and his various family members or between him and his peers at school, each of which describes a particular system of interactions. Whether assessment is concerned with problems at an individual level or at a systems level, similar strategies will be found, namely the concern with a specific practical question, a systematic analysis of the various maintaining and causative factors, and the generation of specific treatment objectives.

(b) Intervention

Psychological interventions are concerned with promoting benefi-cial change using psychological procedures and principles. Much of this book is about change, which ranges from reducing confusion in elderly residents by means of reality orientation, to applying hypnosis to acute burn injury to reduce trauma and tissue damage. Although the specifics of treatment vary according to the type of problem and the population concerned, it is possible to identify several common features.

Firstly, clinical psychologists are very much concerned with teaching specific skills. It requires skills for a mentally handicapped person to learn to tie his shoe laces and equally it requires skill for a haemophiliac child to carry out factor replacement therapy or a brain-damaged soldier to recognize the sounds and names of letters. Skills training draws upon some well-established procedures such as modelling or demonstration of the skill in question, repeated practice, informational feedback, reinforcement or incentives, and homework tasks.

A second common feature of interventions is the reduction of fear or anxiety. The cognitive–behavioural treatments of phobias and anxieties are described in detail in Chapter 2. Similar methods can be found in the treatment of school phobic children (Chapter 4), in reducing the understandable anxieties about hospitalization and surgery (Chapter 9), and in the direct treatment of a fear of falling in an elderly amputee (Chapter 6). Anxiety is a characteristic not only of psychological problems but also of many physical problems, where it can exacerbate the problem and delay treatment. Wallace, for example, makes a strong case for greater attention to the reduction of fear and anxiety in physical medicine where there is evidence of both physical and psychological benefit.

The third aspect of treatment that is worth noting is the emphasis on the role played by cognitive processes such as thoughts, attitudes, and beliefs. This is particularly evident in the treatment of depression by cognitive therapy (see Chapter 2), but is applicable in other problem areas too. For example, the motivation to overcome physical disability will be directly influenced by the extent to which the patient's attitude is positive and expectations realistic. Wallace's description of the case of Gary illustrates how negative attitudes and unrealistic expectations can hinder progress.

Many patients are strongly motivated to seek change. They desperately want to overcome their disabilities. In other cases motivation is itself a problem, as is seen in the apathetic institutionalized behaviour of many chronic psychiatric patients. Some psychological treatments are directly concerned with increasing the patient's motivation for change as in the token economy programmes described in Chapter 3. In psychological terms motivation is not some predetermined state or personality trait, but a product of the various factors that maintain and cause behaviour. The successful treatment of addictions will in part depend upon the person's ability to create and sustain strong incentives for change to counteract those of the addiction in question.

In psychological terms interventions are concerned with four major processess : the change in *behaviour*, such as the acquisition of certain skills; the change in *emotions*, such as the reduction of fear or anxiety and the elevation of depressive mood; changes in *cognition*, such as the modification of attitudes and beliefs; and *environmental* change. In the latter category attention is paid more to the controlling factors in the person's environment and the specific description of the individual's problems. Garland illustrates this with respect to room management in Chapter 7 and Hall in the institutional changes in psychiatric hospitals.

Evaluation

The functional analysis of problems and the specification of treatment objectives makes evaluation a logical component of any treatment programme. By specifying and monitoring treatment goals it is possible to see directly whether treatment has or has not been successful. Thus evaluation is part and parcel of any form of clinical intervention. In addition, the psychologist's research skills can be applied to a much more rigorous evaluation. This is illustrated for example in Chapter 8, where the move of clinical psychologists to general practice has been systematically evaluated by controlled clinical trials.

Evaluation can occur at different levels and with respect to different criteria and measures. Hadley and Strupp (1977) outline a tripartite model for evaluating psychotherapies that embraces the interests of the client, the professional, and of society. The client is primarily interested in personal changes such as reduced distress, increased happiness, or the solving of personal problems. The professional will view change in terms of his or her theoretical model. For example, some therapists regard changes in symptoms or specific problems as of less value than changes in personality or beliefs. In that case a therapy will be judged in terms of its ability to effect these more fundamental changes. From society's perspective therapies are valued in terms of social norms and standards. To what extent are people more 'mentally healthy'? Considerations of cost and efficiency are increasingly significant societal concerns.

The different levels of evaluation are important since they not only contain different perspective and values, but the type of evaluation determines what measures are used. Financial considerations can result in a concern with gross measures of change, such as how many people are admitted and discharged from a hospital or the efficiency of a treatment service in terms of numbers of people treated in relation to staffing. The problem with these measures is that they do not reflect either the client's perspective (being discharged from hospital need not result from psychological improvement) or the professional's perspective. Knowing the logistics of a therapeutic service tells us nothing about its quality and aims. Concern with evaluation therefore is not simply with cost, effectiveness, and efficiency, although these will be important, but with psychological change from the perspectives of both client and therapist.

WORKING WITH OTHER PROFESSIONS

Day-to-day practice of clinical psychology inevitably results in close contact with other professions. This is illustrated in the many examples of collaborative work in the various chapters of the book. In Chapter 10 Hall discusses the different forms such collaboration can take and some of the issues arising out of it.

The most common form of collaboration is that of joint work on clinical cases in which the specialist skills of psychologists combine with nurses, health visitors, physiotherapists, doctors, and other professionals. Wilson and Staples, for example, describe how psychological assessments and interventions combine with the work of physiotherapists and occupational therapists with brain-damaged patients. Mercier's work, described in Chapter 8, indicates how health visitors and psychologists can effectively combine in the group treatment for parents of sleep-disordered pre-school children. In these and other examples successful collaboration depends upon mutual sharing of specialist skills and knowledge. This is of benefit not only to the patient but also to the different professionals who in this way will learn about each other's particular contribution. Collaborative work is particularly valuable since so many problems are multi-dimensional. Wallace's description of her work in intensive care units indicates the value of monitoring and treating a patient's psychological state, in particular their anxieties, which may inhibit their response to prescribed medical treatment such as exercise. There are also ways in which various aspects of physical treatment may have adverse psychological effects, as when the technology of modern obstetric medicine can interfere with the mother's emotional response to her new baby.

In addition to collaborative work there is a clear role for psychologists in training other professions in psychological skills. There are still relatively few clinical psychologists working in the health service in Britain and a recent survey has shown a national vacancy figure of 14 per cent for England (Scrivens and Charlton 1985). Although there is a strong case for training more clinical psychologists, even if the profession were to double in size (an unlikely possibility) there would still be too few psychologists to provide a comprehensive psychological service throughout the country. Moreover, it is clear that the psychological methods and skills that have been developed by psychologists are transferable to other groups. Marks (1985) has demonstrated how nurses can be effectively trained in behavioural skills, for example. Therefore, an important and likely development is that many more psychologists will be involved in training other professions in psychological skills such as counselling and various treatments. In doing this it is important that those being trained are not only given a thorough training in practical skills but also become familiar with the psychological perspectives and theories that underlie those skills. It would be a mistake to apply psychological techniques to clinical problems without a thorough analysis of the causal and maintaining factors. To do the latter requires an awareness of how psychological variables interrelate and this will acquire attention to theory as well as learning practical therapeutic skills. The best training courses involve fairly lengthy and thorough training in both theory and practice. Although this may be expensive at first, there is no doubt that the expense is justified by the results achieved. There is some evidence, for example, that well trained paraprofessionals are equally effective and sometimes more effective than the professionals who train them (Durlak 1978).

FUTURE PRACTICE

It is possible to discern several trends in practice that give some hint as to how clinical psychology is developing. We have already referred to some of these notably the increasing application of psychological methods in various health fields and the increasing emphasis on collaborative work with other professional groups. Two other features are also evident: the move to community care, and changing models of health and medicine.

(a) Community care

There is currently a strong trend towards provision of community care for the mentally ill and the mentally handicapped. This has arisen partly for laudable concern about the low standard of accommodation in large mental hospitals and the documented concerns about the effects of institutionalization on the patients resident there, and partly out of financial reasons, since the run down of such hospitals can lead to immediate savings in terms of both labour and capital costs, even if these savings will have to be offset by the necessary increased costs of a community service. In several areas clinical psychology services have already moved 'into the community' such as is described in their work in primary care in Chapter 8, with the elderly in Chapter 7, and with the mentally handicapped in Chapter 5. One immediate question arises—what consitutes appropriate community care?

One important element of the community care system is that treatment facilities should be as accessible as possible for the person in need. In this way existing community support such as family and friends can remain in contact especially during crisis periods. A second element is that there should be organizational collaboration between different professional and voluntary agencies. This would enable greater continuity of care and the possibility of preventing minor problems turning into major ones. Thus a vital feature of community care is the establishment of close links between specialists, such as psychologists, and primary care staff. There is a need too for the various specialist groups to work together to avoid duplication of skills and contradictory advice and practices. The setting up of Community Mental Handicap Teams in which specialists take a consultancy role to the activities of front-line workers such as social workers and nurses is one example of how a community service can be developed. Similar models for the mentally ill have been developed.

In addition to providing psychological advice and supervision, a clinical psychologist can contribute to a community care programme by working closely with the different groups or teams. This might entail, for example, the setting up of staff support groups or training groups whose function would be to improve communication and provide a forum for the sorting out of interprofessional problems. There has been yet relatively little attention to the psychological problems and stresses of a transition to community care for staff who have acquired specialist skills in other settings. Not only does it involve the acquisition of new skills, but also changes in working practices that may have significant psychological effects, for example the relative isolation of community-based nurses from their own professional group.

There are also some dangers in the move to community care. One danger already mentioned is the belief that a community care system is cheaper than institutional care. There is therefore a real danger that community care will not be adequately funded, and so will become equated with inadequate provision either in terms of accommodation or in terms of staff services.

(b) Changing models of health and medicine

A traditional view of the health service is one in which doctors assisted by nurses apply their skills and expert knowledge to treat illnesses. While this is a large part of modern medicine, it has become increasingly obvious that illness and disease will never be eradicated by technological medicine alone, that much of ill health is a product of the social and economic conditions in which people live, and that many of the most notable improvements in health have come about not from the application of modern treatments but from improvements in social and environmental conditions. Another important factor is the extent to which we as individuals are able to lead more or less healthy lifestyles. All these factors combine to provide a view of health which is more than simply the absence of disease. There is also a growing general public interest in health. A scepticism amongst the public at large about the value of many medical treatments has been fuelled by well-publicized examples of apparently new and effective treatments proving to be ineffective and sometimes harmful. Thus, a model of health emerges which (a) embraces the lifestyle and behaviour of individuals in society, and (b) acknowledges the importance to the individual of good and accurate information about various influences upon health and illness. In the case of coronary heart disease, for example, it is known that individuals are placed at risk by the type of diet they eat, whether or not they smoke, and the extent to which they lead stressful lives (see Chapter 9).

The contribution of clinical psychology to health in general is well described in Wallace's chapter. Perhaps the most important message is that health is intimately concerned with psychological factors not only in terms of general well-being (i.e. psychological state) but in the way that physical illnesses interact with psychological variables. This is illustrated in the case of physical handicap, where a patient's expectations and attitudes will directly influence the nature and extent of their ability to benefit from any individual programme.

The contribution of clinical psychology to health in general could take a number of forms. Firstly, more individual assessment and treatment programmes could be developed, for example stress management for those with coronary heart disease, counselling services for potential AIDS victims, and psychological help for the terminally ill and their relatives. Secondly, more psychologists would be able to offer consultation and counselling services to patients in general hospitals, as illustrated in Wallace's chapter. Thirdly, several authors have illustrated how psychologists can make an impact on the health care system in general. Garland, for example, discusses the way different types of health care make an impact on the elderly and Hall has outlined a role for psychologists in planning mental illness services. At the very least there is a need to promote and support a more psychologically minded approach to health and illness. In addition, there is a role for psychology in the promotion of health with particular focus on the sorts of changes in attitude and behaviour that need to accompany the adoption of a more healthy lifestyle.

The application of psychology to health care should reflect the health problems and needs of a population. If that population and those needs change, then the priorities of the health care system for that population should also change. Kaprio (1979) makes a number of important generalizations about health in Europe.

Europe is becoming healthier, death rates are falling, and patterns of need are changing. With rising living standards have come increases in deaths from chronic degenerative diseases and from such external causes as accidents, violence, and suicide (. . .). Pathological conditions determined by a combination of genetic, environmental, and behavioural factors are beginning to dominate the health scene and intrude into family and community life.

Thus increasing attention needs to be paid to the health care problems of older people, and to the different range of needs they may have, resulting from chronic illness, differing from younger people.

While some congenital abnormalities can be anticipated or detected early, and thus eliminated by counselling parents not to have children or by offering termination of a pregnancy, other abnormalities now have an increased survival rate. There is a growing population of young adults with non-degenerative but irreversible handicaps with considerable expectation of life. These young adults may have received the best surgical and medical attention, but now require specialized help to adapt to their disability and make the best use of their residual abilities.

Changed patterns of family life also have an effect on the care of those with chronic conditions. The increasing proportion of single-parent families, and of families where children have had successive different parents through divorce and remarriage, is likely to reduce the amount of support available to a child within such families. The greater availability of work outside the home for women, and the greater proportion of older people with fewer children to look after them means that care for older people within their own family is less likely to be available. This suggests an increased need for information and guidance to families with a handicapped member, to enable them to cope better and longer with the relative.

The recent development by the WHO of a classification of Impairment, Disability, and Handicap to match the classification of Disease, is indicative of the growing significance to chronic disability in health care. Psychological adjustment of chronic disability has thus become of increasing importance. Adjustment is required not only by the patients but by the staff as well, who are usually trained to care for those improve rapidly, and who may themselves find it hard to cope with long-term problems, and with the much slower rate of improvement common in many chronic conditions.

SUMMARY

Clinical psychology has developed very rapidly as a profession, both numerically and in the range of client problems that are now presented for treatment. A continuing interplay between theory and clinical practice has meant that new areas of psychological research and theory have become of practical significance. The continuing concern of psychologists with assessment has been modified to emphasize those aspects of behaviour and experience more directly related to client problems and treatment. The growing range of effective psychological interventions has increased the interest of both clients and other professionals in them, leading to an important growth in collaboration with and training of other professionals.

Public views of health and illness are changing, and the health needs of that public are changing. Part of that change is a readiness to look at non-medical forms of help, and to take more personal responsibility for health care. The practice of clinical psychology supports both of these changes, and offers many useful concepts and procedures to assist them.

REFERENCES

Barlow, D. N. and Hersen, M. (1984). *Single-case experimental designs. Strategies for studying behavior change* (2nd edn). Pergamon Press, New York.

Durlak, J. A. (1978). Comparative effectiveness of paraprofessional and professional helpers. *Psychol. Bull.* **86**, 80–92.

Hadley, S. W. and Strupp, M. H. (1977). Evaluations of treatment in psychotherapy: Naivete or necessity? *Prof. Psychol.* **8**, 478–89.

Kaprio, L. A. (1979). Primary health care in Europe. Copenhagen, WHO Regional Office for Europe (EURO Reports and Studies No. 14).

Mahoney, M. J. and Freeman, A., ed. (1985). *Cognition and psychotherapy*. Plenum Press, New York.

Marks, I. M. (1985). Controlled trial of psychiatric nurse therapists in primary care. *Br. med. J.* **290**. 1181–4.

Scrivens, E. and Charlton, D. (1985). *The nature and size of clinical psychology services within health districts in England*. Bath Social Policy Paper Series, University of Bath.

Glossary

Agoraphobia. From the Greek 'fear of the market place'. Characterized by fear of being away from a place of safety, usually the home. Low self-esteem and excessive dependence on others are features.

Anorexia nervosa. Loss of weight usually due to persistent fasting or excessive dieting. Amenorrhoea is also common as are fear of fatness and disturbed body-image. Almost entirely found in girls and younger women.

Anxiety. Feelings of apprehension and unease in response to real or imagined threat. Anxiety consists of *physiological reactions* such as increased heart rate, sweating, trembling, *behavioural responses* such as avoidance, and *cognitive disturbance* such as worrying thoughts or frightening fantasies. There are a variety of clinical anxiety states e.g. generalised anxiety, phobic anxiety.

Anxiety management training. The use of behavioural treatments of anxiety in the form of a skills training approach. Anxious patients are directly taught methods of managing their anxiety such as relaxation and planned practice either individually or in a group.

Assessment
Behavioural: psychological measurement procedures which focus on the behaviour which is to be treated, or which is likely to change, at the time it occurs and without making any assumptions about underlying causes or variables.

Psychometric: psychological measurement procedures which measure assumed traits or characteristics, typically involving comparison of the patient with appropriate norms, often conducted in a face-to-face assessment setting.

Baseline. An assessment, or results of an assessment, carried out before treatment has started and normally continued until the measure is stable or steady.

Behaviour therapy. Method of psychological treatment developed in the 1950s, derived from experimental studies of conditioning and learning. The focus of treatment is on overt behaviour using psychological principles to achieve specific behavioural goals. Often contrasted with **psychodynamic** psychotherapies (see below) where the focus is more on achieving insight or personality change.

Between-groups design. An experimental design where two or more different groups are studied, one receiving the experimental treatment and the other(s) receiving control or comparison treatments. In some such designs all groups receive all treatments but in a different order.

Biofeedback. Use of electronic equipment to monitor bodily reactions (e.g. heart rate, EEG) to enable individuals to modify and control these reactions. Usually achieved by the feedback of the response in terms of a visual or auditory signal that varies in intensity according to the subject's control. Clinical applications are in anxiety states, headaches, high blood pressure, and some muscular skeletal disorders.

Bulimia. Disturbance of eating characterized by excessive preoccupation with food, a pattern of binge eating and self-induced vomiting or laxative abuse. Occurs mainly in young women of slightly older age range than anorexics. See anorexia nervosa.

Client-centred therapy. Developed by Carl Rogers in 1940s, CCT aims to help clients explore their feelings in the context of a warm, empathic, and trusting relationship. Therapy is seen as personal growth rather than 'treatment' and the approach eschews specific techniques or procedures.

Clinical psychology. The application of psychological theory and practice to a broad range of problems—mental and physical—for which people seek treatment.

Cognition. A general term to cover all aspects of knowledge—perceiving, thinking, imagining, reasoning, etc. Contrasted with affect or feeling. It is maintained by some that all emotions are cognitively processed and by others that emotions are at times directly experienced.

Cognitive-behaviour therapy. Describes the combination of behaviour therapy and cognitive therapy in which, generally, behavioural procedures are used to change cognitive processes. It is a more liberal form of behaviour therapy in the recognition paid to thoughts and beliefs in understanding and changing psychological problems.

Cognitive therapy. The prime focus is on patient's thinking processes with the goal of changing distorted or unrealistic thoughts and beliefs. Methods vary from Socratic argument to behavioural procedure. Beck's cognitive therapy developed in 1970s is a promising new treatment for depression.

Community psychology. The application of psychological theory and practice to people living in natural communities, and to the problems encountered by people in that setting.

Conditioning. The process by which a particular response comes to be elicited by a stimulus, event or object other than that to which it is the natural or reflexive response.

Classical conditioning: the association in time of a neutral stimulus (e.g. bell) with a reflexive stimulus (e.g. food) so that a conditioned response (e.g. salivation) occurs to the neutral stimulus.

Operant conditioning: the process by which behaviour is modified by systematically varying its consequences (rewards and punishments).

Control group. A group of patients or people in all respects similar to the main group, except that they are not subjected to the treatment or condition that is being experimentally investigated.

Counselling. A helping relationship in which the counsellor seeks to enable the client explore his or her concerns and to find ways of resolving them. Counselling is a form of psychological treatment although generally its focus is on less disturbed clients and often in non-medical settings, e.g. student counselling.

Depression. Feelings of sadness, hopelessness, lowered bodily activity. Clinical depression is characterized by a reduction or increase in appetite, disturbances of thought and movement, usually being slowed down or occasionally agitated, lethargy, poor concentration, feelings of guilt and self blame and general loss of interest in previously enjoyed activities.

Educational psychology. The application of psychological theory and practice to educational methods, and to problems encountered by people in the educational process.

Evaluation. The process of finding the value of a treatment, by formally determining whether it is effective, efficient, and acceptable, in achieving predetermined objectives.

Event sampling. A behavioural assessment technique where only a proportion of the key events are observed thoroughly, although all events are recorded: this technique is particularly appropriate for complex key events demanding very detailed observation.

Functional analysis. The analysis of the relationship between a key event, and the preceding, concurrent, and following events, to see if there is any association between them. If such an association is found this functional relationship can be used to develop a treatment strategy.

Health psychology. The application of psychological theory and practice to the beliefs, behaviour, and experience of people relating to their health, both when they are well and when they are ill.

Hypnosis. A state in which the hypnotized person responds to external suggestions allowing events to be experienced as if they were actually occurring. Successfully used as an anaesthetic and analgesic in selected subjects. Used as a form of psychotherapy and has been closely studied by experimental psychologists.

Intelligence. General mental ability and specialized abilities such as numeracy, verbal reasoning, perceptual skills. There is a long-standing controversy over the extent to which general intelligence (called G) exists over and above a variety of specialized abilities. The Intelligence Quotient (IQ) describes a way of measuring intelligence using psychological tests.

Learning. The process by which knowledge and behaviour are acquired and understood. *The laws of learning* refer to basic principles formulated by psychologists in the scientific study of learned behaviour. *Learning Theory* describes the body of theoretical knowledge on the processes involved in learning.

Milieu therapy. A method of psychotherapy that arose in the context of institutional care of psychiatric patients. The total environment or milieu including staff and patients is designed to be a 'therapeutic community', conducive to the patients' psychological welfare and recovery.

Morbidity. The nature and frequency of specific mental or physical conditions in the population, often expressed as the number of contacts or notified cases for every 1 000, say, of the population.

Neuropsychology. The study of the relationship between brain structure and pathology, and behaviour and experience.

Normalization. A complex philosophy of care advocated by Wolfensberger, which essentially stresses that the objectives and practices of caring institutions or regimes should be socially valued: the philosophy has many detailed implications, and although mainly applied to the care of mentally handicapped people has potential applications for other client groups.

Obsession. Irrational idea or thought that persists against ones will. Often accompanied by ritualistic, compulsive behaviour. Common obsessions are of checking, contamination, and harm to self or others.

Personality. The integrated organization of the physical and psychological characteristics of an individual, including intelligence, emotionality, and social behaviour, in the way that the individual presents himself to others. *Personality traits* describe general characteristics of the individual, e.g. impulsive, sociable, taciturn etc. *Personality types* describe major patterns of personality, e.g. introvert, neurotic.

Phobia. Intense fear and avoidance of harmless events or objects. There are a variety of specific phobias e.g. insects and animals, also social phobias and **agoraphobia**.

Psychoanalysis. A method of psychological treatment, developed from the work of Freud, which focuses on the uncovering of unconscious conflicts by predominantly verbal means. Significant features of psychoanalysis include free association, interpretation, and the development of transference whereby strong emotional feelings experienced in other relationships are 'transferred' to the therapist. Classically a lengthy and intensive therapy lasting several years, although briefer and less intensive forms have also been developed.

Psychodynamic. Derived from psychoanalytic theory, describing the interplay of mental and emotional forces and the way these affect behaviour and mental state.

Psychotherapy. General term for any treatment by psychological means designed to reduce personal distress, raise morale, or help solve personal or social problems. Sometimes used to describe verbal methods of therapy in contrast to **Behaviour therapy**, although this distinction is not consistently used.

Psychotropic. Drugs with an effect on psychological function, behaviour, or experience, which includes a wide range of substances but is usually taken to refer to those drugs most frequently used in psychiatry (e.g. major tranquillizers or antidepressants).

Punishment. Describes the way the probability of a response is reduced by the presentation of an aversive consequence.

Questionnaire. Any list of questions seeking information about a person's attitudes, knowledge, or traits, often self-administered and thus easy to use and often used for surveys. Some questionnaires contain an anti-faking scale.

Rating scale. A list of questions or statements about a person which are judged or rated, typically by another person (the rater) about the extent to which they occur. The observation or rating procedure is usually well-defined.

Rehabilitation. Procedures for helping disabled patients to return to society after illness and to maximize their general functioning. It is applied both to institutionalized psychiatric patients being returned to community settings and to the physically handicapped being helped to recover from or adapt to their disability.

Reinforcement. Describes the process in **operant conditioning** by which a response is strengthened by its consequences.

Positive reinforcement describes the strengthening of a response by presenting a stimulus (e.g. a reward). *Negative reinforcement* describes the process of strengthening a response by taking away an aversive or unpleasant stimulus (e.g. removal of loud noise or shock). Not to be confused with **punishment**.

Reliability. The extent to which a measurement procedure gives consistent or closely similar results when applied more than once, under similar conditions, to the same person or group. When the measure is applied by two or more different users (or raters or testers) the degree of consistency or similarity is a measure of inter-user (or -tester) reliability.

Schizophrenia. A major psychiatric disorder characterized by disturbances of thought, flattened or inappropriate emotions, delusions, and hallucinations usually in the form of imagined voices. Tends to occur in young adults in acute form and can become chronic.

Self-monitoring. Assessment procedures that involve a person in recording his own behaviour by suitable charts or diaries, or by suitable physiological devices.

Single-case designs. An experimental design where one person receives a series of treatments or conditions in a carefully planned sequence, with some conditions possibly repeated (but where the sequence minimizes the effect of early conditions on later conditions).

Social skills training. The use of didactic procedures of modelling, role-playing, and feedback, to train people in 'social skills'. Social skills refers to specific features of social behaviour that result in successful interaction. These range from specific non-verbal behaviours such as eye contact or gesture to complex patterns of interaction.

Statistical analysis. The process of subjecting a number of figures to a particular manipulation (which may include correlation, analysis of variance, calculation of means) essentially to condense the figures to show some central characteristics of the data. *The statistical significance* of the results is the probability that that result could have been achieved by chance, or by random allocation, and is conventionally expressed at probability levels of 5, 1, or 0.1 per cent (or as 0.05, 0.01, or 0.001).

Stress. *Either* unpleasant aspects of the external social and physical environment *or* the subjective response of the individual to threats and challenges arising from that environment.

Tests

Attainment: sets of standard questions or items designed to measure specific achievements or attainments, such as reading, and distinguished from the measurement of more general abilities.

Intelligence: sets of standard problems and materials designed to measure maximum general mental ability, or power of learning and understanding, and typically yielding an intelligence quotient (IQ).

Personality: *either* sets of standard questions relating to a persons own distinctive character, or normal mode of functioning, scored to yield measures of different personality traits; *or* sets of *projective* materials which are essentially ambiguous or neutral in meaning, the responses to which are assumed to reveal underlying traits or characteristics.

Time out. Withdrawal of positive reinforcement for a particular behaviour (e.g. shouting, fighting) by taking the individual out of the environment where such behaviour is being reinforced. Often used in managing aggressive behaviour in children and adolescents.

Time sampling. A behavioural assessment technique involving observation of the patient or setting for only a proportion of the total time possible, by observing according to a predetermined schedule of random or systematically chosen times, thus giving a representative sample of observations.

Validity. The extent to which a measurement procedure assesses what it is supposed to assess. This somewhat circular definition may be clarified by distinguishing between face or content validity—the extent to which inspection of the form or content of the procedure shows it is appropriate; and empirical validity—the extent to which the procedure is consistent with the scores derived from another totally independent measure of the same phenomenon.

Index

accident-prone environments and
people 223, 224
activities
observation and maximization in
chronic pain 226
programmes for elderly 183
remedial therapist providing 249
Activities of Daily Living (ADL) 260
addictions 43
behavioural treatment 43–7, 271
adolescence 85–114
drug and alcohol dependency 90
health promotion 111–13
lack of social skills 106–7
primary prevention programmes 112
smoking in 111–12
adults, psychological problems 34–5
treatment 33–61
Adult Training Centres 118, 123–4
advocacy role 158–9, 268
affective disorders 64–5, 195
aggressive behaviour 65, 109–11
in elderly 168, 180–1
agoraphobia 39–41, 59, 198
group therapy 57
alcohol 43
intake record 45, 46
amnesia, retrograde, anterograde 146
angina pectoris 215
anhedonia 67
Antecedents–Behaviour–Consequents
(ABC) approach 23
antidepressants 48
antisocial behaviour 270
anxiety 36, 39, 194, 199
assessment 228
chest pain and 216, 218, 273
in coronary care units 214–15
in day-care patients, consultation
on 235, 271
in elderly 167, 174–6

helping children to overcome 107–9,
271
obsessional 42
pain detection threshold, effect
on 231
presenting as physical disease
216–17, 271
in primary health care 199–200
anxiety reduction 39, 42, 174–76,
199–200, 265, 271
behavioural treatment 39, 42,
199–200, 265
cognitive therapy 174–6
in physical disease 223, 271
teaching of 202
assertiveness training 41, 58
assessment 1, 18–21, 269–70
after head injury 145–58
basic principles 37–9, 269–70
behavioural, see behavioural
assessment
of childhood problems 96–9
of chronic psychiatric disabilities
71–4, 74, 270
cognitive behavioural 224–5
criterion-referenced 19–20
data base for 185
of elderly 170–2, 185
functional analysis 23, 269–70
in gerontology 180
instruments (validity, reliability)
20–1
major categories 18–21, 22, 269–70
of mentally handicapped 120–6, 269
neuropsychological, see
neuropsychological assessment
in physical health 224–8, 229
of physically handicapped
people 139–45, 198
psychological tests in 227–8
rating, see rating scale
systems approach 270

287